THE YOUNG IRELAND MOVEMENT

The
Young Ireland
Movement

RICHARD DAVIS

GILL AND MACMILLAN
Dublin
BARNES & NOBLE BOOKS
Totowa, New Jersey

Published in Ireland by
Gill and Macmillan Ltd
Goldenbridge
Dublin 8
with associated companies in
Auckland, Dallas, Delhi, Hong Kong,
Johannesburg, Lagos, London, Manzini,
Melbourne, Nairobi, New York, Singapore,
Tokyo, Washington
© Richard Davis 1987
0 7171 1543 7
Print origination in Dublin by Galaxy Reproductions Ltd
Printed in Great Britain by
The Camelot Press, Southampton

British Library of Congress Cataloguing in Publication Data
Davis, Richard
    The Young Ireland movements
    1. Young Ireland. (movements)
    I. Title
    322.4'2'0915   DA950.2
    ISBN 0-7171-1543-7

First published in the USA 1988 by
Barnes & Noble Books
81 Adams Drive,
Totowa, New Jersey 07512
0-389-20773-X

Contents

Acknowledgments

I am indebted to the University of Tasmania for granting me leave, to the Queen's University of Belfast for awarding me a fellowship at the Institute of Irish Studies for 1985-6, and to the other Institute fellows for a stimulating environment to write this book. Individual scholars who provided valuable assistance or advice were Kerby Miller, Desmond Bowen, R. D. C. Black, Tom Power, T. G. McGrath, R. H. Buchanan, Eamon Phoenix, Alan Ward, David Wilson, Nigel Oxley, Sean Ó Lúing, J. C. Beckett, Aidan Clarke, Maurice O'Connell, Kevin Nowlan, Fr F. X. Martin, O.S.A., and Oliver MacDonagh. I also thank Professor John Dillon for permission to quote from the Dillon papers and Anthony O'Brien for his helpfulness in making available the Smith O'Brien papers still in family possession. I am grateful to the staffs of the National Library of Ireland, Dublin, the British Newspaper Library, Colindale, and the Linenhall Library, Belfast for their willing assistance. I also thank my brother and sister and their families for accommodating me in London. My colleagues Asim Roy and Michael Bennett helped me to adjust to the computer age. Finally, I am particularly grateful to my wife for her tolerance and massive assistance with the proofs and index. None of the above, however, share any responsibility for any errors of commission or omission in the text.

Introduction

The Historical
Context of Young Ireland

Today Young Ireland appears little more than a link in the chain of nationalist ideology extending from Wolfe Tone to the Irish Revolution of 1919-21. Its legacy of chauvinist verse, bombastic rhetoric and ineffectual soul-searching has little appeal. Thomas Davis is merely a plaster saint. Only the Provisional IRA takes seriously Young Ireland's role in the tradition it claims to defend. But a closer analysis of the voluminous Young Ireland books and periodicals reveals neglected issues. Perennial problems, such as violent versus non-violent resistance, neo-colonialism and racism, Third World development, and liberation theology emerge. The exhumation of Young Ireland ideas, long buried under the preoccupations of the past, is overdue.

Young Ireland was not a clearly articulated movement but a group of Repealers, working with Daniel O'Connell in the 1840s. They vehemently repudiated sneering comparisons with contemporary movements like 'Young Italy' or 'Young England'. Only when driven out of the Repeal Association in 1846 did the dissidents form their own short-lived Irish Confederation. Immediately before the brief rebellion of July 1848, reunification with mainstream Repealers was almost achieved. Had this occurred the rising might have been more effective.

The movement must be considered in several contexts: the continuity of Young Ireland's ideological links with Daniel O'Connell, its European and trans-Atlantic dimensions, the nationalist sequence of what F.S.L. Lyons has called 'magic dates' — '98, 1803, 1848, 1867, 1916, 1919-21, 1968—? — and the Young Ireland preoccupation with anti-imperialism.

Ireland, by the 1840s a by-word for poverty, paradoxically

produced in Daniel O'Connell a leader celebrated overseas as
the originator of disciplined mass constitutional politics,
while his liberal Catholicism fascinated continental religious
thinkers. Yet O'Connell failed to reform a disastrous land
system before the Great Famine of 1845-48, which ultimately
halved the Irish population of 8 million. Following Catholic
emancipation in 1829 (which enabled middle-class Catholics
to sit in parliament, but disenfranchised the masses),
O'Connell concentrated on parliamentary reformist politics
till 1840. The election of Peel's Conservatives in 1841 in
place of the less intransigent Whigs stimulated O'Connell's
new movement for Repeal of the Act of Union, which had
turned Britain and Ireland into a single constitutional entity
in 1801. O'Connell had previously hinted that justice for
Ireland under the Union would obviate the need for Repeal
and an independent Irish legislature.

The nucleus of the group subsequently described as
Young Ireland was formed in 1842. Late that year, Thomas
Davis, Charles Gavan Duffy and John Blake Dillon established
The Nation as a patriotic weekly to ginger O'Connell's campaign. It soon achieved a remarkable circulation. *The Nation*,
which outlived the Rising of 1848, became almost a synonym
for the Young Ireland movement, speaking in its earlier years
for Repeal in general. As Gavan Duffy, not only *Nation* editor
and proprietor, but in later life the voluminous historian of
Young Ireland, pointed out, more revolutions are made from
editors' chairs than from secret societies or military conspiracies.[1]

According to conventional wisdom, *The Nation* preached a
form of pure nationalism which was opposed to O'Connell's
pragmatic reformism. The exact relationship between the
views of O'Connell and *The Nation* is, however, extremely
complex. To O'Connell, *The Nation* proved a mixed blessing.
It created interest and enthusiasm for Repeal, but inevitably
the 'young men' advocated doctrines sometimes at variance
with the current strategy of the veteran 'Liberator'. Modern
historians emphasise similarities rather than differences.

The split between the Young Irelanders and O'Connell in
July 1846 has long been debated. What were the precise
causes? Gavan Duffy disregarded the ostensible breach over

the Young Irelanders' rejection of O'Connell's absolute non-violence. The real reason, Duffy maintained, was O'Connell's disillusionment with Repeal and desire to renew, in the teeth of Young Ireland opposition, a pragmatic alliance with the English Whigs. First in the field, Duffy's views gained widespread currency after 1883, but were eventually challenged. Denis Gwynn found Young Irelanders like Davis, who were hostile to the Catholic tradition, needling the relatively tolerant O'Connell. Kevin Nowlan denied Duffy's related contention that, after the failure of O'Connell's 'monster meetings' in his 'Repeal Year' of 1843 and a period of imprisonment in 1844, O'Connell became a mere figurehead, dominated by his bigoted son, John. Nowlan has probed Duffy's partisanship, masquerading as self-effacing analysis; he identifies Duffy as a leading conservative influence on Young Ireland. The editor of O'Connell's voluminous correspondence, Professor Maurice O'Connell, argues that the ostensible cause of division, non-violence, was in fact the real issue.[2]

Other problems, non-denominational education in particular, centred on religious pluralism. The British government's legislation for Irish university colleges in 1845 was crucial. Here again, while Duffy's account was strongly critical of O'Connell, modern historians from Denis Gwynn in the 1940s to D. A. Kerr in the 1980s have placed more onus for the dispute on Young Irelanders. Some use Gwynn's strictures on Davis's disdain for the ethos of Catholic Ireland to argue that the country contains two irreconcilable religious traditions. The essential problem of Young Ireland's relations with the Catholic church can now be explored in the light of new material in episcopal and Roman archives, opened up by historians like Desmond Bowen in his account of the seminal figure, Cardinal Paul Cullen.[3]

Young Ireland responded to O'Connell's overseas interests. Young Ireland opinion was often a projection of that of the Liberator. Both O'Connell and Young Ireland were aware of contemporary European nationalism, such as the 'Young' movements stimulated by Mazzini, but their common slogan 'Ourselves Alone' implies introversion. All shades of Repeal opinion were fascinated by the contemporary progress of Canada towards responsible government and the steady advance of British power in India. The plight of other peoples submerged by the British colossus, such as the New Zealand Maoris and the Australian Aborigines, reinforced Repeal rhetoric.

If, however, the Young Irelanders anticipated modern radical anti-imperialism, several have been accused of extreme conservatism. Smith O'Brien, leader of the unsuccessful rebellion in 1848, is portrayed more as an Irish country gentleman than a revolutionary. Was he in reality a high-minded but unintelligent figurehead? Padraic Pearse, who placed the Young Irelanders, Thomas Davis, John Mitchel and Fintan Lalor among the 'Fathers' of Irish nationalism, has been judged by revisionist historians to have had fascist tendencies. Davis, whose moral superiority was once a nationalist truism, has been attacked by Alf MacLochlainn for exhibiting, especially in his poetry, a disastrous Celtic racism. Other authorities, such as Oliver MacDonagh and Maurice O'Connell, agree in criticising Davis's overblown patriotism. Mitchel's writings require no revisionist inter-pretation. Few would now accept Arthur Griffith's preface to *Jail Journal*, which asserted that the slave-owning society lauded by Mitchel was indeed a suitable model for Irish aspirations. If, as has been maintained, Mitchel's *Jail Journal*, echoing Thomas Carlyle's now virtually unreadable rhetoric, was the only great book produced by Young Ireland, modern impatience with the movement is understandable. However, revisionism evokes its own counter-analysis. Can the case for Young Ireland authoritarianism be fully sustained in the light of evidence from its neglected writings?[4]

The present work endeavours to disentangle Young Ireland as far as possible from O'Connell and assess its rôle in Irish history. It poses questions about Irish nationalism in general. Can a community be stirred to patriotism without creating a narrow and intolerant spirit? Is cultural nationalism valuable in a campaign against specific grievances? Can the example and encouragement of other countries and suppressed groups help in a campaign of 'Ourselves Alone'? Is it possible to devise a pluralist political culture in a divided country like Ireland without making existing churches fearful of a rival religion of patriotism? Was there any possibility in the 1840s of reconciling northern Protestants to an integrated nation? Was mixed education a feasible policy? Is there a non-violent way to national autonomy? Can classes be united in a period of economic crisis to work for the benefit of the whole community, or is economic improvement only possible through the victory of one class? Young Ireland did not find the solution to any of these problems, but the interest of the movement lies in the vitality of the debate it generated.

PART ONE

Young Ireland
from Inception to
Dispersion

1

The Establishment of *The Nation*

Daniel O'Connell's Ireland

On 22 September 1842, shortly before *The Nation*'s first issue, the perceptive German traveller and librarian, Johann Georg Kohl, disembarked at Dublin's new Kingstown Harbour. Like other travellers, Kohl was struck by the paradox of a beautiful country full of 'ruin, decay, rags and misery'. Somewhat ambiguous as to whether this was caused by defective Irish character or British misgovernment, Kohl sensed the tension in disturbed counties like Tipperary where agrarian secret societies were active in murder and outrage. He was correspondingly shocked by the repressive activity of the armed constabulary. He considered the discipline of the hated new workhouses very severe and regarded them as inadequate for Irish conditions. Impressed by the Irish devotion to the church, Kohl was shocked by the rigidity of the religious divisions, with separate inns and even stage-coaches for Protestants and Catholics. Though Irish critics sneered at Kohl's survey of the interior of hovels from the top of a stage-coach, his published account was frequently cited by Daniel O'Connell as proof of British misrule.[1]

Kohl, for his part, was fascinated by the two contrasting Irish leaders of the period, the statesman, Daniel O'Connell and the Capuchin temperance reformer, Fr Theobald Mathew. When Kohl appeared at Kingstown, ironically renamed after the roué George IV, O'Connell was a veteran of sixty-seven. His career stretched back to pre-Union Ireland and pre-Revolutionary Europe. As a student on the continent, O'Connell had almost lost his Catholic faith to the currently fashionable philosophy of the Enlightenment. The excesses of the French Revolution, from which he narrowly escaped, and the shock in 1815 of killing his opponent in a duel reinforced O'Connell's hatred of violence. Nevertheless, there was a verbal violence in his forensic and political oratory. After the relief legislation in 1793, a career at the bar was possible for talented Catholics like himself. O'Connell opposed both the United Irishmen's 1798 rebellion and the 1800 Act of Union, when the all-Protestant Irish parliament voted itself out of existence. In the new century Catholics were still denied the right to sit in the United Kingdom parliament. The campaign for 'Catholic Emancipation' lasted till 1829. O'Connell, having ousted more conservative Catholic leaders, established an epoch-making Catholic Association in 1823. For the first time a mass political organisation, based on a Catholic rent of a penny a month collected at church doors, appeared in the British Isles. Despite British attempts at suppression, momentum increased till 1828 when O'Connell himself, technically ineligible as a Catholic, won the parliamentary seat of Clare against a popular Protestant landlord. The Tory government of Sir Robert Peel and the Duke of Wellington partially capitulated. They granted Catholic Emancipation, but disenfranchised the class of forty-shilling freeholders who had achieved it. The Irish electorate was reduced from 200,000 to 60,000. As O'Connell himself said, emancipation 'was calculated to benefit the wealthier classes, and did not do much for the poor'. Nevertheless, O'Connell became 'the Liberator' to the Irish people. Tories, furious at emancipation, helped to defeat Wellington. With Irish assistance the Whigs passed the Great Reform Bill of 1832, which enfranchised the British middle classes, but did little for Ireland.[2]

After the dramatic success of 1829, O'Connell lost momentum in the 1830s. Oscillating between the competing ideals of good government and self-government, O'Connell decided to support the Whig administration. His group of about forty Irish MPs became essential Whig allies. The Whigs gave Ireland more equitable administration, encouraging landlords to recognise their duties to the people and governed impartially between the Catholic majority and the privileged Protestant minority of about 20 per cent, mostly in the north.

Unfortunately, due to the intransigence of the Tory House of Lords, the Whigs failed to effect their major Irish reforms. Tithes paid to the minority church were merely commuted to a rent-charge, not abolished. Municipal 'reform', limited rather than increased the scope of local self-government. The new English system of poor relief, restricted to the grim workhouse, was bodily transferred to Ireland where, as Kohl recognised, it was unsuitable for a population on the brink of starvation. The Whigs dared not reform the land system at the expense of property rights. By the late 1830s disillusionment with O'Connell's apparent 'Whig alliance' was mounting in Ireland. Members of his Irish party accepted government offices; O'Connell rebuffed trade unionists and Chartists who might have shown solidarity with the Irish; the once radical Presbyterians in Ulster, under the guidance of the Rev. Henry Cooke, made common cause with the conservative Anglicans against O'Connell's Catholic resurgence.

Anticipating Tory victory under Robert Peel, against whom he had once nearly fought a duel, O'Connell turned to Repeal of the Union. An earlier 'Precursor' (to justice: in other words, a movement for Repeal) Society in 1838 had proved ineffectual. On 15 April 1840 O'Connell launched a new association for Repeal. The organisation particularly emphasised its 'loyalty', in title and demeanour. O'Connell cherished an obsequious devotion to the young Victoria, 'the darling little Queen'. The Repeal movement rejected violence and any breach of the law.[3]

Unlike the original Catholic Association, Repeal did not gain the automatic adhesion of the higher clergy, though O'Connell's organisational strategy was basically similar. Indeed, Archbishops Crolly and Murray, of Armagh and Dublin respectively, held aloof. The first person of consequence to adhere to Repeal was John MacHale, the fiery archbishop of Tuam. O'Connell hoped to gain Protestant approval. Here he found the task beyond his capacities. The liberal northern Protestant supporters of William Sharman Crawford, already critical of O'Connell, also rejected Repeal. Similarly, the Rev. Henry Montgomery, whose followers seceded from the Cooke dominated Presbyterian church, rejected O'Connell's overtures and his movement. When, in early 1841, O'Connell himself visited Belfast, he was challenged to debate by the hostile Henry Cooke, and could only obtain a hearing from Catholics and a handful of exceptional Protestants. As the initially small Catholic population was reinforced by immigrants from country areas, Belfast, Ireland's sole industrialising city, developed a tradition of bitter sectarian conflict. North-east Ulster remained the only region of Ireland with a substantial Protestant working class.[4]

At the British general election of July 1841 O'Connell's Repeal movement was tested and found wanting. From twenty-eight in the previous parliament, O'Connell's following was drastically reduced and fluctuated between twelve and twenty reliable members. The Liberator was personally humiliated by losing his Dublin seat and having to represent the more faithful Cork County. Furthermore, the relatively friendly Whigs were defeated and O'Connell's old foe, Sir Robert Peel, took over as head of a Conservative ministry. Could O'Connell's Repeal agitation succeed in forcing Peel to capitulate as he had done in 1829? The omens were unfavourable. O'Connell's election defeat was a poor start. Moreover, Peel had made it clear that he would never concede self-government to Ireland.

E. Strauss, writing in the 1950s, perceptively depicted O'Connell as trapped between the demands of the lower classes for fixity of tenure and the insistence by the middle classes and the church on social stability. After 1841 his only option appeared to be the advocacy of purely political Repeal, masked by some quasi-revolutionary rhetoric. Unfortunately, Peel was already determined to call O'Connell's bluff. O'Connell's correspondence in 1842 indicates that he had himself almost despaired of maintaining a strong organisation. The Repeal rent was not as forthcoming as the old Catholic rent. 'Want', lamented the Liberator in July 1842, 'is literally killing me.' Nevertheless, to the observer Kohl, signs of Repeal enthusiasm appeared everywhere.[5]

Punch and other English critics lambasted O'Connell for extorting 'rint' out of the suffering Irish poor. O'Connell easily reassured his followers by a powerful public reply to such criticism. He stressed the large income he had relinquished at the bar and declared a patriotic leader worthy of his hire.[6]

Kohl and other observers were more sympathetic to Fr Mathew, then at the height of his fame as an Irish temperance reformer. The aristocratic Capuchin's crusade began in 1838 and peaked in 1842 when, for the first time he moved out of Ireland to bring his message to Irish communities and others in Britain. An astonishing number of 5 million are said to have taken a pledge of total abstinence in a country long depicted as a byword for drunken misery. Fr Mathew, ironically, had less than the full backing of his own church, some of whose members looked askance at his perpetual pledge and the ecumenical attitude which led him to work closely with Quakers and Protestant temperance advocates. The strong Repealer, Archbishop MacHale, was bitterly opposed and refused Fr Mathew access to his diocese. The Capuchin was non-political, and generally conservative in his attitudes, but O'Connell did his best to associate the Repeal movement with the temperance crusade. Fr Mathew's great success was not destined to last; but the reform, albeit temporary, in public attitudes provided the backdrop for the subsequent Repeal and Young Ireland movements of the later 1840s.[7]

The Genesis of 'The Nation'

In either spring or summer 1842, while O'Connell concentrated on his duties as Lord Mayor of Dublin and allowed the Repeal movement a lull, three aspirant lawyers took a twenty minute stroll from the Dublin Four Courts to the city's adjacent 1700 acre Phoenix Park. They paused under a majestic elm, opposite Kilmainham, in whose grim prison so many patriots acknowledging their influence were to suffer or die. By a coincidence, the companions hailed from three of the four Irish provinces and three important Irish communities. Thomas Davis, a barrister of twenty-seven, represented Munster and the Protestant ascendancy. John Dillon, identical in age, came from the Connacht Catholic community. Their companion, Charles Gavan Duffy, twenty-four, was born into the embattled Catholic community of Ulster.[8]

Under the elm, Duffy, according to his own account, proposed a jointly owned weekly newspaper to promote their country's affairs more vigorously. The others promised contributions, but left it to Duffy, who already owned and edited a paper in Belfast, to provide finance. Davis, however, claimed that the decision was taken earlier on the short walk, thus implying that the proposal was not produced by Duffy out of the blue. The latter had already sounded out O'Connell's close supporter, the Co. Cork landowner W. J. O'Neill Daunt, as a likely collaborator. The sad, drunken misanthrope and gifted poet, James Clarence Mangan, eking out a miserable existence on odd jobs found for him by friends, already wrote for Duffy's Belfast *Vindicator*. Dillon suggested two able TCD students, John O'Hagan and John Pigot, the latter subsequently an intimate of Davis. Davis himself could count on John O'Callaghan, a minor writer whose *Green Book* miscellany had recently achieved considerable success. O'Connell had been impressed by its defence of Irish culture and assertion of Ireland's war-like prowess. Initiative, however, depended on the original triumvirate.

Gavan Duffy in the Making

The chosen editor of the new *Nation* was born in the northern town of Monaghan in 1816. His father exemplified the newly emergent Catholic. He owned a shop, several blocks of land and a bleaching green, symptomatic of the old linen industry which, by mid-century, became increasingly centralised in Belfast. Through his mother, Gavan Duffy had some Protestant Cromwellian settler blood. He grew up a devout Catholic. After his father's death when Charles was only ten, a liberal priest, Fr James Duffy, became his guardian. Fr Duffy permitted Charles to attend an all-Protestant school run by the Presbyterian, the Rev. John Bleckley. Here the instruction was excellent, but Duffy had to endure the gibes of his fellow-pupils resentful of a papist and tolerate the repetition of anti-Catholic jokes, differing little from those purveyed by loyalist papers in the 1980s. He held his own, gained acceptance and even found his Catholic faith strengthened by the experience. After five years, however, an unjust

flogging by the otherwise conscientious Mr Bleckley persuaded Duffy to leave the school abruptly and study at
home. He grew up with the thunder of Orange drums rever-
berating in his ears from June to August each year. The
lesson was continually reinforced that 'to be a Protestant of
any sort was a diploma of merit and a title to social rank not
to be disputed'. Persistent Orange marches 'forbade us to
forget the past'. One of Duffy's earliest memories was the
sight of a Catholic shot dead from an Orange procession.
The crime went unpunished. Raised in a community 'subject
to daily insolence and injustice', Duffy was introduced to
journalism and a more coherent nationalism by Charles
Hamilton Teeling, who had written a personal narrative of
the '98 rebellion. Duffy became convinced that Orangemen
respected only strength. 'If the Orangeman breaks the peace,
thrash him.' Duffy's clerical guardian balked at sending him
to Trinity College, Dublin, where the atmosphere was still
anti-Catholic. Instead, Duffy went in 1836 to work as a
trainee on the Dublin Catholic daily, the *Morning Register*.
He may also have worked on the pro-O'Connell *Pilot* under
Richard Barrett who was to become a bitter rival.[9]

Soon Duffy became sub-editor of the *Register*. Duffy observed O'Connell, who according to the former's retrospective
account, was a great disappointment, failing in his 'fierceness
and vulgarity' to justify the reputation of an heroic leader.
While Duffy at this time was said to have walked out of a
meeting when the Liberator was overbearing, in his youth he
was probably more susceptible to O'Connell's charisma and
bonhomie than he later admitted. In 1839 Duffy became
editor of a new Catholic bi-weekly, *The Vindicator*, in the
heart of hostile Belfast. He later bought out the paper. Decid-
ing that his political future required legal qualifications,
Duffy took terms at the King's Inns in Dublin. There he met
Dillon, ensconced in his own position on the *Morning
Register*, and later Dillon's friend, Thomas Davis. The latter
at first seemed too 'arrogant and dogmatic' for Duffy's taste,
but respect grew before the decisive walk in Phoenix Park.
Duffy admits himself a Catholic nationalist at this stage,
requiring Davis's influence to 'adopt a nationality which em-
braced the whole nation.'[10]

The Emergence of Dillon

In appearance, John Blake Dillon was the most impressive of the three Phoenix Park strollers in that spring day of 1842. In hyperbolic late Victorian style, Duffy described Dillon's 'sweet gravity of countenance, and the simple stately grace of his tall figure', while another colleague, John Mitchel, compared his form and head with the Belvedere Appollo. Dillon's family had originally been substantial tenant farmers in Roscommon. His father, the athletic Luke, a 1798 rebel unable to renew his lease, had been forced to migrate to the Mayo town of Ballaghaderrin. John claimed that he had grown up believing Ireland 'the most degraded country in the world, Mayo the most degraded county in Ireland, and the Barony of Costello [containing Ballaghaderrin] the most degraded district in Mayo'. However, a contemporary English traveller was impressed by the well-dressed people at the town's fair, and some of the latter were probably customers of the thriving Dillon business.[11]

John's second name, Blake, was the maiden name of his mother, a member of an influential Anglo-Irish Galway family. John, like Duffy in his early years, was educated at an old-style hedge school, a relic of the eighteenth-century penal laws making Catholic education theoretically impossible. Urged by his mother, Dillon attended the seminary of Maynooth, established with a government grant in 1795 to protect Catholic priests from continental revolutionary influences. Dillon, however, discovered that he had no vocation for the priesthood and decided to study law. There were no family objections to the Protestant ascendancy ethos of Trinity College, Dublin, which Dillon entered as a poor sizar. Because of his sojourn at Maynooth, Dillon was several years behind his contemporary, Thomas Davis, in both legal and University studies. The two men, however, met and became firm friends. Dillon was one of the first of Davis's contemporaries to detect the latter's hidden merits. Appropriately, Dillon succeeded Davis as president of the College Historical Society. Together they dabbled in journalism. Their letter in the *Morning Register*, condemning the dismissal of the eminent Irish chancellor, Lord Plunket, achieved considerable publicity. Dillon was appointed sub-editor of that paper. From March to June 1841 Dillon and Davis, disdaining the 'old fool' of a proprietor, converted the daily from a Whiggish Catholic organ to 'a hot missionary of insurrection, canvassing the capacity of the country for defence in guerrilla warfare', while asserting the right of revolution and opposition to British advance in India. Such radicalism proved premature; after a few weeks, Dillon and Davis were forced to seek another outlet. According to Davis, the proprietor Michael Staunton's 'timidity and our impatience spoiled the project'. Duffy's proposition, discussed under the elm tree, was particularly welcome.[12]

Dillon, like Duffy, was then essentially a liberal Catholic. Confronted by the abject poverty of Mayo's dense population, Dillon could not share the complacency of Thackeray, who, intoxicated by its wildly picturesque scenery, became indifferent to the rags of the inhabitants. On the contrary, Dillon smouldered with rage at an irresponsible aristocracy which could inflict such privations on the masses. He studied land tenures and social theories, eventually perceiving self-government as the only antidote. Dillon's views were originally as Benthamite as O'Connell's. Like Gavan Duffy, Dillon needed Davis's perspective to appreciate an integrated non-sectarian nationalism. Growing up in an Irish-speaking area John developed a passion for Irish music, especially Carolan.

The Early Development of Davis

Though Duffy had the finance and journalistic expertise, and Dillon was closest to the problems of the Irish majority, it was Davis who eventually took the lead. Like Duffy, Davis's ancestry combined the antagonistic Irish traditions, but in very different proportions. Davis's father, James Thomas, was a Royal Artillery surgeon who had served in the Napoleonic Wars. The family originally derived from Celtic Wales, but long residence in Buckinghamshire had made it identify as English. Davis's mother, Mary Atkins, was descended from Cromwellian settlers. There was a connection with the old Norman family of Howard and intermarriage with the native Irish sept of The O'Sullivan Beare. In reality,

Thomas Davis was as mixed in blood as most of his Irish contemporaries. English opinion, however, stressed the superiority of Anglo-Saxons over Celts, and Davis, signing his first verse contributions in *The Nation* as 'The Celt', was abstracting part of his pedigree to assume the cause of the underdog. John O'Donovan, author of the Irish Grammar, later reproved 'O'Davis' as Cymbric not Gaelic.[13]

Davis's early life is a case study in psycho-history. He was not only the youngest of a family of four, but a posthumous child who never knew a father. This may have accounted for an infant preoccupation with death as 'a very comfortable sort of phantasy and sweet dream'. Born in the garrison town of Mallow, Co. Cork, Davis was brought up, after the age of four, in Dublin. Despite the brevity of his domicile, he retained a sentimental attachment to his 'own dear dear Munster', which he loved 'almost to tears'. His mother was left with some means, and Thomas himself had an allowance. His family had High Tory views, implying strong anti-Catholicism. Young Thomas's dull, stuttering backwardness which made reading difficult may be partly attributed to the absence of a suitable male model and a consequent lack of rapport with his immediate environment. He grew up, a delicate boy, in an abstracted world of his own: 'When boyhood's fire was in my blood, I dreamt of ancient freemen. . . .' Like Dillon, his passion was Irish music.[14]

Davis was originally educated at Mr Mongan's then well-known private Dublin school. As a priggish boy, uninterested in games and sometimes upset by the high spirits of his mates, Thomas made little mark. Later, Davis apostrophised his attendance at 'a mixed seminary' where he learned to love his Catholic fellow-countrymen; given the social polarisation of the period, Mr Mongan's was an important experience. One of the games at which Davis blundered was hurling; he must therefore have obtained a flavour of Gaelic sport and not only cricket, a game tolerated, however, by his subsequent *Nation*. Davis gained sufficient exercise from his love of walking, combined with his delight in local place names and monuments, to give the impression, despite his delicacy, of rude health.

At sixteen, in 1831, Davis enrolled at what he called that

'laughing-stock of the literary world', and 'obstacle to the nation's march', Trinity College, Dublin, an institution which had nevertheless produced Wolfe Tone, the inspiration of the United Irishmen and the 1798 rebellion. At Trinity, Davis's old habits persisted: he read voraciously but appeared colourless and complacent to his fellows. His temperate habits excluded him from the dull and deep potations favoured by many undergraduates. An important influence on Davis was Thomas Wallis, a cynical and indolent if original student who eked out a pittance coaching his juniors. Davis graduated in 1835 with a second-class honours degree, under a reformed system, in logics and ethics, while his friend Dillon achieved first class in the same subjects in 1840. After university Davis read for the Irish bar, being called in 1838.[15]

Thomas Davis's Europe, 1836-38

Pursuit of legal qualifications took Davis to London in 1836. He spent part of the next two years travelling in England and perhaps on the continent. Though details of Davis's peregrinations are lost, biographers who claim that experience of other countries, literary or physical, finally integrated Davis's incipient nationalism are probably correct. He perfected his knowledge of French and German and devoured pertinent literature in those languages. In the late 1830s Europe was in ferment. The conservative forces, inspired by Prince Metternich, the Austrian chancellor, were desperately attempting to hold back the tide of liberalism, nationalism and revolution. The Chartist revolutionaries in 1839 threatened the British establishment with physical force; the French Bourbons had been overthrown in 1830, and opposition to the complacent bourgeois 'July monarchy' mounted. Capitalising on the Italian desire for unity and the end of Austrian control, Guiseppe Mazzini formed his impractical but inspirational 'Young Italy' and other 'Young' conspiracies. Mazzini advocated guerrilla warfare as a means to national regeneration; in his insistence that Italy must achieve its own salvation, he adopted what his Irish contemporaries called 'Ourselves Alone'. Mazzini's Young Europe in 1834 proclaimed an 'act of brotherhood' defining nationality as a sacred mission for the benefit of humanity. Meanwhile the progress of popular education encouraged European vernaculars in place of élitist languages like French and English. All this was a heady brew for Thomas Davis who ironically came from the only country where, under O'Connell, a mass proto-nationalist sentiment existed. O'Connell, often cited by European radicals, struck fear into Metternich. Even Mazzini who, dependent in exile on British goodwill, denied that Ireland had a national 'mission', frequently invoked the Liberator.[16]

European thinkers taught Davis to modify substantially the Benthamite utilitarianism, which he too shared with O'Connell. Davis now read the strongly anti-clerical Jules Michelet and Augustin Thierry. They helped to transform his romantic interest in old Gaelic society and song into a potent agent for reactivating Celtic Irish resistance to the Anglo-Saxons. Montesquieu's writings further encouraged reflection on individual national characteristics. An important precedent was the Prussian dominated German customs union, or Zollverein of 1834, which, by opposing industrial protection to the free trade demanded by England's manufactures, eventually destroyed British industrial supremacy. Thomas Carlyle, whose contempt for the entire laissez-faire philosophy was as vigorous as his low opinion of the Irish character, provided more food for Davis's thought.

Davis's Conversion to Repeal

Towards the end of his journeying years Davis prepared himself for a new phase in his career. Never a complete recluse, but always delighting in constructive sociability, Davis, according to a friend, 'passed in one stride from speculation into action, and never exhibited any deficiency in the most practical or mechanical of its duties'. Before his call to the bar in 1838, Davis had presided over a small law students' history society where he advertised Irish history. After his election in January 1835, Davis also participated less prominently in the famous College Historical Society, formerly patronised by the great Edmund Burke and Wolfe Tone. When the then frivolous and worldly society was reconstituted in early 1839, Davis became a leading member, and as its auditor closed the session in June 1839 with an address on the constitutions of England and America.[17]

A year later, in June 1840, Davis, now president, delivered a more significant farewell address. Gavan Duffy claims this as the watershed in Davis's development. Two years earlier, a friend, D. O. Madden, considered him an Englishman rather than an Irishman. In 1837, Davis had self-published a dull pamphlet on reform of the House of Lords. Davis, like O'Connell, made the relatively conservative demand for election of the Lords, not abolition of their veto.

In June 1840, Davis treated the 'Hist' to a full-scale attack on Trinity College itself, though the president had 'not, personally, one sad or angry reminiscence of old Trinity'. Davis complained of the predominantly classical curriculum of dead languages and dead societies. The traditional 'ancients v. moderns' dispute buttressed his plea for Irish identification: 'BUT, GENTLEMEN, YOU HAVE A COUNTRY.' Irish history should no longer be neglected, and the Irish language emphasised second to English. The merits of the latter, the language of seven-eighths of the country, were strongly asserted. The address advocated no political solution, but presupposed Ireland as a nation distinct from England. Davis revealed his anti-imperialism by contending that Britain's alien civilisation had ruined the natives of India. He developed this theme in a number of articles in *The Citizen*, a little magazine owned by W. E. Hudson and controlled by Thomas Wallis and other members of the 'Hist' set. Davis appealed to the professional classes to give a lead to peasants currently gaining education through the new National schools. All energy should be committed to raising Ireland from her misery. Davis insisted that Irish regeneration could only be achieved by her sons. He was as sensitive as any foreign visitor to the fact that 'the poor and the pest-houses are full, yet the valleys of her country and the streets of her metropolis swarm with the starving.' Despite a Polonius-like tone, he pricked the consciences of some of his privileged listeners.[18]

Davis's next step was crucial. Dare he now, in the teeth of local Protestant prejudice, identify openly with O'Connell?

Given his unionist background and the fact that his elder brother, Dr John Davis, showed no magnanimity to Thomas's nationalist friends, it required considerable courage to overcome his 'natural repugnance' and enter 'the big beggarman's' Repeal headquarters in the Corn Exchange Building, Burgh Quay. The Rubicon was duly crossed on 19 April 1841 when Davis and Dillon attended to enrol in the Repeal Association.

O'Connell was delighted. His efforts to give Repeal a non-sectarian image had so far achieved little success. Earlier in the year the 'rash and perilous' experiment of a visit by the Liberator to Belfast had ended in his hurried departure by ship to Scotland and the shattering of every window in Duffy's *Vindicator* office by outraged Orangemen.

Admitting Davis and Dillon to the Association, O'Connell eulogised the former: 'Mr Davis was a gentleman who had distinguished himself by opposing the abuses of Trinity College. He had already written his name on the page of Irish history and he [O'Connell] had no doubt that it would come out in bright and brilliant characters [*loud cheers*].' On the following day's meeting, Davis was accorded the honour of being voted to the chair. Though Dillon was then equally, if not more, distinguished, his accession as a Catholic to the movement passed without comment. O'Connell's hyperbole was typical of his tactics. Davis had not achieved anything exceptional at that time, though the address to the 'Hist' had clearly impressed the Liberator.[19]

The new recruits were not asked to serve any Repeal apprenticeship, but were immediately placed on the organisation's general committee. Davis himself retained some ruling caste arrogance. Barely a month after his accession to Repeal, he questioned the Liberator's handling of Michael Doheny. The latter, a self-educated but successful barrister of Tipperary peasant stock, later became one of Davis's most devoted admirers and imitators. O'Connell, unruffled by Davis's presumption, mildly asked his son, John, to assure Davis that funds were insufficient for effective agitation, and that Doheny received great delicacy of treatment. The future relations between Davis and the O'Connells on both sides saw respect mingled with frustration. Though O'Connell him-

self was pleased to acquire Davis, the latter inspired con-
temptuous banter from the Liberator's veteran agitators, two
of whom, Richard Barrett, editor of *The Pilot*, and Tom
Steele, 'the Head Pacificator', were Protestants. To such men
Davis was a simpleton who had nearly bankrupted the
Register.[20]

As O'Connell recovered from his serious reversal in the
general election of July 1841, the onus fell on Davis and
Dillon to produce a new initiative. They had just suffered
a setback in July on their resignation from the *Register*.
Fortunately, they had also met Gavan Duffy, the ultimate
answer to their problem. Meanwhile, Davis continued his
lengthy treatises in *The Citizen*, which in 1842 became the
Dublin Monthly Magazine. By 1842, British reverses in
Afghanistan and the subsequent British reprisals against
Afghan rebel groups, created passionate partisanship in
Ireland.

Davis produced an erudite, fact-packed background to
Afghan society and history. He believed these *Dublin Monthly*
articles 'very treasonable' and later claimed that opposition
to British policy had at this time been pressed to the margin
of legality.[21]

From the Phoenix Park Ramble to The Nation's First Number

All was not quite plain sailing after the Phoenix Park
meeting. Davis still favoured other projects and the differences
between him and his two colleagues were considerable. Moreover, while Davis prevailed in securing the name 'Nation' in
preference to the less dramatic 'National', several of his other
friends were unhappy. Wallis scorned the new paper as likely
to become 'the wash hand basin of O'Connell'. Educated men,
declared Wallis, never read weeklies. Far better was an
equivalent of the famous *Edinburgh Review* which provided
the intellectual underpinning of the Whig party. Old ascendancy scruples about a final descent into the Repeal mire
with the coarse-tongued O'Connell died hard. A suggestion,
worrying to O'Connell, for a Liberal party, unconnected
with Repeal, was mooted. Davis, partly influenced by his
friend Daniel Madden, a Protestant convert from Catholicism

somewhat sceptical of Repeal, prevaricated. Perhaps the unsuccessful *Evening Freeman* could be acquired for the cause to replace or reinforce the projected *Nation* weekly? Reorganisation by the *Freeman's Journal*, now partly owned by the clever young Protestant doctor, John Gray, fortunately prevented any such diversion. Davis, however, still hankered after reviving the unprofitable *Dublin Monthly Magazine*.[22]

John Dillon now forced Davis into line with some frank speaking. Dillon bluntly rejected Davis's vague suggestion that, without actually abandoning *The Nation* idea, the latter should concentrate on the formation of a social club linked with the *Dublin Monthly Magazine*. The *Magazine*, said Dillon, had been losing money for three years and was a spent force. Dillon proved correct. In June 1843 Davis sadly wrote the *Magazine*'s obituary. Dillon further deflated Davis by politely disapproving of the prospectus that Davis had written for *The Nation*: 'I think it would not answer the purpose for which it was intended.' On the other hand, a letter by Duffy in his *Vindicator* of 23 June was 'a first-rate production. A weekly paper conducted by that fellow would be an invaluable acquisition.'

Davis was chagrined at Dillon's attitude: 'We all agreed to write prospectuses. I alone wrote one.' Though Dillon's letter to Davis does not specify the precise objection to the prospectus, he probably thought Davis too tendentious. Had the obstinate fellow learned nothing from his failure to attract subscribers for the *Register*, *The Citizen* and the *Dublin Monthly Magazine*?[23]

In August 1842 Davis took the prospectus to Duffy in Belfast. There Davis wrote a new version. Duffy insisted on changing only one sentence and adding the names of the main contributors. Davis later claimed that the prospectus and an article he wrote for Duffy's *Vindicator* 'were certainly the first comprehensive expressions of a national policy printed in Ireland'. The new prospectus achieved the desired results. *The Nation* boasted in its first issue that no paper had previously started with such a huge number of subscribers. The Davis-Dillon-Duffy combination had at last produced the right formula, appealing to hitherto untapped reservoirs of idealism and curiosity.[24]

Davis's prospectus justified the publication of another weekly by suggesting that a 'NEW MIND' had grown in opposition to 'sectarian ascendancy'. *The Nation* would be more 'racy of the soil', and, 'unshackled by sect or party', lead the educated classes of all parties towards Nationality. This Nationality would not only alleviate poverty by securing self-government, but would 'purify' the people 'with a lofty and heroic love of country', embracing manners, literature and deeds. Such Nationality, comprehending all races and creeds, Protestant and Catholic, Milesian and Cromwellian, 'would be recognised by the world'.

The new nationality clearly extended beyond the utilitarian constitutionalism generally attributed to O'Connell, and the prospectus asserted an independence which appeared to distance *The Nation* from the Repeal organisation. Barrett of *The Pilot*, refused to publish a passage in the prospectus which rejected 'all services and gratitude for the past'. Nevertheless, O'Neill Daunt suggested incorporating the Liberator's son, John, as one of the signatories of the prospectus. This was done and John O'Connell MP took pride of place in large letters at the head of the contributors. Objection by rival Repeal journals is said to have persuaded John to withdraw. But Duffy's *Vindicator* in fact published the 'John O'Connell' prospectus from 31 August to 1 October 1842. It never printed the 'revised' version. There is no evidence that John O'Connell was offended by the prospectus. He was then demanding that Repeal papers put 'a little pepper into their articles'.[25]

Davis claims to have educated his collaborators in nationalism. Lip service to sectarian unity, usually traced to Tone, later became a republican cliché. In 1842, however, its implications may not have been fully realised by its advocates. When Davis went to Belfast to meet Duffy, he was full of enthusiasm for Catholic-Protestant union in 'the Athens of Ireland'. Duffy set out to initiate him into the realities of a city 'as sordid as Manchester', full of 'noisy fanatics' soured by their own bigotry. For their part, Duffy's Catholic friends were bemused by Davis, a Protestant who accepted the national tradition of the majority, and asserted the right of a Protestant to share it.

This Protestant assertion was no theoretical pose. Davis was no evangelical. Indeed, it has been said that he was a Protestant only in culture. Duffy defended him against charges of irreligion, arguing that Davis's apparent scepticism was simply a debating tactic. Davis's religion, he admitted, was more akin to the bloodless rationalism of the eighteenth century than to any more modern piety. Sometimes Davis showed an interest in Unitarianism, the most freethinking variant of Protestantism. Ironically, latitudinarian Protestants were more likely to have co-operated with O'Connell than crusading evangelicals. Davis considered English utilitarianism and 'sensualism' a greater danger to Ireland than papal supremacy, reversible within twenty years in an independent Ireland by 'a few of us laymen'. Davis's poetry, however, often celebrated the Catholic tradition, and an unpublished poem, 'Pilgrim's Hymn' appears Catholic in inspiration.

O'Connell, despite his perennial rejection of Catholic ascendancy and Catholic sectarian advantage in the Repeal Association, privately assured a future Catholic primate that ten years after Repeal the entire Protestant community would have disappeared. This was the antithesis of Davis's expectation. The Liberator was sometimes unable to maintain a non-sectarian posture. In 1839, for example, he created considerable controversy by rejoicing in the advance of English Catholicism over a 'Reformation' pronounced by some of the world's richest men. O'Connell was then supported by Duffy's *Vindicator*. Though recent critics have found Catholic triumphalism in Duffy's Belfast paper, his contemporary Barrett accused *The Vindicator* of indifference to both Catholicism and Repeal. The former criticism appears more justified, and Davis's influence does appear to have played an important part in drawing Duffy towards an all-embracing nationalism.[26]

Davis's mid-1842 visit to Belfast, when he was introduced to the Catholic bishop, was a beneficial experience for both him and Duffy. Duffy, reared as a Catholic, emphasised the need for popular education, while Davis considered that progress demanded the conversion of the educated Protestant community. Duffy, no doubt with some vehemence, insisted that there was little hope of winning Ulster Protestants to

Irish nationality. A common policy was eventually agreed. Duffy then set out to discuss the issues with Dillon. Duffy emerges as a mediator between the two original friends.

All now seemed settled. Duffy extricated himself from *The Vindicator*, from which he had saved sufficient capital to start a new paper, proposed successfully to his Belfast sweetheart, Emily McLaughlin, and moved to Dublin in the autumn of 1842. *The Nation*'s first issue was due on 8 October. This proved impossible. Davis, despite all the talks, still appeared less than fully committed. He and Dillon 'agreed at first to write one political article a week each'. Davis was out of town when an initial crisis occurred. An SOS from Duffy brought him scurrying back to Dublin. He found himself responsible for four articles, not one. Ill-wishers, like Barrett, whose *Pilot* was already attacking Duffy and hoping for the collapse of another of Tom Davis's ventures, were confounded on 15 October when the new paper finally appeared and the first impression was snapped up before noon.[27]

'This October Fifteenth, Eighteen Forty and Two'

Modern readers, straining over the dense, deteriorating print of the fourteen packed pages of *The Nation*, require an imaginative effort to recapture the excitement it created in October 1842. There were no illustrations. Articles were generally unsigned. Advertisers then relied on printed promise. Perry's Pills undertook to relieve venereal disease and virtually everything else for 2/6, while *The Nation* itself cost 6d, a high price. *The Nation* did not eschew ordinary popular news. It repeated a recent titillating *Freeman's Journal* article on 'An Elopment Extraordinary', and gave copious details of Repeal Association proceedings.

Interest centred on the editorial page where the original triumvirate of Duffy, Davis and Dillon anonymously expounded their views. As editor, Duffy led off. He demanded national feeling in place of Ireland's 'mendicant spirit' towards England, and ridiculed the swaggering English visitor. *The Nation* was not going to allow traducers of Ireland to escape with impunity. Dillon followed with an orthodox utilitarian attack on Irish landlords. If laws were intended for human happiness what was the justification for this class, 'the real cause of this unnatural, monstrous combination of poverty and profusion?' Then came Davis, reinforcing his articles in the *Dublin Monthly Magazine* with more attacks on the English invasion of Afghanistan, which had 'no pretext save a lie, and no design save aggrandisement'.

The Nation's objectives were appropriately expressed in verses contrived by J. C. Mangan and T. M. Hughes, former editor of the *London Magazine and Charivari*, *Punch*'s predecessor. Mangan's doggerel, '*The Nation*'s First Number', exuded whimsical self-confidence:

> 'Tis a great day, and glorious, O Public! for you —
> This October Fifteenth, Eighteen Forty and Two!

Mangan, writing no doubt to order, epitomised the respective messages of the three progenitors. For Duffy there was popular education:

> Be it ours to stand forth and contend in the van
> Of truth's legions for freedom that birthright of man.
> Shaking off the dull cobwebs that else might encumber
> Our weapon — the pen — in *The Nation*'s First Number.

Dillon's agrarian preoccupation received due consideration:

> We assume a New Era — be this our first news —
> When the serf-grinding Landlords shall shake in their shoes.

As for Davis, his wider perspectives were noted.

> Whereso'er TRUTH and LIBERTY's flags are unfurl'd,
> From the Suir to the Tweed, from the Boyne to the Humber,
> Raise one shout of Applause from *The Nation*'s First
>   Number.

When he wrote of 'a bloodless yet mighty reform' emerging 'from the flood of the Popular Storm!', Mangan was talking the language of O'Connell, rather than Mazzini. Hughes reinforced the message with a poem, 'We Want no Swords':

> With conquering MIND alone we fight —
>   'Tis all we need for freedom!

When Hughes scorned 'a victory stained with blood — barbarian blood or Roman', he outdid O'Connell's repeated declarations that Repeal was not worth a single drop of blood. Whatever their subsequent misgivings, there is no doubt that the triumvirate saw *The Nation* as an integral part of O'Connell's Repeal movement, and remained a loyal auxiliary for the first year of publication.

O'Connell and the Early 'Nation'

Duffy later maintained that *The Nation*'s immediate achievement was to introduce critical discussion of hitherto unchallenged statements of O'Connell and his entourage. His rival Barrett, whose circulation was only one-tenth of *The Nation*'s, partly endorsed Duffy's assertion, by arguing that Repeal was not mentioned in *The Nation*'s first five issues and that the new paper had only jumped on the bandwagon when the cause appeared in the ascendant. Conflict between *The Pilot* and *The Nation* began in early 1843, when the former accused the latter of being a clone of the anti-Repeal *Monitor* in whose office it was printed. To Daunt, *The Nation* versus *The Pilot* was a 'Damascus sword against a billhook'. Such rivalries between Repeal papers, though he sometimes tried to check them, did not worry the Liberator unduly. However, there was a basic difference between *The Pilot*'s discovery of 'two Nations on one soil', which identified Irishness and Catholicism, and *The Nation*'s all-embracing nationalism.[28]

The vital difference was at first neglected and *The Nation* followed the same pattern as other Repeal journals, borrowing articles from them. Moreover, early *Nation* leaders addressed topics previously ventilated in papers like *The Freeman's Journal* and *The Pilot*, or at the weekly meetings of the Repeal Association. There O'Connell, after receipt of subscriptions and membership applications from around the country, gave his inspirational lay sermon. The Liberator skilfully wove recent events into a standard discourse emphasising the economic disaster of the Union, England's current difficulties at home and abroad, the iniquities of the land system, the demand for security of tenure, and the traditional perfidy of the 'Saxon'. While exalting the potential power and moral authority of the Irish people, the Liberator repudiated crime, physical force and Ribbonism, and demanded temperance and discipline in Irish ranks. Within such comprehensive parameters *The Nation* editorials vigorously developed the flights of O'Connell's rhetoric. Dillon's concern with land tenure and Davis's with British imperialism followed established Repeal lines. Even historical nationalism received a boost in early 1843 from O'Connell's *A Memoir of Ireland, Native and Saxon*.

Inevitably, differences of emphasis appeared. Duffy's concentration on popular education and uplift as opposed to the Liberator's tactical flattery of the Irish people's physical and moral strength was a good example. O'Connell was sceptical of local Repeal reading rooms and associated programmes of national training. Repeal wardens he saw mainly as fund collectors. Eventually the Liberator voted Repeal funds for reading rooms, but baulked at systematic rules for their organisation.[29]

Different conceptions of Irish educational needs led to O'Connell's irritation at *The Nation*'s praise of writers he deemed anti-national, such as William Carleton, William Maxwell, William Maginn, 'Fr Prout', and Charles Lever. Several of these writers painted unflattering portraits of their fellow-countrymen which could be interpreted either as pro-British propaganda, or a call to self-improvement. However, when Duffy complained that Samuel Lover's *Handy Andy* provided stage Irish stereotypes for English ridicule, the Liberator upheld Lover as an excellent novelist.[30]

If O'Connell was ambivalent between satisfaction at *The Nation*'s stimulus to Repeal and fear that it would preach extremism, Duffy and his friends were no less ambivalent in their attitude to O'Connell. Duffy claimed that from the outset his group feared O'Connell's ruthless record of crushing supporters and periodicals who demonstrated too much independence. The Liberator's coolness to Repeal reading rooms, likely to increase *Nation* circulation, is relevant here. Duffy's subsequent assistant, Thomas D'Arcy McGee, maintained that O'Connell criticised *The Nation* from its first issue, 'but not very much' as he considered it unlikely to last. But Daunt, the mediator, early told Duffy that the Liberator feared that *The Nation* writers were trying to undermine him. Duffy completely rejected the suggestion. Nevertheless, he rejoiced that *The Nation*'s success made suppression by O'Connell impossible.[31]

On the other hand, Duffy portrays a different O'Connell operating in the large Repeal committee, which included the chief writers of *The Nation*. There the Liberator was tolerant and reasonable, listening to diverging viewpoints and accepting gracefully those majority decisions which went against him. John Mitchel, another critic of O'Connell, remembered the Liberator at the centre of a jovial group 'with his fatherly smile for all around, his cordial greeting and kind word to everyone who comes up, especially to the young.'[32]

The Nation organisers played a fully supportive role at the weekly Repeal public meetings at Burgh Quay. The editors of the Repeal journals were clearing agencies for subscriptions, donations and applications for new membership. These were presented with the maximum publicity and written up in detail in the press. Duffy claimed uniqueness in publishing Repeal proceedings free of charge. At the Repeal Association meetings he had a special brief, as former *Vindicator* editor, for contributions from Ulster. Invariably, the progress of the movement in that province was exaggerated, even by Duffy, with frequent reports of Protestant conversion to Repeal.

Davis, *The Nation* spokesman on Protestants, acted only as Duffy's understudy at open Repeal meetings, processing subscriptions and membership applications in the latter's absence. He spoke briefly and infrequently, not considering himself an orator and vastly preferring action in the committee room above the hall. As a mark of respect, Duffy was voted to the chair at a weekly Repeal meeting in late 1842 and Davis in early 1843.[33]

There was, despite the persistent antagonism between *The Nation* and *The Pilot*, relatively good Repeal teamwork in 1842-43. The chief *Nation* contributors, nicknamed 'The Clique' by *The Pilot*, secretly attended 'frugal' supper parties in their different houses on Saturday nights. The original triumvirate was joined by John Pigot, 'a bright handsome boy', who proved very influential behind the scenes, and John O'Hagan, 'modest and reticent', as an inner core of management, but other contributors were also invited. At supper each individual submitted his ideas to constructive criticism. Though the responsibility of contributors for their own opinions was advertised, the weekly suppers, often followed on the Sunday by rambles to places of historical interest, created intellectual cohesion. It was not all journalism: 'we chaffed a little — joked a little — and Americanized a little'. Fr Mathew's influence ensured that no stimulants beyond witty conversation were required. The intoxicating influence of Thomas Carlyle's literary style and scorching denunciation of humbug later led to the suppers being dubbed 'tea and Thomas'. Here Davis was in his element and became the recognised leader of the group.[34]

Duffy, though some colleagues found him selfish, was almost as fertile in ideas. On *The Vindicator* he had discovered the value of patriotic verse in consciousness raising. He proposed the same tactics to Davis and Dillon when planning *The Nation*. At an early supper Duffy read his poem 'Fag an Bealach' (clear the way). Taking his theme from the cry of traditional faction fighters, Duffy converted it to a call for unity against the invader:

> Know, ye suffering brethren ours,
> > Might is strong, but Right is stronger.
> Saxon wiles or Saxon pow'rs
> > Can enslave our land no longer;

Davis had published no verse before being approached by Duffy. Like Dillon he agreed to try some. While Dillon was dissatisfied by his own initial efforts, Davis threw himself into the manufacture of patriotic verse with gusto, translating Goethe, Stolberg and other continental writers when his own invention failed. His first poem, 'My Grave' a fey evocation of place and patriotism, was published in *The Nation*'s third number with Duffy's trend-setting 'Fag an Bealach'.

Shortly before the deadline for the issue of 19 November 1842, Davis thrust the manuscript of a full-scale ballad, 'Lament for the death of Owen Roe O'Neill' into a surprised

Duffy's hands. The story of Owen's poisoning by the 'Saxon' who feared his cold steel established Davis as a patriotic poet. Celebrating Davis's centenary in 1914, W. B. Yeats saw real inspiration in this poem; he suggested that Davis could have been a great poet in Elizabethan days when the common language was sufficiently vigorous to enable men of action to achieve results obtainable later only by full-time writers. After Owen Roe, verse poured from Davis's pen. Meanwhile, Dillon's contributions petered out in early 1843, as he concentrated on his legal practice, and Duffy became increasingly preoccupied with the paper's management. Davis found himself writing most of the prose. His 'fertility', as Duffy said, 'made us independent of help'. For his efforts Davis received about 400 pounds a year, twice the great T. B. Macaulay's payment as a regular contributor to the famous *Edinburgh Review*.[35]

Like O'Connell, Davis was an admirer of Thomas Moore and set out to create a more popular version of Moore's poetry for the masses. Other models were Burns, Berenger and T. B. Macaulay, whose *Lays of Ancient Rome* were published in late 1842 and reviewed critically but appreciatively by Davis. Macaulay, in fact, accepted the beauty of *The Nation*'s verse, though not its sentiments. Duffy, Davis, Mangan and volunteer poets soon built up so effective a body of verse that it was published in early 1843 as *The Spirit of the Nation*. The collection sold rapidly and aroused a storm of controversy as a clever but pernicious attempt to foment rebellion by stirring up anti-English feeling. Samuel Ferguson, then a sympathetic unionist, complained that 'some of these fellows long to stick their skeans into the bowels of the Saxon'. *The Nation* retorted that 'we sup not on pickled Saxons' and rapped excessively bellicose volunteer poets in its 'answers to correspondents' column.[36]

Though O'Connell later claimed to have been embarrassed by *The Nation*'s warlike sentiments, clear differentiation was difficult in 1843. His sons, John and Maurice, contributed to *The Spirit of the Nation*. *The Pilot* also contained its quota of militant verse, and poets like the prolific Jean de Jean Frazer published in both outlets. John O'Connell, who had signed the original *Nation* prospectus, eventually contributed some prose in 1842 when, according to Duffy, the paper's future was already assured. His father preceded him with 'A Repeal Catechism' in several instalments. Davis, irritated at the exclusion of his own articles, agreed that the Liberator's participation would increase circulation. Later instalments appeared first in Richard Barrett's more loyal *Pilot*. However Daunt's two *Nation* articles, which Davis considered bad, ardently defended O'Connell's acceptance of the Repeal tribute.[37]

By early 1843 therefore, despite tension between O'Connell's veterans and the new men, most of the differences appeared fairly minor. There was concern at *The Nation*'s support for anti-national or anti-Catholic Irish writers, bellicose poems, Davis's advocacy of a French alliance, and the stand of Duffy and Dillon against O'Connell on the principle of a poor law. But the most potentially divisive issue was religion.

Several small incidents indicated trouble to come. When Duffy's former paper, the Belfast *Vindicator*, now edited by Kevin Buggy of Kilkenny, an occasional *Nation* poet, declared Protestantism 'a miserable heresy', there were rumblings in the Repeal Association. Even Duffy played down the idea of censure against his friend Buggy, who had to operate in a 'hot moral atmosphere'. Repealers tried to be fair, but non-sectarianism was difficult in practice. On the other side, Davis aroused ire by a chance remark equating Muslim and Christian crusades. Surely *The Nation* was not going to pander to rationalism? Later full-scale denunciations of its 'infidelity' were levelled against *The Nation*.[38]

First Steps in Secular Nationalism

Davis, however, had already begun what he considered *The Nation*'s first comprehensive examination of nationality since the prospectus and *The Vindicator* article. His 'Letters of a Protestant on Repeal', were published anonymously in *The Nation* between December 1842 and December 1843, and developed in other articles. Davis not only exalted Irish nationalism as 'a spiritual essence', transcending mundane considerations, but stressed the need for Protestant participation to make it a reality. His almost arrogant assertion of Protestant strength and influence, making Catholic ascendancy impossible, was repudiated by *The Pilot*. It maintained that Protestantism was dying out, even in Ulster.[39]

Despite his private letters to prelates, in the public Repeal Association meetings the Liberator's views resembled those of Davis. O'Connell persistently denied, in his speeches and in his *Memoir*, that Catholics had ever persecuted when they had the power in Ireland. Davis fully supported this view; his best piece of historical writing, 'The Patriot Parliament of 1689', was written to support the non-persecution doctrine. On the other hand, O'Connell anticipated Davis's 'Letters of a Protestant on Repeal'. In November 1842 the Liberator, after his usual examples of Catholic tolerance in Ireland and elsewhere, insisted: 'But were not the Protestants of Ireland a strong body in themselves, capable of maintaining their own right, if necessary, and would they not have an immense majority in the [Irish post-Repeal] House of Lords, as well as the monarch in their favour?' This approximated Davis's view that Protestants 'are and will be right well able to take care of themselves'. A few days later, a Repeal Association report, signed by O'Connell, but doubtless influenced by Davis, informed Irish Protestants that Ireland was also their native land, and called on them, instead of sharing English hostility to the land of their birth, to participate in 'a communion of benevolent affection, and genuine Irish patriotism'. O'Connell similarly asserted preference for the pre-emancipation Protestant-dominated Irish parliament of the late eighteenth century to the union. For his part, Davis refused to condemn the late eighteenth-century Irish Protestants who wrung independence for themselves by 'the terror of arms' while denying emancipation to the Catholic majority, then slaves corrupted by domination. He believed that only in 1828, when the Irish masses proved themselves by their resolution, not by their numbers, did they make themselves worthy of emancipation. Davis, who cited Leonidas, Brutus, and Washington as examples of great spirits served by helots, seemed to be approaching an élitism, if not racism, modified by his axiom that a corrupted people was capable of regeneration through education.

O'Connell also implied racism in his view that 'the Irishman who consented to be governed by Englishmen was a slave, and ought to be blackened by a burnt cork, as nature had not made a negro of him already'.[40]

In several of the later 'Letters' Davis also remained very close to O'Connell's preoccupations, denouncing, for example, England's deliberate campaign to provide 'an unjust and falsely disparaging account of the resources, military achievements, character, and abilities of the Irish'. Again, despite his later claim that it was spirit, not numbers, that decided a nation's claim to freedom, Davis's February letters recapitulated O'Connell's demonstration that Ireland's population was greater than a number of contemporary European states. These views were somewhat inconsistent with the criticism that the Liberator emphasised existing Irish purity, rather than the need for national regeneration.[41]

If Davis showed too much arrogance as a Protestant Repealer, he was also taking literally the Liberator's political exaggeration in the euphoric Repeal year. Problems were to occur when views privately expressed had to be reconciled with public rhetoric. Even Davis's first expressions of cultural nationalism, as in his declaration of the Irishman's duty 'to discard all Anglicanism — all the peculiarly English notions of England, of Ireland, and of other lands, as they are, and as they were', did not seriously conflict with O'Connell's current oratory.

Towards Confrontation — Old and Young Ireland, 1843-45

The Repeal Year

While Davis composed his early 'Letters of a Protestant', O'Connell at the first Repeal Association meeting of 1843 boldly declared it the Repeal Year. The omens seemed excellent. According to the Liberator's principle of 'England's difficulty is Ireland's opportunity', England was strained. France and the USA appeared hostile; Britain was over-committed imperially in India, China, Syria, and elsewhere; hostile tariffs were appearing on the continent, and Britain's own economy was sagging. O'Connell outlined a programme of agitation in the country instead of parliament, the recruitment of three million Repealers and the eventual carrying of Repeal by moral force. He accompanied his ultimate objective with five reforms: abolishing tithes, establishing fixity of tenure, protecting native manufactures, extending the franchise and introducing the secret ballot, and uprooting the poor law, itself rendered redundant by the encouragement to manufactures. The *Nation* group, though in general agreement, was not entirely happy with this programme; some sympathetic Protestant gentry might be alienated. The young men also opposed the total elimination of a poor law. Duffy, refuting his rival Barrett, believed the present system better than no poor law at all. A *Nation* leader by Davis claimed that O'Connell had compromised by agreeing to amelioration of the poor laws.[1]

As the leading members of the *Nation* staff were members of the Repeal Committee, the provenance of certain ideas is obscure. Dillon, for example, editorially endorsed O'Connell's strategy, maintaining that a distracted England could not resist Irish demands. O'Connell's decision, to guage support by visiting the whole country, was upheld as preferable to ten years of futile parliamentary debate. Davis emphasised England's difficulties overseas, imperial and foreign (the USA and France). He quoted O'Connell's recent *Memoir* showing Ireland's gain from past Anglo-French conflict. With 42,000 Irish in the British Army, coercion of Repealers was hazardous.[2]

The new Repeal campaign took fire after a late February debate in the Dublin Corporation. O'Connell, no longer lord mayor, rejected, in a celebrated oration, the legality of the 1800 Act of Union and lamented its economic effects. He reiterated his non-sectarianism: 'I include all — Protestant, Presbyterian, and Catholic. My object is to benefit all — to do good to my countrymen of every persuasion alike, and to confer on every man the advantages that I seek for those who agree with me in religious opinions.' Like Davis's most recent 'Letters of a Protestant' the Liberator demonstrated that Ireland's resources were greater than many independent European powers possessed. On the other side, Isaac Butt accepted that Repeal was not synonymous with Catholic ascendancy. However, he probed the inconsistency of O'Connell's contention that a House of Lords would defend Protestant rights, while Repeal was committed to a five-point social programme which no conservative would accept without revolution. This endorsed the young men's original criticism; soon afterwards O'Connell, confronted by a Repealer objecting to commitment to other policies, declared 'give him a Repealer, even if he be an Orangeman, and he would honour and respect him.' Davis, both publicly and privately, delighted in the Corporation debate which appeared proof of Ireland's self-governing ability. He detected patriotism even in Repeal opponents.[3]

Monster Meetings: Prelude to Insurrection?

More Catholic bishops joined the Association as the movement 'caught the public's fancy'. O'Connell continued his travels throughout Ireland. The crowds grew. At Limerick on 19 April the audience was estimated at 120,000; four days later O'Connell gathered 150,000 at Kells. At Cork on 21 May the press reported half a million. The Repeal rent peaked at £2000 a week. *The Nation*, whose leading figures rarely attended these demonstrations, exulted. All O'Connell's speeches appeared in detail. In late April Davis rejoiced that Munster, which Wolfe Tone had said would be difficult to organise for nationality, had shown itself solid for Repeal. A week later Davis in 'Something is Coming' warned the Irish people to avoid premature insurrections and concentrate on meetings, organisation and the collection of funds. O'Connell's plan for an unofficial Council of 300 to draft a Repeal bill was 'the wisest, the boldest, and the most pregnant with great results' of all his policies. Davis reiterated the lesson that past Irish victories depended on England's troubles, and detailed her current embarrassments. Peel's threat of coercion and insistence that Repeal was out of the question did not dismay *The Nation*. Davis denounced the proposed disarming bill and published an open letter to the the Duke of Wellington warning him of England's American and Chartist troubles. Like O'Connell, Davis suggested the suitability of Ireland for guerrilla warfare. The landowner, Shine Lawlor, then rejected Repeal as certain to end in bloodshed.[4]

Was Davis as confident in private as he appeared on paper? Correspondence with his sceptical friend, D. O. Madden, indicates that he was. The latter appeared to Davis to underrate Ireland's resources: a united and bold Catholic population, sympathetic bishops, a neutral Protestant working class, educated Protestants whose fear of Catholic ascendancy alone separated them from Repeal, American assistance, and Irish soldiers in the British Army. The movement, Davis believed, would not fail through its leadership; 'even O'C. [onnell] has looked very far ahead this time and knows he cannot retreat.' Madden, however, remained unconvinced, pointing out that Peel, fully backed by English public opinion, was awaiting the right moment and would be ruthless in his use of force. 'Depend upon it that O'Connell will be defeated in this business.' Davis retorted that Madden underestimated the extent of the Irish gentry's movement towards Repeal and had no proof that 'England is dead against us.' On the contrary, he believed half the English population would support Ireland's peaceful protest. Davis still anticipated O'Connell's success as in 1829, 'by the power of fighting, not the practice of it'. If a fight did nevertheless come, Davis expected England to be much weakened in the contest. Though hindsight shows Madden closer to the truth than Davis, contemporary Irish unionist journals were furious at Peel's comparative inaction and sometimes suspected him of conniving at revolution.[5]

Duffy's subsequent comments on the exchange with Madden suggest that Davis wished to avoid war, but if not 'to wage it to the last gasp.' The public and private views of *The Nation*'s promoters differed little in 1843. When the issue of absolute non-violence was raised by Ebenezer Shackleton, a Quaker Repealer, who objected to the commemoration of Irish battles on the Association membership card, Davis answered with an editorial, 'The Morality of War'. Davis repudiated any desire to encourage war, but claimed that in a just war there was 'more of self-restraint, more contempt for bodily suffering, more of high impulse, more of greatness achieved for its own great sake — more, in short, of heroism, in war than in almost any other human occupation.' He quoted Dr Thomas Arnold's view that 'a sound military system is no mean school of virtue.' Davis might technically wish to avoid war, but his mind was full of warlike images and he was fast becoming a keen armchair strategist. A few days after Davis's justification for war, O'Connell significantly uttered 'the Mallow defiance' when he challenged the British government to stride to victory over his dead body. Throughout the Repeal movement in 1843 there was an ambivalence between the conscious objective of a strong and efficient passive resistance organisation, and an impulse to war and military victory.[6]

The events and statements of 1843 led to the prosecution of the leading Repealers later in the year and, ostensibly, a Repeal split in 1846. In the campaign of what were described by the horrified London *Times* as O'Connell's 'monster meetings', there was close liaison between the *Nation* group and O'Connell's family and closest advisers. Duffy suggests that the young *Nation* men 'bore the same relation to O'Connell as the heads of the public service bear to the cabinet. They projected much of the work announced from the platform, executed a liberal proportion of the agenda authorised in committee, and constantly brought the supreme stimulus of imagination to the cause.' He credits them with planning monster meetings at historic sites, bands, banners and the mustering of the people into ordered ranks. His colleague, Michael Doheny, excluding Duffy from the inner circle, claimed that the monster meetings had long been a design of Davis, Dillon and himself. They were intended as secret military manoeuvres, not unlike those of the pre-1916 Irish Volunteers, manipulated by a secret IRB group while nominally under moderate control.[7]

The Cashel monster meeting on 21 May is particularly important in this context. Though there had already been several larger demonstrations, Cashel is sometimes claimed as the first real 'monster' meeting. Michael Doheny, as one of the most influential Repealers in the area, was a leading organiser. The significance of the gathering, estimated at 300,000 and exceeded at the time only by Cork, lay in the organisation which brought out each parish in an orderly display of quasi-military might. O'Connell's speech on the occasion contained the usual repudiation of violence, but opponents were not convinced. Doheny claimed that the men of Tipperary had defied the hostile former Chancellor, Lord Brougham, and threats of physical force to put down Repeal. The unionist *Warder* greeted the demonstration with an article, 'The Repeal Insurrection'. 'This chronic rebellion spreads far and wide through this country.' It lamented that the government allowed treason to thrive. Davis's rough and ready doggerel, never anthologised, 'The March to Tipperary' was considered almost as menacing as the demonstration itself.[8]

> We carry no gun,
> Yet devil a one
> But knows how to march in Tipperary.

As the unionist Frederick Shaw said in the House of Commons, *The Nation* was proving Dr Johnson's aphorism, 'I don't care who makes the laws, if I could but write the ballads.' Isaac Butt, in an anti-Repeal meeting in Dublin, castigated such verse to encourage a county renowned for its agrarian crime. It was, moreover, only a few weeks since *The Nation*'s anonymous publication of J. K. Ingram's glorification of the United Irishmen, 'Who Fears to Speak of '98' ('Memory of the Dead'). For his part, Davis only thinly veiled the military significance of the demonstration. 'The silent and stern assemblage of orderly men, like the myriads of Tipperary, or like one of Napoleon's armies, is a noble sight and a mighty power.' Davis later showed considerable concern that Irish demonstrators march in step at such meetings. Cowardly, undisciplined 'scolding mobs' were a different matter.[9]

Events moved quickly after the Tipperary meetings. Seven Repeal magistrates, including Lord ffrench, were dismissed as Justices of the Peace, and the 'Radical Whig' MP for Limerick, William Smith O'Brien, who, according to the unionist *Dublin Evening Mail* on 17 April had 'always hitherto shown himself to be a strenuous anti-repealer', resigned his own commission in protest. The Repeal rent rose sharply from £600 in that month to over £2000. Archbishop Murray of Dublin denied that all the Catholic bishops were Repealers, but this failed to reduce the growing enthusiasm. In early April, the Lord Lieutenant, Lord De Grey, had already informed Peel that Ireland was on the brink of disaster.[10]

The Nation group had clearly played a large part in these developments, but as so much evidence comes from their own sources, it is important not to exaggerate. The *Dublin Evening Mail* quoted Barrett's *Pilot* frequently as one of the most seditious and violent journals of the time, though the more intellectual *Warder* had a preference, quoted by Duffy in his history, for *The Nation* as the most dangerous disseminator of treason. The other prominent members of the Repeal committee, such as John O'Connell, Tom Steele and Captain Edward Broderick, were hardly as lacking in resourcefulness as Duffy claims. When serious divisions arose, *The Nation* men did not always succeed in carrying things their way. Nevertheless, they were reinforced at the end of April by several very able newcomers.

Michael Doheny now formally joined the Repeal Association on Davis's invitation. Doheny, who, according to John Mitchel, had 'a broad, honest Milesian face', was born in

1805, the son of a poor farmer in Fethard, Co. Tipperary. He was almost totally self-educated with a mere nine months at school after reaching the advanced age of 21. He scraped together sufficient money by tutoring and journalism to study law in Dublin and London, where he was called as a Middle Temple barrister in 1838. Returning to Cashel, Doheny married and developed a reputation defending poor tenants against exacting landlords. Writing poetry and prose for *The Nation*, Doheny was criticised for clumsily modelling his style on Davis, but, unlike Davis, he had the Irish language. Doheny was always particularly ardent in his assertion of Catholicism.

Another member of the group, joining on 29 May 1843, was Thomas MacNevin, an almost exact contemporary of Davis who, born in either Dublin or Galway, went up to Trinity College, Dublin in 1831 as a Catholic, graduated BA in 1839 and was called to the bar a year later. MacNevin preceded Davis as auditor (1837-38) and president (1838-39) of the College Historical Society. He had, however, no contact with Davis or *The Nation* writers before joining the Repeal Association. He was to prove a brilliant, if florid, orator, and demonstrated a flair for patriotic history and *Nation* journalism. Short in physique but agile, MacNevin's auburn hair was traced to Danish ancestry. He died in 1848 after a tragic battle against brain disease.[11]

Denny Lane and Michael John Barry hailed from Cork. Both were barristers, the former an 1839 graduate of Trinity College. Barry, though ultra-cautious in action, proved himself an exceptionally vigorous poet, writer and speaker. He abandoned Repeal after 1848. Lane in 1843 had the advantage of being the only child of a Cork distiller, not yet required to take over the family business interests. Another important Repeal acquisition was John O'Hagan, Catholic, lawyer and Trinity graduate. Born at Newry in 1822, he moved ultimately from patriotic poetry to high judicial office.

Meanwhile excitement mounted at the monster meetings. Altogether there were 37 demonstrations. The 'Mallow defiance' was followed, amongst many others, by historically resonant meetings at Tara, seat of the ancient high kings, and Mullaghmast, where 400 Leinster chieftains had been murdered in 1567, allegedly by the viceroy, the Earl of Sussex. The Tara gathering was conveniently calculated at exactly one million, but 750,000 is a more likely number. Mounted marshals patrolled them, O'Connell significantly remarked, 'as if they were in battalions'. In *The Nation*, Duffy also drew military analogies. 'It was a sight, not grand alone, but appalling — not exciting merely pride but fear. Such an army — for they had the steadiness and order of trained men — no free state would willingly see on its bosom if it were not composed of its choicest citizens.' The Irish Volunteers who had exacted independence for the Irish parliament from Britain in 1782 were one-third of their number.[12]

Not all, however, saw the meetings as warlike. The Quaker, Ebenezer Shackleton, who had clashed with Davis on absolute non-violence, felt 'inexpressible delight' at another August monster meeting at Baltinglass. Like Duffy, however, Shackleton attributed the good order to Fr Mathew's ministrations.[13]

O'Connell invariably denounced violence and Ribbonism; his rejection of a single drop of blood became wearisome through repetition. But what did he really mean? Was his movement true passive resistance or was it merely a prelude to a military campaign? The Liberator himself obscured the issue by accepting violence in defence, not the pure Quaker doctrine of turning the other cheek. Unionist papers like *The Warder* assumed that, while *The Nation* writers were in fact dangerous revolutionaries, O'Connell himself was too cowardly to hazard any form of violence; hence the verbal qualifications to his apparently militaristic statements.[14]

Such militancy was reinforced at Mullaghmast, which *The Nation* promised would be 'the monster of the Monster Meetings'. Mullaghmast, a symbol of Saxon treachery, was intended as a practice muster of Leinster towns. O'Connell was duly crowned with a Repeal cap designed by the sculptor, John Hogan, and the painter, Henry McManus.[15]

The Clontarf Anticlimax

Peel's government now decided to strike. The next meetings,

for which Duffy was one of the secretaries, was planned for the site of Brian Boru's victory over the Danes at Clontarf. An advertisement in *The Nation* spoke of 'Repeal cavalry', thus giving the government a pretext to ban the demonstration, which O'Connell immediately called off. Before the proclamation was certain, Duffy in *The Nation* ambiguously advised its receipt 'without dismay'. The Boston Tea Party, he suggested, was not the work of a passionate mob. When the proclamation was published and the arrests of O'Connell and leading Repealers were imminent, *The Nation* lamely suggested: 'trust in O'Connell and fear not'. The paper, despite criticism of its religious indifferentism, gladly committed the safety of the country to the Catholic clergy, who had never failed the Irish people in their time of peril. It praised the Repeal organisation for averting the 'Peterloo massacre' desired by the government. Elsewhere, Davis complacently surveyed a year's work, congratulating *The Nation* on its unique non-sectarianism and resolute pursuit of nationality: 'We succeeded because we were in earnest.'[16]

This passive acceptance of the ban complicates the claim by Duffy and Doheny that *The Nation* group had, on the Repeal committee, demanded resistance. They were overborne by a small majority influenced by the Liberator. The actions of Davis evoked bitter controversy in 1848. *The Pilot*, partly supported by John O'Connell, accused Davis of cowardice, maintaining that he had fled in terror to the west of Ireland at the prospect of indictment. John O'Connell reported how Davis, in great agitation, had begged his father to destroy all papers before inevitable arrest. The Liberator, according to John, had coolly refused to concede his rights. John Dillon defended Davis. The latter had expected insurrection on the arrest of O'Connell. Davis, a student of military tactics, secretly visited Castlebar to spy out the land. He naturally concealed his presence. But such a temporary withdrawal would not 'have prevented prosecution. The Dillon and John O'Connell accounts are quite compatible. If Davis really anticipated rebellion, excitement, agitation, and a demand for the destruction of papers were natural. *The Nation* articles earlier in the year, and the subsequent arguments of his colleagues, after their break with the O'Connells, indicated that the young men expected O'Connell to resist arrest. The Liberator's own insistence on the legitimacy of defensive violence seemed clearly applicable to an unjust prosecution. But in his emphasis to Davis on his legal rights O'Connell finally dropped tactical ambiguity and opted for a defence in the courts, not a 'battle line'. The Liberator had misled, not only the public, but even close associates on the Repeal committee. The young men may have been willingly misled in the face of much evidence, but their delusion could have been quickly terminated by O'Connell had it suited his purposes to do so.[17]

The disillusionment of Davis and his friends was heightened by the delirious exaltation of the unionist press at the discomfiture of the Repealers. 'A bold and decisive blow has been struck, and Repeal, if it be not extinct, is breathing its last.' For months the unionists had lamented the effusion of rebellious verse and militant oratory. The time for ridicule and parody had at last arrived. Moore's *Irish Melodies* provided a new cue:

> The tongue that once through Tara's halls
>   The soul of treason shed
> Now hangs so mute, for fear of squalls,
>   That Dan, poor soul, seems fled.

and,

> Believe me if all those red coats and bright arms,
>   That I tremblingly gaze on to-day
> Got the rout by to-morrow, to ease our alarms
>   Like last year's rent passing away,
> I would fool thee again as I fooled thee before,
>   Bully, swagger, and lie as of old;
> Talk treason as loud as I did at Lismore,
>   As at Mallow, be haughty and bold.

The 'Spirit of the Nation' was similarly lampooned.

> The 'Freeman's' prose, the 'Nation's' muse,
>   Have spread our boastings far and wide;
> Through Gallia rang our wild halloos,
>   That boomed across the Atlantic tide. . . .

> Give back our shillings, craven Dan;
>   We'll serve no mean-souled Beggarman.[18]

Most galling was the fact that the unionist press had apparently been closer to the truth than *The Nation* group in its contemptuous insistence, throughout the period of monster meetings, that O'Connell would never hazard his own personal safety. In attacking O'Connell's cowardice the unionists were partly correct; the Liberator's fears, however, lay in the world to come. As he told a Repeal meeting, with obvious reference to his fatal duel in 1815, he had too much blood on his soul already to risk responsibility for shedding more.[19]

Like it or not, *The Nation* writers had to accept the situation. Not only were O'Connell, his son John, T. M. Ray, the Repeal Association secretary, Tom Steele, and two priests amongst the nine men arrested for sedition, but the editors of the Repeal newspapers were included. Duffy had therefore to assume total responsibility for the verse and political articles, many of which had been written by Davis. 'Something is Coming' and the answer to Ebenezer Shackleton's pacifism, 'The Morality of War', were certainly by Davis. This vulnerability of Repeal editors led in 1844 to their formal resignation from the Association. Duffy, though he had apparently suggested the idea, was unhappy to leave the Association where he had been very active. Gray of the *Freeman's Journal* and Barrett of *The Pilot* also retired. Though in close touch with other members of the Repeal Committee, Duffy's physical absence from the Association was a setback for *The Nation* group. Not till 1845 did Davis participate more frequently at general Association meetings. In 1844, the young men's viewpoint was usually given by Thomas MacNevin.[20]

As the 'traversers' were all released on bail, there was no immediate change in the Repeal routine after Clontarf, apart from the abrupt abandonment of the monster meetings, the Council of 300 (or Preservative Society), and the arbitration courts, established in the wake of the dismissal of Repeal JPs. The young men strenuously resisted O'Connell's attempt to follow his old tactic of disbanding a threatened movement and establishing a new society, possibly based on the muted objective of federalism, in its place. Such action might have prejudiced the case to be fought in the courts to maintain the boasted legality of all O'Connell had done in 1843.

The movement was drifting, despite *The Nation*'s efforts to maintain patriotic spirits. When Davis declared in a December editorial, 'we are on the right road', the *Evening Mail* sarcastically enquired, to what? Prison? It wrote the epitaph for the Repeal Year which had secured Ireland neither a parliament, nor even a Council of 300, but had certainly filled the Association coffers. Davis now admitted that even those who considered liberty worth 'a sea of blood' would have to agree with the Liberator that 'it is neither needful nor politic for you to embark in a war with your oppressor.'

What had gone wrong? In one of the last editorials of a fateful year *The Nation* suggested that there was 'too much menace for our state of preparation'. Numbers had been exaggerated, and far from showing military discipline the crowds attending demonstrations had failed to keep in step, often broke ranks and were not organised in divisions. The prosecutions were in fact fortunate as they 'sobered the giddy and overweening'. The young men concentrated on popular education. As MacNevin reported from a *Nation* supper in 1844, fairly general agreement was reached that 'our plan was to let this agitation work its own sweet will — be as boisterous or brutal as it please — whilst we continued with our pens (in one sense pickaxes) working the fresh mine of nationality.' Davis appealed to conservative federalists who sought some autonomy short of Repeal.[21]

The Accession of William Smith O'Brien

The only bright star on the Repeal horizon was the long-delayed accession of William Smith O'Brien, MP for Limerick. The second son of Sir Edward O'Brien, Bt, of Dromoland Co. Clare, who claimed descent from King Brian Boru, William was born in 1803. He was thus eleven years Davis's senior. 'From my boyhood I have entertained a passionate affection for Ireland.' He was deeply indignant at the wrongs suffered by its people. Unlike Davis, O'Brien was educated as a country gentleman in England at Harrow and Trinity College, Cambridge, graduating from the latter in 1826. In about 1820 he modestly told his parents that though 'my talents are moderate' he had considerable enthusiasm and application. It was decided that he should read for the bar. O'Brien's mother had endeavoured to bring him up as a keen evangelical Protestant, but not with complete success. O'Brien's professional problems were solved when he inherited the Cahirmoyle estate of his maternal uncle, William Smith, and added the latter's name to his own, thus laying himself open to the gibe that there was too much Smith and not enough O'Brien. He married Lucy Gabbett and the couple produced seven children. In very trying circumstances, she contrived to preserve her looks and her sense of humour:

> And in that never failing smile
> Playful and arch, yet free from guile.[22]

O'Brien turned naturally to politics; he was first nominated for the pocket borough of Ennis in 1828. With considerable courage he joined O'Connell's Catholic Association. Nevertheless he refused to stand against the newly appointed minister, Vesey Fitzgerald, in Clare, arguing that as Fitzgerald supported Emancipation such action would interfere with the legitimate political influence of the local gentry. Fitzgerald was in fact O'Brien's patron in Ennis. O'Brien could hardly endorse O'Connell's decision to stand against Fitzgerald. When O'Brien claimed that O'Connell's return, rejecting the unanimous wishes of the gentry, had deluded the people with false promises, he was called out by O'Connell's faithful ally and future 'Head Pacificator', Tom Steele. The two Cambridge educated Protestant landowners duly met at Kilburn, near London, and exchanged shots at twelve paces. No damage was done but honour was satisfied. For many years O'Brien remained alienated from O'Connell's party. While refusing 'to be in the smallest degree controlled by Mr O'Connell', O'Brien admitted in 1837 that there was 'a general coincidence of views upon questions of public policy'.[23]

Smith O'Brien has appeared in recent history as a stiff-necked, and not very intelligent gentleman of prickly honour. He had, however, considerable presence, tall with a figure 'as lithe and active' as a youth half his age. O'Brien's claim that he would soon have achieved political office had he not taken up the Repeal cause seems justified. In the early 1830s he produced an Irish poor law bill, wisely circularising a number of Catholic bishops. He received general, if constructively critical support, from the great liberal prelate, James Doyle of Kildare and Leighlin. The bill failed but O'Brien ultimately voted for the government's alternative. Interested in emigration, he promulgated Edward Gibbon Wakefield's views on systematic colonisation in the House of Commons. Another O'Brien preoccupation was education at all levels. A close ally of the liberal Catholic educational reformer, Thomas Wyse, O'Brien supported the Irish National System of education, which since 1831 attempted to provide common primary schooling for Catholic and Protestant. He was also a keen advocate of provincial colleges, especially for Limerick, to break the monopoly of Trinity College, Dublin and provide professional qualifications for the Catholic middle classes.[24]

By 1843, O'Brien grew increasingly disillusioned with the government of Peel, of whom he had once considered himself a supporter. His resignation as a JP in May did not, however, bring him immediately into the Repeal Association. He continued to work for reform in parliament, opposing the prohibition of arms as an insult to the Irish, worse treated than the savage New Zealand Maoris.

In May O'Brien had told his wife Lucy that it was a good sign that people in England were beginning to be frightened about Repeal. 'There is never any chance of getting anything in the way of conciliatory government from England unless she becomes alarmed.' The Repeal Association did all it could to woo him with reports of its congratulatory motions and the publication and wide circulation at its own expense of O'Brien's 4 July speech. John O'Connell wrote in 'admiration of your conduct throughout this session'.[25]

The arrests of O'Connell and his allies finally convinced O'Brien that neutrality was no longer possible. He sent a £5 subscription to the Repeal Association. The accompanying letter, formally read by O'Connell who proposed O'Brien's membership, traced the latter's ideological development. O'Brien, opposing Repeal after Emancipation, came to see that English anti-Catholic feeling was too strong to permit Irish reform. The 'calumnies and invective' emanating from the government press had created more animosities than

O'Connell's strongest language. Ireland, instead of taking its rightful place as 'an integral part of the great Empire which the valour of her sons has contributed to win, has been treated as a dependent, tributary province'. Visits to Belgium and Germany highlighted Ireland's exceptional poverty. O'Brien considered O'Connell's monster meetings perfectly legal; active resistance could be justified only in an extremity. Finally, the new recruit admitted that his decision had almost separated him from his family.[26]

The latter was no exaggeration. His mother, Lady O'Brien, outraged at reading her son's decision in *The Times*, wrote immediately to her 'dear child' to warn him against joining the forces of confusion and bloodshed, intent on separating Ireland and England. She wanted to 'clasp your knees and hold you fast until you gave a promise that you would separate yourself from these ungodly men.' As a precaution against conviction for treason, which would lead to the confiscation of his property, Lady O'Brien deferred the final settlement of her father's estate on her younger son. O'Brien, like other Protestant Repealers, was not deflected from his purpose by the need for a considerable personal sacrifice; even the smiling Lucy was less than enthusiastic about her husband's new political orientation. However, O'Brien's sisters, Grace and Anne Martineau, were supportive if critical, the latter admiring Davis and corresponding with *The Nation*. The unionist *Warder* sneered that O'Brien's conversion to Repeal was due to O'Connell's threat to deprive him of his parliamentary seat unless O'Brien, 'pitifully mean, unstable and contradictory' in his public life, cooperated.[27]

While his mother verged on political and religious hysteria, O'Brien's 'ungodly men' were overjoyed. Ray, the Repeal secretary, reported that 'nothing could equal the enthusiasm' with which the Association received the Liberator's reading of his 'eloquent and powerful' expressions of O'Brien's station and influence, plus the fact that he had joined Repeal after a full trial of all other resources, made his accession valuable 'beyond estimate'. The Liberator, in words similar to those with which he had greeted Davis, declared that 'no man ever deserved better of his native country than he does of Ireland.'[28]

A less impassioned reading of O'Brien's letter than was possible either for his family or the Repealers indicates that he was not relinquishing either his religion, his status as a country gentleman, or his belief in the British Empire. O'Brien insisted that he reserved his independence of judgment, 'while no remains of personal estrangement shall impair the cordiality of my co-operation with Mr O'Connell.' The reality of this independence became clear later. Like Davis, O'Brien was not required to serve any apprenticeship. He was asked by John O'Connell to sit on the Repeal standing committee and its financial committee for the consideration of the post-Repeal economy. Not expected to attend in person, O'Brien was invited to send written submissions.[29]

But O'Brien's self-recognised enthusiasm and application allowed him no figurehead role. He took his place on the committees at a difficult time for the Association. Most of the energy of the O'Connells was focused on the state trial. O'Brien, unconnected with the monster meetings of the previous year, had the experience and personal authority to assume the Liberator's role, not only in committee, but as principal speaker at the weekly public meetings of the Repeal Association. He was, however, a shy and diffident man, quite unused to popular politics.

On 23 January 1844 O'Brien was accorded the honour of chairing the session, but subsequently he proposed other chairmen, previously decided in committee, acting in fact as prime minister in the alternative Irish parliament. Even in the Liberator's presence, O'Brien spoke at length and introduced important business. On 5 February O'Brien secured the appointment of a new Repeal parliamentary committee, whose object was to watch the Westminster proceedings and produce its own reports and proposals for Irish legislation. The committee not only exposed the deficiencies of British administration in Ireland, but also demonstrated Ireland's fitness for self-government. Dillon, Davis, Doheny and Duffy, before his enforced resignation, served on this committee. Here the 'young men' were in their element. Davis proved an inexhaustible compiler of reports, while O'Brien was an excellent chairman. By May M. J. Barry had produced a long document on British aggression in Sind, the heartland of modern Pakistan; Davis had examined the failure of the government to publish the great Ordnance Survey with its invaluable data on Irish population and resources; John O'Connell had compiled a detailed study of tariffs; his brother Maurice was preparing another on fisheries. The advent of O'Brien gave new life and vigour to the Association, mobilising the energies of the O'Connell family itself. In open meetings O'Brien appeared a model of tact. When John O'Connell moved for tough action against Glasgow Repealers who had exhibited an anti-Protestant placard, O'Brien, speaking as a Protestant, secured their reprieve. On another occasion he declared that he would never regret joining Repeal, 'if my countrymen retain the same peaceful attitude of moral dignity which they have lately sustained.' By the time the traversers were finally removed on 30 May 1844 to their comfortable retreat in Richmond Prison, O'Brien had established himself as an active Repeal leader, second only to the Liberator himself.[30]

The State Trial

Meanwhile the trial of O'Connell and his fellow defendants began in late January and lasted twenty-five days while an indictment, nearly one hundred yards long, with a diversity of accusations against different traversers, was tried by an all-Protestant jury. Seditious speeches and articles were the essence of the government's case, but a somewhat far-fetched theory of general conspiracy was also introduced.

O'Connell was now on his mettle as a celebrated barrister who had assured Repealers of the total legality of their actions. His speech was a failure. The religious composition of the jury, however, rendered all forensic oratory for the defence academic, though it certainly created renewed interest in the Repeal cause which had been flagging since Clontarf. The trial was also important in fuelling intra-Repeal division, as it aired the question of violence and provocation during the Repeal Year.

Duffy occupied a key position at the trial as *Nation* editor. He insisted that 'the authority and responsibility were in him alone', denying that he was simply the figurehead in

an editorial collective and that *The Nation* would be much
the same without him. *The Nation* had been projected, established and edited, apart from a period of sickness, by Duffy
himself. He therefore had no desire to place any of the onus
on Davis.[31]

The prosecution allegation of a general conspiracy required
a demonstration that there was no difference between
O'Connell's speeches and the articles in the Repeal press.
Subsequently, this led to accusations that *The Nation*'s
irresponsibility had placed the entire Repeal movement in
jeopardy. However, Barrett's *Pilot* was also indicted. There
seems, moreover, to have been considerable truth in the
attorney-general's comment on the reports of O'Connell's
speeches and *The Nation* editorials: 'I say you can read
nothing which may be on one side of the paper that has not
some reference to the other.' Davis's 'The Morality of War'
and 'Something is Coming' were interpreted as anticipatory
of a violent revolution. In reply, Whiteside, Duffy's counsel,
claimed that *Nation* poems, such as 'Memory of the Dead'
('Who Fears to Speak of '98?') were no more seditious than
Moore or Scott. The former had also attacked 'Saxons'.
Whiteside denied that there was definite proof of treason in
the articles. Inaccurately, he maintained that Duffy simply
transmitted subscriptions at Repeal meetings, never spoke
and attended no demonstrations in the country.[32]

Such arguments did not prevent the Protestant jury dis-
covering conspiracy. All the traversers, save one who had
died since the indictment, were convicted. At this stage
O'Connell was narrowly prevented from dissolving the
Repeal Association by a strong adverse reaction from the
younger men, with Smith O'Brien, according to Duffy,
acting as umpire, but generally favourable to O'Connell.
Doheny, on the other hand, saw O'Brien as leading the
resistance to dissolution. The new Association was to be
purged of its 'illegal' attributes, presumably all hints of
violence of which so much had been made in the trial.
Duffy claimed that on his suggestion the separation of the
Repeal editors from the Association was put forward as a
compromise. An assurance was apparently given by the
Liberator to Duffy against the espousal of federalism.[33]

John Mitchel Joins 'The Nation'

The Nation tried to rebuild momentum. It advised its readers to 'Hoard up your passions as though they were coined gold.' It intransigently printed another exchange on 'Moral Force', very like the original between Davis and Shackleton which had been so effectively used in the trial. Once again *The Nation* refused an 'unqualified censure of war'. Another leader on 'The Convicted Conspirators' pointed out that Jesus had been one too. This 'horribly blasphemous article' was condemned by *The Warder*. 'Is this the way *The Nation* proposed to amalgamate Protestant and papist in one common bond of infidelity and devilship?' *The Nation* had now succeeded in eliciting charges of infidelity from both extreme Protestant and Catholic sources.[34]

The blasphemer was the son of a northern Unitarian minister who had been on the fringe of the United Irishmen and who had seceded from the Henry Cooke dominated Presbyterian church with the liberal minister, Henry Montgomery. John Mitchel was born in Co. Derry in 1815, but despite his more favourable background, took longer to mature as a nationalist than his near contemporary, Thomas Davis. He grew up mainly in Newry where, at Dr Henderson's school, he met the slightly older John Martin. The latter, born in 1812, formed a lifelong friendship with Mitchel, finally cemented in matrimony when Martin, towards the end of his life, married Mitchel's sister, Henrietta. Mitchel and Martin both received Arts degrees from Trinity College, Dublin, in 1834. While Martin then made a desultory study of medicine before inheriting a tidy estate at Loughorne, near Newry, Mitchel was constrained to find a profession. After an unhappy acquaintance with banking, he settled down as a solicitor in Banbridge. Martin remained for the time a complacent bachelor; Mitchel's dealings with the opposite sex were more romantic. After the respective parents had foiled one attempt at engagement with a young lady in 1835, Mitchel secured approval for marriage in 1837 after eloping with Jenny Verner, aged 17.

Two years later, Mitchel and Martin helped to organise a public dinner for O'Connell in Newry. They were impressed by the early *Nation*. When visiting Dublin on business,

Mitchel sought out Davis, contributed to *The Nation* in February 1843, and on 8 May 1843 was proposed for Repeal Association membership by Duffy. Mitchel joined because of 'the butchery and assassination which appear to be the means of opposing Repeal, contemplated by the Northern Orangemen, and recommended by certain Thug newspapers.' A few weeks after admission to Repeal, he and Davis collaborated on a *Nation* editorial, 'The Anti-Irish Catholics', Mitchel pointing out that Irish Catholics had successfully asserted themselves in the past, despite the opposition of their aristocracy. After Clontarf, though far from the scene of action, Mitchel took the militant line which was to characterise his entire nationalist career. If Ireland, he declared, 'be not ready to achieve repeal with a strong hand, she ought to make herself ready without delay, and if she be worthy of the place she seeks among the nations, she will do that.' Mitchel's penetrating style made him a valuable acquisition for *The Nation*, but his job in Banbridge prevented him from writing regularly. Controversy dogged his steps from the start.[35]

Young Ireland Christened

'The initial sacred few' as *The Nation* facetiously called its directors, or 'The Clique' according to *The Pilot*, soon absorbed Mitchel, as a result of Davis's influence. Other regulars were Doheny, Dillon, MacNevin, Barry, Duffy, David Cangley, O'Hagan, Lane and the poets Denis F. MacCarthy and R. D. Williams, plus one or two others. O'Brien, far from being intimate with the 'Circle', did not even hear of its existence till informed by Duffy in late 1846. In September 1844 John O'Connell spoke approvingly of Young Ireland's ability to link Milesians and Presbyterians. By March 1844 unionists distinguished between the listless policy of O'Connell, not yet imprisoned, and the more vigorous 'Young Ireland'. Smith O'Brien, declared *The Warder*, was difficult to classify. Falling in age between 'young Ireland' and 'old Ireland', he might well be depicted as 'middle-aged Ireland', a description O'Brien himself adopted in the following year and retained till he relinquished his mediating role at the end of 1846. Though MacNevin desired it, the title, 'Young Ireland', had not been assumed by *The Nation* group itself, still averse to public difference from O'Connell. Mazzini was sometimes mentioned as an Italian patriot in *The Nation*, and some support from the Young England group at Westminster was acknowledged, but there was no attempt to adapt their general views to Irish conditions. In early 1845, on the contrary, Davis, in a poem, 'The Cruisgin Lan', called for Old and Young Ireland to unite. Nevertheless, from this time it is no longer an anachronism to refer to 'Young Ireland'. There is some truth in *The Pilot*'s complaint that *The Nation* group inconsistently accepted and rejected the 'Young Ireland' title to suit their needs.[36]

Three and a half months separated the verdict against the traversers on 12 February and their actual imprisonment on 30 May 1844. O'Connell conducted a campaign of public meetings in England. Davis feared that the Liberator might betray the movement by descending into a new Whig alliance. In the Repeal Association, John O'Connell was compelled to explain away the so-called 1834 Lichfield House Compact between O'Connell and the Whigs. Against probing from Young Irelanders like MacNevin and Barry, he claimed that the Whigs were supported only when they were right. There was still no real desire to attack the Liberator. *The Nation* congratulated the people on their patience, and advised them to wait till the right moment. There was always educational and constructive work to be done on Repeal committees and the projected shilling Library of Ireland, for which all the prominent Young Irelanders were allocated a historical volume.[37]

O'Connell's Captivity: O'Brien in Control

The Repeal rent, a sure index of public interest, slumped. The final imprisonment of the traversers on 30 May was, *The Warder* gloated, the fall of the curtain on O'Connell:

> Poor Dan is gone to gaol
>   Says the Shan Van Vough;
> With six members of his tail,
>   Says the Shan Van Vough.

> Oh, where is all their boast
> How they'd whale the Saxon host,
> And that he would rule the roost?
> Says the Shan Van Vough.[38]

But far from being a quietus, imprisonment produced a remarkable revival in Repeal fortunes, the rent rocketing upwards from £500 per week to over £3,000. *The Nation* extracted full propagandist advantage by appearing in mourning bands and dating each week from the beginning of 'the captivity'. It still advised caution and restraint. Meanwhile, O'Connell, in a final attempt to rehabilitate his tarnished reputation as a constitutional lawyer, appealed to the ultimate authority of the House of Lords.

No leadership vacuum occurred in the Repeal movement. On the first Monday after the Liberator's imprisonment, when William Smith O'Brien entered the Association's new Conciliation Hall on Burgh Quay at 1 p.m. 'the scene that ensued . . . is beyond description. The cheering, and the hurraing, and the waving of handkerchiefs continued for about ten minutes.' Leading the protest against O'Connell's imprisonment, O'Brien firmly took control. His tall, distant and austere figure contrasted with O'Connell's bluff populism, but O'Brien identified with O'Connell's general policy, and was regarded as a member of the 'peace party' rather than the young men's 'war party'. He promised to 'sustain any extemity of personal endurance in a peaceful struggle', but rejected civil war: 'I am not prepared to shed one drop of Irish blood.' As a gentle rebuke to *The Nation*, which continued such discussion, O'Brien rejected speculation on the ultimate right of resistance by force as unprofitable. The following week, the Association recorded its highest subscription.[39]

In the three months before the House of Lords judges by a narrow and largely partisan Whig majority reversed the convictions and freed the traversers, O'Brien gave the Association a leadership appreciated by Young Ireland. O'Connell's own views were submitted through his younger son, Dan, but O'Brien's opinions were always, even when transmitted by letter, treated with particular respect. Pressure was now exerted on those Irish MPs, nominally for Repeal, but in practice often absent from both Westminster and Association meetings. Davis prepared a committee report on the matter, and *The Nation* reinforced the message in its editorials. The detailed analysis of division stirred sluggish and resentful MPs. One of those who had clashed with *The Nation* was R. Dillon Browne, Member for Mayo. Browne was particularly concerned that the Repeal Association should commit itself to opposing the government's Charitable Bequests bill, which, though an improvement from the Catholic viewpoint on existing legislation, nevertheless included insulting provisions. It was a difficult issue, as will be demonstrated later. Both the Repeal Association and the Catholic hierarchy were divided. Even the Young Irelanders themselves saw it in different ways: Doheny considered the bill 'obnoxious in all its provisions', but recognised that Davis and O'Brien, who endorsed the Catholic grievance without foisting his views on the Association, were mainly concerned with combating a device for splitting the nationalist movement.[40]

Such problems could not detract from the excellent impression made by Repeal directed by O'Brien. A unionist friend of O'Brien knew hundreds in the north distressed by English legislation, who retained their 'mistrust of your association'. Educated people were impressed by calm reasoning and statistics, not vapourings about the year of captivity and other sentimental matters. 'I admit the tone of the Association is altogether more practical and better since the two O'Connells' absence'. *Tait's Magazine*, quoted by *The Nation*, asserted that O'Brien had most of O'Connell's qualities without his faults. As a Protestant, he might win over the liberal Protestants whom O'Connell was unable to reach. O'Brien's brainchild, the parliamentary committee, was doing 'great work in a quiet way' in providing a training in business and political knowledge. Repeal, *Tait's* argued, now had a momentum of its own. 'We believe that O'Connell's life or death, imprisonment or liberation, is now a matter of the smallest practical consequence to the further progress of this national movement.'[41]

Such opinions were certainly a boost to O'Brien's ego, but what of the O'Connell camp? The Liberator had wel-

comed O'Brien's temporary leadership. He only feared that
O'Brien might be overburdened. In February 1844, O'Connell,
through Daunt, told O'Brien they had not intended to
encumber him with 'the troublesome task of remodelling the
whole of the arrangements of our Association', the chief need
being to disembarrass the movement of arbitration courts.
A few weeks later O'Connell was effusive with his 'most
emphatically cordial thanks for the manner in which you
have conducted the Repeal cause since I left Dublin.'
O'Brien's accession was 'providential'. His rank and religion
made him the 'beau ideal' of Repeal. 'I never felt half so
grateful for the exertions of any other political colleague in
my long experience.' Politically, the Liberator was 'delighted
that you are a Protestant', as 'it is impossible that any Protestant who calmly thinks can imagine that you would be a
party to any political movement which could deprive Protestants of their legitimate station and due sway in the
state.' Even O'Brien's former duelling antagonist, Tom
Steele, wrote to 'my dear William with great admiration for
the course you are pursuing.'[42]

Inside Richmond Prison

The Liberator subsequently discovered that O'Brien
possessed a strong Protestantism at variance with other
O'Connellite strategies. In gaol, the two O'Connells cannot
have entirely relished the popularity of the Smith O'Brien
regime. The comfortable incarceration which allowed the
state prisoners to receive their friends and undertake a
number of useful pursuits left the Liberator open to hostile
propaganda. Before his departure to Richmond, the widower
O'Connell had fallen in love with Rose McDowell, a Protestant
from Belfast, forty-six years his junior. To the Liberator,
she was 'one of the most superior women I ever met with in
intellect, sound judgment and fascinating sweetness'. He
arranged for her to visit him in gaol. Though *The Nation*
studiously avoided the subject, the unionist press was less
reticent, giving full details of the affair and anticipating 'a
bride obtained in Bridewell'. Alas, the Liberator was unlucky
in love. Years later, Duffy, who shared his imprisonment,

spoke contemptuously of the distracting influence of 'a passionate love for a gifted young girl who might have been his granddaughter', arguing that this incarceration marked the beginning of the Liberator's decline as a national strategist. The moderate Repealer, Sir Colman O'Loghlen, agreed with this estimate, but modern historians are more sceptical.[43]

Leaks from the gaol prevented the discomfiture of O'Connell from being hushed up. Duffy, whose wife was too ill to visit frequently, was himself at this time the subject of a verse lampoon by John O'Connell. Ostensibly addressed to Mrs Duffy, the skit warned her that her husband was ogling the lady visitors:

Well, then, first I've remarked he was never so gay
As he has been since Wednesday when you went away.[44]

Duffy, whose wife died after a long wasting sickness in the following year, was scarcely amused by John O'Connell's wit. In gaol Duffy himself took ill and was unable to attend cele-bratory banquets after release. Though efforts were made to argue the contrary, the relations between Old and Young Ireland were strained by Richmond Prison, where Duffy was in a minority. Gray of the *Freeman's Journal* sometimes sympathised with Young Ireland, but the others were hard core O'Connellites, including the hated Dicky Barrett. The later subsequently asserted that his Richmond experience confirmed his suspicions of the Young Ireland clique.[45]

Repeal after O'Connell's Release: Federalism

The passionate enthusiasm and demonstrations which greeted the release of the traversers masked for a time the fact that Repeal was now floundering without any real policy. Moreover, it was obvious that Daniel and John O'Connell would have to reassert their leadership very firmly in the face of O'Brien's success. At O'Connell's triumphant return to the Conciliation Hall on 9 September, he scarcely endeared Duffy or the Young Irelanders when denouncing the original adverse verdict: '*The Nation* was read against me — passages I disapproved of and condemned were read against me.'[46]

The first new sign of serious dissent was caused by the federalist controversy. Back in Conciliation Hall, O'Connell rejoiced that before the House of Lords' verdict, he was 'frequently laughed at and ridiculed for having boasted that no man was ever entrapped into a prison who followed my advice.' He therefore rejected implementation of the 1843 idea of a Council of 300 as too likely to breach the Irish Convention Act. Instead, he delighted in conservatives turning to federalism. People like Sharman Crawford, a northern Protestant MP and land reformer, Bishop Patrick Kennedy of Killaloe and others were federalists. To maintain momentum, especially in conciliating Protestants, so important a feature of the O'Brien period, O'Connell's move towards federalism after his release seems tactically sound.[47]

It proved a sensitive issue. Federalism appealed to some liberal Protestants as it gave Ireland limited self-government, while retaining Irish MPs in the Westminster parliament, legislating on foreign, imperial and other matters of general concern. Simple Repeal in theory meant a total independence for Ireland retaining only its link with the crown. Yet this had not existed before the Union; O'Connell was frequently challenged to declare the precise meaning of Repeal. Adherence to federalism did not disqualify candidates from Association membership. Indeed, as demonstrated, Fr Thaddeus O'Malley, believed that O'Brien, with his strong views on Ireland's share in British colonisation, would naturally join as a federalist. Hitherto, the Young Irelanders had been very flexible on federalism. In one of his rare interventions in Conciliation Hall public debates, Davis declared that, despite his own fervent belief in absolute independence, 'he did not think that it would be a bad way to get at it by first obtaining a local legislature that would combine all parties to work for Ireland, and by which they would get the Protestant party, whose assistance he looked upon as invaluable, into harness for the country, for then they would be qualified for total independence.' It was John O'Connell who reminded Davis that they must carefully avoid any suggestion of abandoning total independence, while considering a local parliament as an instalment. Davis concurred. But Davis used federalism to woo unionists.[48]

In *The Nation*, Davis persisted in this stepping-stone approach. A *Nation* editorial, probably by Davis, on 6 January
1844 declared that though the federalists asked for less than
Repeal, they asked a great deal, and if successful would have
done 'infinite service to Ireland'. O'Brien partly disagreed
with Davis, in that he felt that federalism would actually
be harder to obtain than Repeal because the British would
be reluctant to accord Ireland her fair share of MPs in the
imperial parliament. Responding to O'Connell's remarks on
federalism in September, *The Nation* agreed that federalists
should be welcomed, but warned, as John O'Connell had
done to Davis in 1843, that pure Repealers should not give
up their own ideals. Thomas Davis, whose prospective father-
in-law, Thomas Hutton, was a Dublin federalist, journeyed
north to talk to Ulster federalists. Meanwhile, O'Connell
proceeded to do exactly what he had been warned not to do.
He declared in a letter to the Association read on 14 October
that 'I do at present feel a preference for the federative
plan.'[49] Duffy now 'rushed into print without giving O'Connell
any opportunity to explain.' Davis was still away and so were
Dillon, Barry, Lane and MacNevin. Duffy acted on his own
authority. In retrospect, he insisted that the Repeal Association would have committed suicide had it then descended
into federalism. He also regarded O'Connell's statement a
breach of a private undertaking a year earlier. Duffy therefore addressed a signed remonstrance to O'Connell in *The
Nation*.[50]

This was the first clear and avowed public criticism of
O'Connell by 'Young Ireland'. A contemporary cartoon
showed *The Nation*, wielding a sword marked 'Young Ireland',
threatening O'Connell who had dropped the staff of federalism. Duffy admits that Davis in his place would have confined himself to private remonstrance. Certainly, his criticism
of the Liberator was widely quoted in Ireland, England and
the continent.[51]

What exactly did Duffy say? With tongue in cheek, he
claimed that prison experience had demonstrated the
Liberator's respect for opinions other than his own. Furthermore, Duffy could not use the Repeal Association forum as
he was no longer a member. He also pointed out that *The*

Nation (Davis in fact) had in the previous year insisted on tolerance for federalists within Repeal. Federalists were useful allies, but Repeal and federalism were entirely different things. The imperial parliament would work in England's interest and distract Irish attention from their own country. Most Repealers were committed to simple Repeal and the Association committee was not entitled to weaken its moral position. The most important of Duffy's arguments, which separated nationalists from reformists, was his fear that the link with British imperialism would continue the dominance in Ireland of British manners and culture. O'Connell had laid great stress on a pamphlet by a young northern Protestant, Grey Porter, who flirted with Repeal and talked of a 'Hiberno-British Empire'.

To the unionist *Warder*, whose ability Duffy fully accepted, Duffy's letter really meant: 'O'Connell, you apostate villain . . . you have sold Repeal to the Whigs . . . and deserted to the colours of federalism, which must make our country eternally the province of English legislation.' *The Warder* considered *The Nation*, despite all its fiery articles and poems, 'doomed' for the simple reason that their masters were the priests, for whom O'Connell was simply a man of business. Attacks on *The Nation*'s 'infidelity' were then increasing, stimulated partly by Davis's tactless defence of his Protestant convert friend, D. O. Madden. But *The Pilot* had long asserted Catholic nationalism against *The Nation*.[52]

O'Connell was surprised at Duffy's reaction to his statement on federalism. He assumed that Smith O'Brien and Davis favoured it. The Liberator complained bitterly about *The Nation*'s onslaught when 'Tom Davis actually went down to Belfast himself to get up a federalist party there.' This seems to endorse *The Pilot*'s later contention that Davis and his allies in the Repeal committee had persuaded O'Connell that they could win over the north if he declared for federalism. When the Liberator complied they accused him of apostasy. O'Brien, not then associated with Young Ireland, appeared the decisive voice in wooing non-Catholics. As O'Connell told O'Brien, 'years upon years would elapse' before any Protestants came round the Repeal without him. But the latter, though his position could easily be confused with it, was not in fact a federalist. Davis's position was similarly ambiguous. He originally believed O'Connell's letter 'very able of its kind, but it is bad policy, if not worse, to suddenly read his incantation.' Davis wrote to John O'Connell suggesting that the Liberator should not raise the issue again till the federalists 'do something'. O'Connell did appear to act on this advice when he subsequently retracted by claiming, inconsistently, that there was no federalist plan before the public. Eventually, when he achieved support neither from federalists nor from most Repealers, apart from the ever faithful *Pilot*, O'Connell dropped the whole matter. Ironically, after breaking with O'Connell, Duffy strove to persuade federalists like William Sharman Crawford to join the Young Ireland organisation.[53]

The damage had nevertheless been done. As Doheny said, 'a blow had been given to the Association from which it never recovered.' Duffy admitted his breach with the Young Ireland policy of not openly challenging O'Connell, and especially in the absence of his leading colleagues. Duffy's reaction seems based on personal pique rather than reason. Private representation was surely wiser than advertising the division between Young and Old Ireland. Davis, adhering to his stepping-stone policy, was critical of O'Connell's blatant and unconvincing somersault, rather than his attempt to appeal to Protestant opinion. He now fell into line behind Duffy. After a week of silence, both Davis and Duffy wrote *Nation* editorials on the subject. Davis related O'Connell's federalism, which he hoped would not last long, to other apparent difficulties of the Repeal movement, such as the decline in Repeal rent and the good relations between the French and English monarchs. Duffy, denying that the temporary silence was due to O'Connell's threats, still maintained the federalism was but a Chapel of Ease to St Stephen's, the Westminster parliament. Significantly, the same issue carried a long letter by MacNevin to the Belfast *Vindicator*, replying to an 'Irish Priest' who had charged Young Ireland with religious indifferentism. MacNevin totally disclaimed any difference between Young and Old Ireland. All worked together: 'what O'Connell was doing in the forum, they resolved to do in literature, the arts, and society.' When Davis asked the Liberator to prevent attacks on *The Nation*, he was advised to 'lessen a little your Protestant zeal' and curb his 'Protestant monomania'.[54]

Leadership and Religious Contention

Duffy's challenge thus occurred at a particularly unfortunate time. The Charitable Bequests bill had infuriated those Catholic bishops, led by MacHale, who were most supportive of the Repeal Association. Was it to become the type of secular political organisation, demanded by MacNevin, which would eschew purely religious issues likely to divide Protestant and Catholic members? MacHale and the supportive bishops accepted no such interpretation.

Behind this difference lay an unspoken consideration. By late 1844 Smith O'Brien had clearly emerged as the unequivocal second-in-command to O'Connell. Indeed the Liberator liked to assert that they were joint leaders and that his position would be untenable without O'Brien at his side. Yet what of the movement on the ageing O'Connell's death, now that Repeal was unlikely to be achieved for some time? Catholic bishops might have been dubious about a Protestant leader. Smith O'Brien clearly envisaged the Repeal Association as a secular body. He was also well known as a longtime advocate of mixed education, though he tactfully accepted that conscientious objectors like Archbishop MacHale, with whom he maintained a courteous correspondence, should not be deprived of school grants.

The only alternative to O'Brien was the Liberator's son John. *The Pilot* quoted a French paper upholding John O'Connell against the 'vain, frivolous and crotchety' O'Brien. O'Connell, it insisted, was hypocritical in advertising O'Brien as his successor. According to Daunt, who knew both sides, the Young Irelanders, fearing that John O'Connell was being groomed for leadership, demanded an elective leadership, favouring O'Brien, rather than a hereditary monarchy.[55]

John O'Connell had more ability than Duffy's derogatory portrait suggests. Lacking his father's imposing presence, John, a smallish man, attempted to remedy the deficiency by assiduous application to detail. He made himself the financial expert of the Association, and received much praise for his reports and other publications. He produced a 'Repeal Dictionary' which, though criticised by Young Irelanders, was serialised in *The Nation*. The latter paper had welcomed his name in its early prospectus. Though Duffy fell foul of his verse, his two poems in 'The Spirit of the Nation', exuded romantic nationalism, one hinting at revolution when depicting a storm which laid the 'tyrant' low. Born in 1810 and trained as a barrister, John had sat in parliament continuously since 1832. In the early years of Repeal he showed little sign of Catholic exclusivism. In fact John firmly disciplined Repealers insulting Protestants. By the end of 1844 and the beginning of 1845, when O'Brien obtained the initiative, John's approach became markedly ecclesiastical. His father still occasionally demonstrated his old pragmatism, but John, who considered changing the Repeal Association to the Catholic Association, appeared to be totally devoted to the interests of the MacHaleite prelates.[56]

The hierarchy was then divided into three antagonistic factions. The traditionally independent 'Gallican' bishops, led by Archbishops Crolly and Murray, favoured accommodation with the British government in matters such as education and charitable bequests. MacHale's new nationalistic Gallicans supported Repeal and opposed any liaison with the government. From Rome emanated Ultramontanism, insistent on rigid obedience to the Vatican, and the elimination of all Irish Gallicanism, though originally MacHale's was preferred to Murray's. The pivot of Irish Ultramontanism was Dr Paul Cullen, rector of the Irish College in Rome and ultimately successor to Archbishops Murray and Crolly in turn. Meanwhile, the British government, with some apparent assistance from the traditional Gallican bishops, sought Vatican support against Repeal. In early 1845, O'Connell disputed with Archbishop Crolly the validity of a papal rescript criticising the involvement of Irish clergy in politics. O'Connell, under the Primate's rebuke, retracted his initial insistence that the rescript was uncanonical. There was then considerable Repeal fear that a concordat would be signed between the British government and the pope. A *Nation* leader, probably by Davis, dismissed the rescript as 'a very harmless homily, irrelevant to Repeal, and idle against the agitation.' In the Repeal Association, O'Connell emphatically agreed and used that forum to appeal to Murray and Crolly to quit the Charitable Bequests Board. Thus the Repeal Association, contrary to the wishes of Davis, who had long been wary of control by prelates like MacHale, was drawn into agitation for purely Catholic issues, and adopted a particular side in an intra-Catholic dispute. Denis Gwynn argued that *The Nation* was becoming vulnerable because of its 'growing and definite estrangement from the Catholic tradition of the movement which O'Connell had created'. Yet this begs a number of questions. The exact nature of the Catholic tradition was still contested between the bishops, and O'Connell had himself done much to build up a non-sectarian image.[57]

The real issue was rather different. The MacHale bishops would not support Repeal unless the Association acted as their instrument against both the British government and their hierarchical rivals. The O'Connells were well aware of this fact. If Daniel could still afford pragmatism, his son John, who needed the full support of the clergy and bishops to ensure succession to the leadership, could not. This helps to explain the virulence of some of his attacks on 'infidel colleges' and the religious indifferentism of the Young Irelanders which was to characterise his politics till 1848. Similarly, *The Pilot*'s attacks on *The Nation*'s latitudinarianism were intended to win the battle for Repeal circulation.

The Colleges Dispute

Mixed education, stimulated by Peel's Colleges bill, dominated the first half of 1845, and persisted long afterwards. The dispute, which led to the first full-scale confrontation between Old and Young Ireland at Conciliation Hall on 27 May, had kindled for some time. Smith O'Brien was an advocate of the mixed education of Catholics and Protestants in the National Schools. The Liberator appeared to hold the same opinion, which was closely related to the ideal of a non-sectarian national movement.

The Repeal committee discussed the College issue in the

autumn of 1844. In the absence of the O'Connells, resolutions favourable to mixed education were drawn up. According to Davis's account, 'on Johnny's first appearance in the Committee they were read to him, and he gave them a flat negative', preferring education under the Jesuits. The Liberator, arriving an hour later, admitted his advocacy of mixed education but insisted on consulting the Catholic bishops. Sir Colman O'Loghlen, a Catholic barrister sympathetic to mixed education, endorsed Davis's account, perceiving that O'Connell, led by his son, had used the bishops to ensure rejection.

The Liberator's episcopal correspondence in early 1845 certainly indicates strong hostility to the projected Colleges. He told Bishop Cantwell, for example, that the Irish National System of primary schools was acceptable only because the Protestants rejected it; the Catholic middle and upper classes, however, could not be trusted in undenominational institutions. The Liberator's only concession was, he told MacHale, to allow Protestants to attend institutions where the professors were appointed by canonical Catholic authority. The dispute was intensified by O'Connell's contest with the pro-government Archbishop Crolly on the papal rescript.[58]

After a preliminary clash in the Repeal Association on the principle of mixed education between Smith O'Brien and his fellow MP, Dillon Browne, a moratorium on debate was decided until the publication of Peel's bill in May 1845. Discussion persisted, however, in the papers, with *The Nation* and *The Pilot* taking diametrically opposed positions. Peel offered three non-residential Irish Colleges on the model of London University. The initial professors were government appointments and some institutional control of student lodgings was included. As there was no religious provision, apart from private endowments, the O'Connells echoed the cry of a Tory reactionary MP that these were 'Godless Colleges'.

In the Repeal Association there was early confrontation between the Young Irelanders, led by Davis, and the O'Connells. John was extremely vehement. Davis refused to condemn the bill utterly. He admired its lack of sectarianism, and believed it possible to add religious safeguards. Even the

Liberator admitted that his son had provoked Davis's comments. The faithful *Pilot* duly condemned the bill as 'execrable', and insisted that Protestants were only auxiliaries in the Association.[59]

So serious was the situation that the Repeal committee appeared on the verge of disintegration and a general split loomed. O'Brien, absent on 12 May, endorsed mixed academical education by letter and deprecated 'the very strong and unqualified language of condemnation' at the Association. In committee, Davis and O'Loghlen, hearing that John O'Connell was preparing for a showdown at the next general meeting, accepted deferral of the public reading of O'Brien's letter till the Catholic bishops had spoken. Davis assured an irritated O'Brien that 'the danger was terrible and pressing and there was no other possible arrangement to avoid a break up.' Davis, realising that the hierarchy was divided, anticipated a more balanced reaction than that of John O'Connell, committed to the strong views of Archbishop MacHale. 'Crolly', said Davis, 'is for mixed education and so are others, I am told.' Davis refused to accept 'the unresisted triumph of blind bigotry in a National Association'. The factions in the hierarchy, on the other hand, made Repeal Association endorsement essential to the MacHale group.[60]

The divided Catholic hierarchy, meeting on 23 May, opted for an inconsistent compromise, which asserted a readiness for co-operation on fair and reasonable terms. According to Fr Thaddeus O'Malley, no doubt deriving his information from Archbishop Murray, a majority of bishops favoured co-operation. They insisted on a fair proportion of the professors under episcopal supervision, the appointment of chaplains, and representation of the bishops on a board of trustees. To appease the minority of the hierarchy, separate instruction was required in a number of disciplines, including history and medicine. As O'Malley said, this latter demand was incompatible with acquiescence in the principle of mixed education. It therefore became possible both to insist and deny that the bishops accepted the principle of mixed education.[61]

Davis in Tears

The crisis came at the Association meeting on 26 May. Though commentators have concentrated on the clash between O'Connell and Davis, it was in fact O'Brien, often regarded as a mediator, who set out the Young Irelanders' position. O'Brien, not Davis, first asserted that the bishops had given 'tacit sanction' to mixed education in their demand for safeguards. O'Brien was conciliatory, repeating his opposition to the Charitable Bequests Act and reaffirming his belief that conscientious objectors to the National Educational System, like MacHale, should receive public funding. The Middle-Aged Irelander, as he regarded himself, denounced the lack of religious provision in the new Colleges and the government appointment of professors. However, O'Brien strongly supported the principle of mixed education as a social emollient.

The Liberator and John O'Connell ignored O'Brien's olive branch and denounced the 'execrable' bill in unmeasured terms. Davis tried to interject O'Brien's contention that the Catholic bishops had accepted its principle. Tempers rose. When Michael Conway, editor of the *Newry Examiner* and little renowned for either piety or consistency, denounced another Young Irelander as a hypocrite and bad Catholic, Davis sarcastically referred to Conway as 'my very Catholic friend'. O'Connell interpreted this as an insult to Catholicism, but Davis continued to argue effectively for mixed education and the need to amend the bill according to the demands of the bishops. O'Connell in reply rejected 'Young Ireland' and its 'pranks'. 'I shall stand by Old Ireland; and I have some slight notion that Old Ireland will stand by me.' Davis, rebutting the Liberator's suggestion that there was a 'Young Ireland' opposition group, broke down and wept. O'Connell proffered his hand and reconciliation was ostensibly achieved.

The Colleges Issue Persists

Far from ending the struggle, the debate inaugurated a conflict which persisted into the 1850s. Young and Old Ireland were agreed that Peel's bill required amendment, especially on government appointment of professors. No improvement was, however, achieved in the next weeks. O'Brien finally voted against the third reading. But this did nothing to lessen the internal Repeal wrangle. Old Irelanders, led by John O'Connell, stepped up their rhetoric against infidelity. The Liberator again wavered, admitting in mid-1845 that his earlier endorsement of mixed education continued for literary and scientific subjects. Davis sought to obtain signatures for a petition demanding amendments to the Colleges bill, while accepting the principle of mixed education. He obtained the support of 170 members of the Dublin intelligentsia, but John O'Connell's antagonistic petition was considerably more effective. As the sympathetic Dr William Griffin said, Davis's petition was too controversial for Limerick. John Dillon, while favourable, thought Davis should let the Colleges issue sleep for fear of provoking O'Connell.[62]

The threat of a Repeal split was still grave. In committee Protestants were sharply advised to keep out of the education debate. According to Davis, 'O'Connell seemed anxious that the supporters of mixed education should secede from the Association; but none of us did so, nor ought we under any circumstances short of impending expulsion.' As a contingency plan against a proposal by the Liberator to commit the Association to separate education, and thus compel the withdrawal of the integrationists, Davis suggested an amendment against motions on issues dividing the Repeal committee. He hoped that lengthy discussion would force the withdrawal of the original motion. Davis's perception of John O'Connell's strategy was supported by the persistently provocative rhetoric of the Old Irelanders which made it difficult for mixed educationalists to remain honourably silent. In late 1845 the educational separatists established a new periodical, *Old Ireland*, also edited by Barrett of *The Pilot*, specifically directed against mixed education. Davis's last intervention in a Repeal Association debate in July 1845 was provoked by the assertion that there could be no advocates of integration present. He abstained from motions expressing Catholic views on the Colleges, rejected the words 'a gigantic scheme of Godless education', and tepidly endorsed agitation for church superintendence of student lodgings. Shortly before Davis's death some weeks later, John O'Connell challenged the Repeal Association to name a single patriot advocating mixed education, in contrast to numerous integrationists apathetic or 'criminally active against their country'.[63]

In the late summer of 1845, when John O'Connell dominated the Repeal Association in his father's absence, many Young Irelanders preferred to remain away. Though Smith O'Brien had earlier lectured Davis on the need to maintain their fight against the unamended Colleges bill alongside the educational separationists, on his return to the Repeal Association in November, he refused to condemn the Colleges in toto. John O'Connell, who privately told O'Brien he regarded separate education as 'uncompromisable', declared that he was unable to 'speak temperately on this subject.' The Liberator, though admitting that O'Brien had been conciliatory, also tilted against infidelity. Younger mixed educationalists were more brutally silenced at the Association meetings.[64]

The witch-hunt against educational integrationists was not necessitated by opposition to Peel's Colleges bill, which dissatisfied all Repealers. Indeed, as O'Brien argued, Irish divisions assisted the government in refusing amendment. The need for John O'Connell in particular to buttress the MacHale prelates against the Crolly-Murray group, still working with the unamended Colleges, was a different matter. Here, as *The Warder* had earlier pointed out, Young Ireland was in an impossible position. Duffy's colleagues knew as well as O'Connell the importance of the priesthood to the movement, especially when the Protestant gentry refused to supply an alternative leadership for the masses. To O'Connell, his 1844 approach to the federalists, stymied by Young Ireland itself, seemed as far as he could travel along this road. His failure drove him into the hands of MacHale. The Young Irelanders in their principled pursuit of national unity through inter-denominational schools had to endure the attacks of the MacHaleites without any hope of receiving the support of the anti-Repeal Murray-Crolly integrationists. Doheny, like other Young Irelanders a supporter of undenominational education, discovered in attacking the Charitable Bequests Act a 'monstrous coalition' between Peel and Archbishop Murray.[65]

Though the Colleges increasingly absorbed Repeal attention in 1845, the Young Irelanders, for whom O'Connell himself was still prepared to cheer in February, continued an optimistic pursuit of Repeal in several directions. Early in the year Davis became more prominent in the Repeal Association public meetings. From the chair on 13 January he tacitly criticised some Repeal colleagues by advertising his object as self-government to cure Irish misery, not personal applause. Anticipating subsequent Young Ireland battles, Davis promised persistence, even if applause was accorded to his enemies and curses to his friends. Davis was ably supported in Association meetings by Barry and MacNevin, but still preferred quiet constructive committee work. 'I do not often attend meetings in this hall, being much too occupied to make speeches.' In March *The Warder* referred to MacNevin's complaint that the Liberator was too conciliatory over a projected royal visit: 'these youngsters beard the old lion in his den with singular audacity' but O'Connell, because of the decline in Repeal fortunes and his fears of another spell in gaol, 'takes their snubs with patience, and disappoints their malice' while attempting to match their rhetoric. During the same month Dr Cane of Kilkenny told Davis to cultivate his oratory alongside his journalism. In May Davis challenged the Liberator on slavery as well as education. This unstable situation seemed unlikely to last indefinitely. Young Irelanders, endlessly hoping for war between England and America, were becoming a nuisance to the veteran agitator.[66]

The Eighty-Two Club

Early 1845 saw the inauguration of a new organisation, mooted during the imprisonment of the traversers. The Eighty-Two Club, intended as an élitist auxiliary of the Repeal Association, provided a centre for the 'intelligence, rank, and wealth' of Repeal and attracted super-class sympathisers, estranged by the Liberator's rough demagoguery. According to *The Warder*, 'the literally "unwashed" do continue to attend at Repeal Hall with astonishing perseverance.' Protestants in particular might be drawn to a more gentlemanly associ- ation. Again, the Eighty-Two Club could be seen as a sub- stitute for the Council of 300, or Preservative Society, which to the annoyance of the Young Irelanders, O'Connell had now definitely abandoned. Davis, working with Sir Colman O'Loghlen, was instrumental in designing an impressive and costly green and gold quasi-military uniform for the Club, which evoked memories of the success of the Irish Volun- teers in 1782 in obtaining a temporary freedom for the Irish parliament. This followed up the attempt in 1843 to turn the monster meetings into practical lessons in drill and dis- ciplined deployment. A leadership cadre, if not an army, was created. As Smith O'Brien declared in Kilkenny, 'I am not sorry that the government should feel that the dress we wear wants nothing but the sword attached to it to con- stitute us as officers of the Irish people [*great cheering*].' It was good for governments to remember the ultimate redress of the sword. The Club's object was not to invite physical force but 'to generate in you that feeling of con- fidence which ought to belong to a great nation'. The sword was omitted not out of fear but because it was unnecessary. Similarly ambiguous language had characterised the Liber- ator's utterances in the Repeal Year. In 'A Song for the '82 Club', *The Warder* pilloried this green triumphalism:

> Then, hip, hip, hurrah! for young old '82
> Though they call it a sham, quite a regular 'do',
> It may keep green Repeal, boys, from looking so blue,
> Which nobody can deny.[67]

A splendid banquet was held in April at the Rotunda to commemorate the anniversary of Grattan's declaration of Irish independence in 1782. O'Connell, an uncomfortable septuagenarian in his green-gold uniform, delivered the presidential address. Young and Old Ireland were equally represented amongst the hundred spectacularly attired members who awed the humbler classes watching in the streets. Davis himself contributed to the abundant oratory, making one of his rare public addresses on the nationalisation of art. Smith O'Brien ominously applauded the lack of arms — at present, and quoted Barry's poem, 'Bide Your Time'.[68]

The Eighty-Two Club, for all its bombast, encouraged divisions in the Repeal Association. O'Connell grew tired of the new organisation which, it was said, he could not control; bitter struggles between Old and Young Ireland ensued over admissions to membership. The Young Irelanders certainly wished to blackball their opponents, but, though they may have succeeded in some instances, their dominance was hardly as great as some accounts suggest. Doheny claims that when inefficient members of the committee were voted out, these included, to the Liberator's indignation, Dicky Barrett of *The Pilot*. Doheny also points to the paradox that 'without having yet performed any distinctive service, or realised the promise involved in its establishment, the club became a very important and imposing body.' The dangerous notion, deriving partly from France and influencing Young Ireland and *The Nation*, that Irish independence could be won by public banquets and spellbinding oratory, regularly reported in six tight columns of newspaper print, was encouraged by the Eighty-Two Club.[69]

The Club reinforced the Young Irelander wing of Repeal by recruiting several able men, and two rhetorical wizards, T. F. Meagher and Richard O'Gorman Jr. John Mitchel and his friend John Martin had been hitherto on the fringe of Repeal and the Young Ireland circle. Thomas Francis Meagher, son of a wealthy Waterford merchant, was born in that city in August 1825. Young Meagher was educated by the Jesuits, first at Clongowes and then at Stonyhurst in Lancashire. He left school in the heady days of the Repeal Year and gravitated towards Conciliation Hall when nominally studying for the Bar. Despite an English accent and a voice lacking richness and flexibility, Meagher made himself into a speaker whose wealth of historical allusion and torrential metaphors captivated even hostile audiences. According to Mitchel, who originally considered Meagher 'rather foppish', the Lancashire intonation evaporated in Davis's presence. Richard O'Gorman Jr, another merchant's son, was born in Dublin in 1826 and took his BA from Trinity College in 1842. He subsequently practised as a barrister. Almost as powerful an orator as

Meagher, O'Gorman likewise specialised in the florid and heavily ornamented rhetoric so popular in his day. Such men, despite their value to Young Ireland, confused the rhetoric of revolution with the substance of revolution itself.[70]

The oratory of the Eighty-Two Club and its thinly disguised physical force implications supported the Liberator in a new round of monster meetings in the summer of 1845. The anniversary of O'Connell's imprisonment was celebrated on 30 May with a solemn oath to continue the battle for Repeal at all costs. The cause appeared to be reviving, despite internal divisions, Peel's determined resistance, and the lack of foreign distractions to weaken Britain.[71]

The Last Days of Thomas Davis

Davis tried to turn attention from the Colleges to Stanley's new Land Bill, which might destroy the relative prosperity of Ulster farms by eroding the tenant right which gave them an advantage over the rest of the country. He prepared a report for the Repeal Association, and attended public sessions to support it. In late June he was forced to apologise three times for the weakness of his voice. The strain of his numerous activities was clearly affecting a constitution which, outwardly robust, was in reality delicate. Before 1845 Davis had done little public speaking, apart from his earlier College Historical Society orations. Though deliberately keeping his speeches short and to the point, Davis became more loquacious in that summer.[72]

Despite his labours, Davis gladly edited *The Nation* while his friends took their summer holidays. In late July or early August he became engaged to Annie Hutton, daughter of the Dublin federalist. Possibly, as J. Hone suggests, Annie's mother reconciled herself to the match after Davis's public confrontation with O'Connell at Conciliation Hall. Annie herself had strong patriotic feelings, regretting, before meeting Davis, that she was not a man able to work for Ireland. She was influenced by Protestant Evangelicalism. Her love and admiration for Davis was unbounded: 'May I write it, Oh! how dearly, passionately I love you. Somehow I'm afraid to say it when you are by, but I will the next time I come.'

She could be playful as well as intense: 'I haven't quite forgiven you yet your impertinent note, about being obliged to write gibberish, gibberish forsooth . . .'[73]

Thinly disguised as 'Fanny', Davis, in well-known lines, drew his handsome, graceful and intelligent fiancée:

> Her eyes are darker than Dunloe,
> Her soul is whiter than the snow,
> Her tresses like arbutus flow,
> Her step like frightened deer.

Annie's fear that Davis would be disappointed in her when he got to know her better was, unhappily, never to be disproved, but Davis's priorities are shown in the couplet:

> Oh! love is more fair than the moonlight,
> And glory more grand than the sun.

While Davis approached personal happiness in August, Duffy, whose wife Emily was dying slowly and painfully from consumption, arranged, as a brief respite from sickbed attendance, a holiday tour of the north with Mitchel, John O'Hagan and Martin. The pleasure of visiting a series of historical sites of nationalist interest in different parts of Ulster was marred by letters complaining bitterly that John O'Connell, the 'Young Liberator', was rapidly turning the Repeal Association into a purely Catholic organisation as he established his 'Vice-Tribunate' deputising for his father. The American Repealers were dismayed by his attacks on slavery, the French by insults, and Young Ireland by accusations of infidelity. Duffy was eventually called away from his holiday when his wife's illness suddenly worsened. It was found to be a false alarm, and, on Davis's insistence, Duffy proceeded with his holiday. This time he went south to Wicklow with Thomas D'Arcy McGee, a potential new recruit from the United States, very young but full of 'original thought'.

McGee, with a United Irishman grandfather, was born at Carlingford in April 1825. He emigrated to the United States in 1842 where an eloquent speech on Repeal in Boston won him a job on the *Boston Pilot*, a powerful organ of Irish America. In 1845 he returned home to become London correspondent of the *Freeman's Journal*, but was sacked for contributing simultaneously to *The Nation*. In April 1846 he offered himself full-time to the latter. Duffy did not find McGee immediately prepossessing. Slovenly in dress and with almost African features, McGee's manner at first seemed too obsequious. Davis, on their only meeting, thought McGee too Yankified in manner and too pushing in seeking his acquaintance. Duffy, however, was so impressed by McGee's intellect that he invited him to Wicklow soon after their introduction.[74]

Duffy relieved Davis from *The Nation* editorship in early September. On 9 September Davis caught scarlatina, and, after a brief rally when he emerged to encounter John O'Connell by chance, relapsed. His family and friends were horrified by his death at the family home in Baggot Street on the 16th. Tributes, sincere and less sincere, poured in. The old Liberator, probably spontaneously, declared that 'my mind is bewildered and my heart afflicted.' Davis had such 'transcendent qualities of mind and heart', such learning and 'such incessant energy and continuous exertion' and 'his loss is indeed irreparable'. According to O'Loghlen, O'Connell in fact 'had a great personal hostility to Davis', whom he believed to be eroding his leadership. O'Loghlen had had to work hard to maintain relations between the two men till the crying episode cleared the air and restored the O'Connell-Davis friendship.[75]

Davis's own circle was distraught. The staid Smith O'Brien felt unable to make a public tribute for fear of dissolving in tears. Dillon felt the news 'like a thrust from a dagger' and wondered if his own life was worth preserving. The ailing MacNevin was left sleepless in 'the greatest agony'. Duffy appeared a pitiable object to the Repeal secretary, T. M. Ray. Davis's family intensified 'the crushing sensation of woe' by refusing to release an unfinished biography of Tone. Dr J. R. Davis threatened a biography of his brother demonstrating that he had been cruelly coerced into Repeal. The unionist *Warder*, which hated O'Connell, was more magnanimous in its 'deepest sorrow' for a man of 'absolutely prodigious scholarship' who was also 'guilelessly honest'. It saw him as second only to O'Brien in 'upholding the go-ahead principles of the Young Ireland party, and administering an unmistakable stimulus to the selfishly cautious dodges of the O'Connell clique.'[76]

Could Davis achieve a new unity over his grave in Mt Jerome cemetery? His huge funeral was attended by all, Old Ireland, Young Ireland, unionists and literary and artistic figures. To the annoyance of *The Warder* some mourners attended in Eighty-Two Club uniforms. Davis would have delighted in the paramilitary gesture. The funeral helped to recruit a replacement poet, 'Speranza', when Miss Jane Francesca Elgee, born in Wexford to a highly conservative Protestant family, but already inspired by anonymous *Nation* articles and poems, first heard the name of Davis. However, John O'Connell, for all his condolences, was clearly aware that Davis's demise removed an important obstacle to the conversion of the Repeal Association into a basically Catholic organisation. Initially, Davis's name was excluded from the infighting between Old and Young Ireland, but, led by *The Pilot* in October 1845, derogatory remarks became a stock-in-trade of the 'Old Ireland' controversial arsenal.[77]

Davis's Significance

Davis's death concluded Young Ireland's first phase. The name itself had only recently passed into general currency, being still disliked by many members of the group and totally rejected by Davis himself as late as May 1845. Enormous claims have sometimes been made for Davis. P. S. O'Hegarty, for example, maintained that had Davis lived, he would have prevented a split in Repeal, a subsequent split amongst the Young Irelanders, national impotence during the potato famine, which shortly followed his death, and the failure of the abortive rebellion. It is unlikely that Davis would have achieved any of these. If argued that the Repeal split was the root cause of the other disasters, it is difficult to see how his presence could have averted divisions which were widening rapidly. Davis himself feared a split. Other writers, diametrically opposed to O'Hegarty, insist that Davis's uncompromising arrogance was itself a major cause of division. This obscures Davis's assertion of a comprehensive ideal of undenominational, or secular, Irish nationalism, against Catholic nationalism. The contentious secularism of Davis has too often been submerged under a nebulous collection of patriotic platitudes in tawdry verse and tedious prose. Even the less attractive features of the real Davis, his 'Protestant monomania', as O'Connell called it, were significant in that they demanded a political pluralism that has always proved difficult to contain within Irish nationalism.[78]

But Davis, whatever his long-term achievements, was no Moses who died after leading his people to the threshold of a promised land. When Davis died, Repeal was little more than a distant possibility. The Association itself approached a dangerous crisis. As for the group of young men recognising Davis's unofficial leadership, could they continue without him, or was it true, as MacNevin lamented, that 'our bond of union is broken'?

Though O'Brien had already been identified by *The Warder* as the Young Ireland leader, he was still socially aloof from the young men and desirous of steering an independent course. He had occasionally accompanied Davis on walking tours and later sometimes dined with Duffy. Duffy, as *Nation* editor, was the natural replacement for Davis but he was outside the Repeal organisation. He had always been controller of *The Nation*, glad to have Davis as a supportive alternative. His difficulty lay in the fact that Dillon had almost dropped out and MacNevin was already suffering from the mental disorder that caused his death in 1848.

Repeal Splits, 1845-46

The Reorganisation of The Nation

The unfortunate Duffy, suddenly bereft of the services of his chief collaborator, was soon struck another painful, if less unexpected blow. Davis was scarcely in his grave, when Emily Duffy, after grim parturition, died on Tuesday morning, 24 September. Duffy, with two tiny children, might have been pardoned for a long withdrawal from Irish politics, but it was not to be. *The Nation* was almost immediately embroiled in another bout with Barrett's *Pilot*, this time in defence of the primate, Dr Crolly, leader of the anti-MacHale bishops. *The Pilot*, which had denounced *The Nation's* infidelity, published an attack on the sanity of the archbishop, who persisted in doing business with the government on the Colleges. Duffy, despite John Pigot's belief that Barrett had hanged himself, retaliated against his rival: 'He is a Protestant, and he assails the very creed which he professes to hold, and audaciously puts himself forth as the champion of a faith whose tenets he does not believe. What is most exalted and sacred is beyond that reach of his calumny. His trade is hypocrisy — his life a continued and consistent lie.' The Liberator, however, continued to have faith in Barrett as his mouthpiece.[1]

Personal difficulties, partly relieved for Duffy in 1846 by his second marriage — this time to his cousin Susan Hughes of Newry — and political disputes paled before the major calamity of the potato famine which persisted till 1848. With tragic irony, the first signs of the dreaded blight appeared shortly after Davis's death. *The Nation's* poetry, leaders and general articles repeatedly addressed the disaster.

However, it was unfortunate that the Repeal Association was distracted by clashes between Old and Young Ireland and the bitter denunciations of 'Godless Colleges'.

According to his own account, Duffy's friends convinced him after Davis's death that the struggle to maintain Repeal purity required him at his post. McGee endorsed the conception of Duffy as the great organiser. Duffy's difficulties were formidable: Dillon was recuperating from illness in Madeira; MacNevin had brain disease; Pigot and O'Hagan planned legal studies in London. Duffy was unimpressed by Barry and D. F. MacCarthy, the poet; Doheny appeared a speaker rather than a writer. Duffy placed Meagher and O'Gorman in the same category. Meagher, able to stir 'the emotions at will' in a public meeting, seemed to Duffy of little use in conference. Daunt, one of the last signatories of the original *Nation* prospectus, was a helpful moderate, but an Old, rather than a Young, Irelander.[2]

Duffy endeavoured to follow the advice of Dillon, now beset with coughs and blisters, to rally round himself 'an efficient little band'. Ruling out the suggested Doheny and MacNevin, Duffy brought in relatively new men. John Mitchel, the Banbridge solicitor with whom *The Nation* editor had spent his interrupted holiday, was employed fulltime as a writer-manager of the paper, and moved to Dublin. He was aided by the 'Irish Gascon', Thomas Devin Reilly. Born in 1824, the son of a Monaghan solicitor, Reilly, who, according to Mitchel, 'had red lightning in his blood', was educated at Trinity College, Dublin. Reilly was soon at loggerheads with D'Arcy McGee, who joined *The Nation* in April 1846. Mitchel and Reilly ultimately proved too radical for Duffy, who came to distrust their judgment, while McGee generally sided with *The Nation* editor on the conservative wing of the movement.[3]

Post-Davis Poetry

As for poetry, Davis's death provided an opportunity for Mangan, who had remained in the shadows during 'The Celt's' supremacy. With 'queer puns', witch's hat, flax-coloured wig, false teeth, dark green spectacles, tar-water bottle for perpetual use, and persistent importuning of his friends for money, Mangan became the proverbial stage-Irish versifier. Eccentricity notwithstanding, Mangan was, as Duffy admitted, a greater poet than the austere Davis. Specialising in free translations of Irish and other poetry, Mangan published his 'Dark Rosaleen' on 30 May 1846. Based on a sixteenth-century original, it is considered one of the finest poems produced by the Young Ireland movement. Though more subtle than some of the 'pretty looking stuff', which Davis told Miss Hutton he wrote for common readers, 'Dark Roseleen' clearly presages a violent revolution with foreign aid:

> There's wine from the Royal Pope
>   Upon the ocean green;
> And Spanish ale shall give you hope,
>   My Dark Rosaleen!

The outcome,

> Oh, the Erne shall run red
>   With redundance of blood:
> The earth shall rock beneath our tread,
>   And flames wrap hill and wood;
> And gun-peal and slogan-cry
>   Wake many a glen serene,
> Ere you shall fade, ere you shall die,
>   My Dark Rosaeleen!

Mangan's poetry was greatly influenced by the Famine, as can be seen from his 'Siberia'. If Mangan was now indisputably *The Nation*'s first poet, praised even by *The Pilot*, he was bravely supported by D. F. MacCarthy, R. D. Williams, the prolific Jean de Jean Frazer, who wrote for many other periodicals, including the detested *Pilot*, and Francis Davis, 'The Belfastman'. Most of the regular male contributors to *The Nation* in this period, with the exception of Mitchel, wrote some poetry.[4]

Poetesses to the Fore

The new *Nation* incorporated an important innovation, the

Repeal Splits, 1845-46 85

lady poet. In Thomas Davis's time there had been verses by 'Maria', but this turned out to be another pseudonym for the prolific cabinet-maker, Jean Frazer. In 1846 a number of real women appeared. The best known was Miss Elgee, 'Speranza'. Duffy was very impressed by her unsolicited contributions. He was furious when Mitchel, in temporary charge, rejected one of Miss Elgee's poetic translations. She became almost as prolific as 'The Celt' himself. If she lacked the literary genius of her son, Oscar Wilde, Speranza was concerned like Davis to arouse patriotism rather than to write poetry. Her poems were filled with images of war and slaughter:

> Be it blood of the tyrant or blood of the slave,
> We'll cross it to Freedom, or find there a grave.

Speranza also expressed the movement's attitude to the Famine in an effective, if somewhat turgid poem that has since appeared in Irish school anthologies:

> There's a proud array of soldiers — what do they round
> your door
> They guard our master's granaries from the thin hands of
> the poor.
> Pale mothers, wherefore weeping? — Would to God that
> we were dead —
> Our children swoon before us and we cannot give them bread.

Other notable poetesses were 'Eva' (Miss Mary Eva Kelly), 'Finola' (Miss Elizabeth Treacy), 'Ethne' (Miss Marie Thompson), and 'Mary' (Miss Mary Downing). They likewise used martial images on occasion, but dwelt with slightly less gusto than Speranza on scenes of carnage.

Amidst this galaxy of feminine talent, *The Nation* remained a little patronising. An article on female education supported women's colleges, but deplored 'pedants in petticoats'. It agreed that some women would do as well as men if they devoted the same amount of time to abstract sciences, while pointing out that in the present state of society women were required mainly as wives and mothers. But there was no need to fear equality of intellect and give women a superficial education.[5]

Mitchel's Railway Article

If Duffy had no reason to fear that the poetic inspiration of *The Nation* would flag on Thomas Davis's death, there were greater problems concerning the political articles. Heavily committed to his Library of Ireland volume, he left Mitchel in control and took a few months sabbatical. In late November 1845, Mitchel responded to provocative English press suggestions for using the new Irish railways to put down Irish revolt. In a *Nation* editorial, 'Threats of Coercion', Mitchel showed how railways could easily be neutralised. Rails could be wrenched away and used for other purposes, presumably pike-making. Troops on trains could be ambushed in numerous places; Andreas Hofer recommending defiles. Hofer (1767-1810), the Che Guevara of the day, had been executed after thrice driving the French from the Tyrol. Repeal wardens, said Mitchel, could take the lead in such defensive activity. 'But 'tis a dream.' There would be no attack.[6]

The article raised a storm of protest. O'Connell personally remonstrated at *The Nation* office. He insisted on a total dissociation of the paper from Repeal. Opinion in England was incensed, yet the Protestant poet and former unionist, Samuel Ferguson, pointed out privately that the offence had originally come from the English journalists. O'Brien, sidestepping expediency, declared the article 'morally and legally justifiable', but was prevented from raising the subject in the Association by the Liberator's son, Maurice. Mitchel, who privately admitted his mistake, tried to rectify matters in the following week, agreeing with O'Connell that *The Nation* had no connection with or control over Repeal wardens. He maintained, however, that his suggestion applied only to an attack on their peaceful movement. In the Repeal Association, O'Connell, reporting on the incident, attempted to distinguish between the old and new *Nation*: 'I admire its talent, and I admired it still more in the time of the illustrious deceased [Davis] [*hear and cheers*].' He denied any personal intention to discourage railway building, being in fact the first shareholder in the Dublin and Cashel Railway. O'Connell's speech was widely considered to have set up *The Nation* for prosecution, which soon followed. Duffy, as the responsible editor, had again to stand trial in June 1846, with Mitchel, the actual author, acting as a solicitor for the defence. Duffy publicly endorsed Mitchel's position in a subsequent *Nation* article. The editor maintained that it was 'most natural and proper' to demonstrate that railways were for peaceful Irish purposes. If a seditious libel it was in the tradition of Swift and Molyneux. Far from being 'imprudent young men', *The Nation* writers, including the honoured Davis, had always advised the Irish people to watch and wait.[7]

Duffy's chief counsel was Robert Holmes, a veteran nationalist and rival of O'Connell's who had defended United Irishmen. His speech in court, far from mitigating the offence, was a ringing declaration for absolute Irish independence. With three Catholics on the jury Duffy was acquitted when it inevitably failed to agree. Young Ireland hopes that the Repeal Association would publish Holmes's speech as a pamphlet were not realised. A crisis between Old and Young Ireland loomed. Before the trial of the railway article, Duffy was offended by O'Connell's attempt to force *The Nation* to pay the legal costs of a radical priest, Fr Davern, whose cause against the landlord, Lord Hawarden, the Repeal Association had previously taken up. Duffy refused outright, though Davern had published in his paper.[8]

A New Pattern Emerges

By early 1846 the new Young Ireland group gained greater coherence. Duffy and Mitchel controlled the paper, with regular poetry from Mangan. In the Repeal Association, Doheny and Barry were backed up by the young orators Meagher and O'Gorman, who had little connection with *The Nation*. Mitchel played an active role in the Association where he spoke for *The Nation*. On 16 March he was voted into the chair for the first time after three years' membership. O'Brien was still not a Young Irelander. Though Duffy claimed that after Davis's death, O'Brien transferred to him the close personal relationship he had previously enjoyed with the dead patriot, a considerable distance, physical and psychological, remained. Duffy and Mitchel became very irritated with O'Brien in early 1846.

In the Association Young Ireland soon confronted
O'Connell, who snubbed young Richard O'Gorman for supporting mixed education. The unionist *Warder* marvelled
that, after all the efforts to destroy *The Nation* it should still
persist in the struggle, now demanding that the Repeal
accounts be published. As its satiric column declared: 'the
dickens such charges of atheism, and heathenism, and Protes-
tanism, for that matter, as we have already cooked up to
cram down the fine peasanthry's throats. . .: but now all the
fat is in the fire, . . . and, signs by, there's that same *Nation*
and not a soul to silence it.' Accounts had long caused
embarrassment. In the past, *The Nation* had been prepared
to trust O'Connell absolutely. Now criticism, from disillusioned supporters like Grey Porter, was reinforced by the
need for careful husbandry of diminished resources.[9]

O'Brien the Cellarman

A bitter new conflict arose. While O'Connell was in gaol,
Davis suggested the withdrawal of Irish MPs from Westminster.
O'Brien was attracted by the proposal. During the Repeal
Year O'Connell had virtually withdrawn from Westminster.
In spring 1845 Davis proposed and carried a motion in the
Repeal Association committee demanding parliamentary
abstention by all Irish MPs. *The Nation* had previously
demanded that Repeal MPs either boycott Westminster completely and work for Ireland at Conciliation Hall or attend
assiduously to parliamentary work in the House of Commons.
The issue came to life in 1846. The Repeal committee undertook a survey of the legality of parliament's control over
members who had already taken an oath of allegiance. The
report, written by Doheny, suggested that parliament did
have such rights. O'Connell, however, brushed these arguments aside. According to Doheny, it was then considered
daring to challenge O'Connell's opinion. A co-ordinated plan
was accepted. Smith O'Brien resisted parliament in London,
while John O'Connell announced defiance at home. The
crisis blew over when Joseph Hume, the English MP who
wished to penalise the Irish, withdrew his motion.[10]

In spring 1846 O'Brien was strongly attacked in the

English press for obstructing Peel's Irish coercion bill in the Commons. O'Brien's repudiation of Westminster, except when Ireland was directly affected, was deplored by the English press; Young Irelanders applauded. Anticipating Parnell in the 1870s, *The Nation* remarked that, as parliament was impervious to argument, the factious opposition of 'interminable speeches', incessant divisions, discussion of every conceivable clause by a group acting in concert was perfectly legitimate. Davis had advised Thomas Wyse, a leading Catholic proponent of mixed education, to use such parliamentary means to forward federalism.[11]

The House of Commons soon replied to Irish obstruction in which even John O'Connell participated. O'Brien was nominated on a Scottish railway committee and John O'Connell received similar duties. O'Brien refused point blank to serve Scotland during an Irish famine. At the same time, O'Brien disagreed with O'Connell in preferring outdoor relief, maintained by taxes on the landowner, to Peel's repeal of the Corn Laws as a remedy for the famine. This division was widened by the ensuing struggle.[12]

When the Commons debated O'Brien's intransigence, O'Connell again contended that parliament had no legal rights over Irish MPs. He did not, however, move an amendment demanded by O'Brien and admitted that the latter had thought his handling of the case unsatisfactory. On 30 April the Commons committed O'Brien to the sergeant-at-arms. The Irish MP was confined to an improvised dungeon in a lean-to shed against the wall of the Chamber, 'a low, small (15 by 8 and 7 feet high), damp-looking and miserable room, with a tressle bed and little deal table.' It was inaccurately described as a cellar. O'Brien's diet, unlike the Liberator's choicer fare in Richmond gaol, apparently consisted of tea and dry toast.[13]

Serious division threatened the Repeal movement. *The Nation* publicly supported O'Brien's 'captivity', the equivalent of O'Connell's after 30 May 1844. O'Brien was implementing Repeal policy, and could not have honourably withdrawn. But John O'Connell, telling O'Brien he agreed with his stand but wanted to oppose the Irish coercion bill, meekly sat on committee as demanded. For the Old Irelanders,

The Pilot dismissed O'Brien's protest as a 'miserable bye-battle', weakening the Irish members' opposition to the coercion bill. Chairing an Association meeting on 27 April, Tom Steele refused three cheers for O'Brien on the same grounds.[14]
A struggle ensued on the Repeal committee. The Young Irelanders, led by Doheny, Barry, O'Gorman, Meagher and what T. M. Ray called 'a vain young man', Patrick James Smyth, supported O'Brien. Smyth, born in 1823, was the son of a Dublin tanner and educated like his friend Meagher at Clongowes. Though the Young Irelanders had a clear majority, a group of Old Ireland leaders warned that endorsement of O'Brien's actions censured his colleagues. To avoid a split the Young Irelanders allowed Doheny to propose a compromise motion in the Association which, despite Meagher's objection, simply offered sympathy to O'Brien.[15]
This put O'Brien, as he told Lucy, into a 'towering passion'. Not only had O'Connell's *'creatures* paralysed the expression of opinion', but his own friends had deserted him. O'Brien determined to resign his seat. The friends hastened to reassure the prisoner. Led by Duffy they pointed out that the compromise resolution was designed simply to avert dissolution of the Association. *The Nation* openly asserted that the Association had not done its full duty by O'Brien, and reprisals against the paper from O'Connell were feared. Dr William Griffin of Limerick urged O'Brien to control his natural inclination to speak out.[16]
John Pigot, who hinted at Old Ireland treachery beyond even O'Brien's suspicions, correctly anticipated that O'Brien would be mollified by strongly supportive motions from his constituents and the Eighty-Two Club. In the latter, the Young Irelanders defeated their opponents, 35-5. A delegation presented the address to O'Brien in his 'cellar'. Invited to participate, the Liberator stalled with a succession of irrelevant jokes and anecdotes.[17]
The Old Irelanders and unionists considered the O'Brien episode a serious challenge. Martin Crean, Repeal acting-secretary, reported anxiously to O'Connell 'that the open and avowed drift of the majority at this meeting was to set up the "Golden ____" in your stead, but this the people will

never submit to.' Old Ireland apparently regarded O'Brien as a 'golden calf', distracting attention from the true deity of the Liberator. Tom Steele likewise thought O'Brien the 'plastic instrument' of 'the machinations of a perfidious clique', and recalled O'Brien's refusal to contest the Clare election in 1828. The unionist *Warder*, considered O'Brien's protest 'selfish and absurd', but believed that it had enabled 'the stormy spirits of *The Nation*' to gain ground hourly on 'the salaried old stagers'. The MP's incarceration gave Young Ireland courage to 'desert the ranks of effete expediency for the banner of active and youthful enterprise.'[18]

O'Brien was clearly of vital importance to Young Ireland, irrespective of the merits of his protest. Some Young Irelanders were dubious about his challenge to the Commons. *The Nation* acknowledged that parliamentary opponents, concerned at his obstructive action, had played on his known 'inflexibility of character' in placing him on the railway committee. The coercion bill, it averred, would have passed in any case. *The Nation* ambiguously denied that O'Brien had been imprudent. Earlier in 1846, John Pigot had deprecated the dissatisfaction of Duffy and Mitchel with O'Brien. Accepting that O'Brien was 'a cold man — a nervous man — a man of no fire or individual intensity', Pigot upheld the Limerick MP as 'a really honest man and inflexibly true to what he says.'[19]

On 25 May, when an Irish unionist, Frederick Shaw, moved that the House's authority had been vindicated, O'Brien was released after 25 days incarceration. O'Connell, who had endured 100 days at Richmond, had intended to move for unconditional discharge. Resolutions of various municipalities in O'Brien's favour and the expulsion of the uniformly hostile *Pilot* from Limerick and Rathkeale made it difficult to sustain the illusion that there was no dissension in the Repeal movement. The Liberator nevertheless, with characteristic hyperbole, declared that 'I would not consent to continue a member of the Association one hour unless William Smith O'Brien was my comrade, my colleague, and my co-equal in the struggle [*Renewed applause*].' *The Nation* tried again to play down the 'Young Ireland' tag as an invention of their enemies. It had no desire to sack O'Connell from the leadership, as *The Pilot* consistently asserted. Duffy's paper nevertheless presented a formidable list of differences, ranging from the legalistic approach of the Association to the 'ecclesiastical character' of its language and proceedings. O'Connell replied in the Association by declaring that he intended 'upon every occasion to place religion as a basis of our proceedings'. *The Nation* mildly agreed, but insisted that no political society should aid clergy to defend faith and morals by distinguishing bad Catholics and bad Protestants. *The Warder*, with more conviction now that the division was public, also emphasised religion. The issue, it declared, was who should govern Ireland after Repeal: 'O'Connell and the priests under a system of hypocrisy and slander' or 'O'Brien and a secular clique of enthusiastic latitudinarians'. The Young Irelanders had long looked to O'Brien as an alternative leader.[20]

The O'Brien imprisonment thus activated a number of issues fermenting within the Repeal movement. One of these was violence. Before O'Brien's release, Michael Doheny, who had particular reason to feel aggrieved, attended a pro-O'Brien Repeal meeting in Liverpool. On the platform were Terence Bellew MacManus, a wealthy Liverpool shipping agent, born in Monaghan in 1823, and another local leader, George Archdeacon. Doheny, later decrying division, openly declared himself a Young Irelander, but not opposed to O'Connell. When Doheny explained himself in the Repeal Association, O'Gorman also admitted acceptance of Young Ireland views, based on the teaching of Davis. Barry generally agreed. The latter, making light of labels, dangerously praised Davis's generosity in his confrontation with O'Connell. Barry alluded to slanders against Davis, before and after his death.[21]

The Liberator easily obtained the expulsion of Archdeacon, accused of declaring that 'even with their physical strength' Liverpool Repealers could beat two million Saxons. O'Connell, using it as a test case, asserted that those talking of physical force handed themselves over to the attorney-general and were traitors not only to their country, but also to the queen. Archdeacon's letter, denying that he had ever incited to violence and complaining that he had been set up for a treason indictment, was summarily rejected by the Liberator. Though Barry agreed with O'Connell's action, the Young Irelanders were soon to suffer likewise. Doheny had already been challenged for reading letters in the Association too favourable to O'Brien, and Captain Seaver, a former Orangeman converted to Repeal, was silenced for the same offence. Ray, writing to O'Connell on Archdeacon, deplored the Liverpool Repealers' declaration that the Commons had no *right* to imprison O'Brien: 'Coupling all together, the Young Ireland principles so far as they exist seem to be avowed and not of any very pacific character either.' *The Nation* prosecution for Mitchel's railway article underlined this message, especially as the latter admitted authorship.[22]

The Whig Alliance

Meanwhile Peel, having carried the repeal of the Corn Laws against the wishes of many of his party, was finally defeated on the Irish Coercion Bill. The spectre of a new Whig alliance was raised when, on 6 June, O'Connell attended, with his son John and other Repeal MPs, a Whig meeting at the house of Lord John Russell. The Young Irelanders turned out in force at the Association to protest against any hint of such a Whig alliance. Meagher, indirectly criticising O'Connell by condemning the Whig administration of 1835-41, used Davis's name so freely as 'our prophet and our guide' that the faithful Steele insisted that they had no prophet other than 'the almost sanctified peaceful moral force revolutionist', Daniel O'Connell. *The Nation* was accused of spreading the rumours of a deal. O'Connell himself wrote to the next meeting against the 'juvenile orators' who were creating so much dissension. The 'juvenile orators', reinforced by Doheny, previously absent, enthusiastically defended themselves. Still denying opposition to O'Connell, O'Gorman asked if they were traitors and liars for criticising the Whigs. Mitchel was tactful, expressing views at some variance with his subsequent vitriolic prose. *The Nation*, he said, had never aimed at separation; he agreed with Doheny that there was no suspicion of O'Connell, merely of Whigs outside the Association. Such soft words seemed to calm the disputants. The chairman hoped no further division would occur. Then John Reilly, an unsuccessful barrister and Town Councillor, made a provocative speech denouncing *The Nation*, and by implication, John Mitchel. The latter's stylistic model, Thomas Carlyle, was irrelevantly repudiated as an infidel influence. *The Pilot* applauded Reilly's 'modest and discreet' lesson to The Clique.[23]

Meanwhile Lord John Russell's government assumed office. *The Nation* stood alone amongst the Repeal press in its opposition. An editorial by the fiery Devin Reilly, dissociated from O'Connell in emphasising national liberty before individual life, 'Mr O'Connell thinks each priceless.' Then Reilly lamented O'Connell's rejection of physical force patriots, such as Washington, Tell and Hofer, but accepted that all Repealers worked willingly with the Liberator as 'a great political experimentalist.'[24]

O'Brien appeared a changed man. On 30 June, for the first time since his imprisonment, he attended the Association. Russell's administration had recently assumed power. The battle lines between reform — in the shape of a Whig alliance — and Repeal were gradually drawn. O'Brien stigmatised reform as more dangerous to Repeal than the Tories. He would even accept O'Connell in the cabinet — but only as a Repealer. Clearly O'Brien was solidly behind the Young Irelanders in their fears of a Whig alliance, which effectively excluded Repeal.

Dungarvan

Meanwhile, the Young Irelanders focussed on the immediate practical question of a candidate for the Dungarvan by-election which O'Connell's former ally Richard Sheil was contesting as a prelude to his assumption of office under Russell. By June 1845, the Liberator was announcing that he had thrown the Whigs 'completely overboard'; he threatened to take Sheil's seat unless he declared for Repeal. A survey had shown that there would have been a majority of 70 for a pure Repealer. O'Brien urged that the contest be fought.[25]

Yet the Liberator promised a Repealer only if one could be found, and concentrated on pressing a list of propositions on the ministry. *The Nation* clearly showed its concern, pointing out that 'to receive laws, good or bad, from the hands of strangers, is the authentic mark of slavery'. Like O'Connell, however, it was willing to challenge the Whigs to implement their system of reforms. Another article approached an outright attack on the Liberator. If, it declared, O'Connell accepted Lord Milltown's suggestion for an Irish party which would merely extract concessions, he would be 'the basest and blackest traitor that ever poisoned God's air, even in Ireland.' The Liberator's oft repeated pledge of 17 October 1842, never to abandon Repeal in his lifetime, was emphasised. A third editorial condemned the cowardice, 'or something worse', of the Association committee for declaring that there was no candidate offering. 'There is yet time to turn back from a path that tends to inevitable ruin and everlasting shame.'[26]

Duffy had certainly thrown down the gauntlet to the Liberator. In retrospect the former argued that O'Connell's behaviour over the by-elections was final proof of a deal between O'Connell and the Whigs. He cited a damning letter of 8 July 1846, published in Fitzpatrick's collection of O'Connell's correspondence, to D. R. Pigot, the Whig father of the Young Irelander, John. Here O'Connell openly admitted that 'I am glad to tell you that I have stifled opposition to Sheil in Dungarvan. The election will not cost him a shilling, and that is what he likes — among other things.' Even worse, O'Connell had 'been working in an under channel' for J. H. Monaghan, who became solicitor-general. Duffy believed, though there was no precise documentation, that O'Connell had come to a clear secret agreement with the Whig leaders. This was also the view of Mitchel, O'Brien and Doheny in their retrospective accounts. As the modern editor of O'Connell's correspondence puts it, 'Sheil's election was a virtual necessity: he would be O'Connell's "hot line" to the incoming Whig prime minister.'[27]

The Peace Resolutions

After *The Nation* outburst, O'Connell at the Repeal Association on 13 July formally minuted a letter from O'Brien which insisted on challenging all Whigs at the polls. As Duffy told O'Brien, O'Brien's communication was completely ignored. Instead the Liberator introduced two momentous resolutions. The first abandoned the Dungarvan contest on the grounds of cost and likely division in Repeal. The second reaffirmed the Association's rejection of physical force. A full discussion in committee had accepted the latter with Mitchel and Meagher dissenting. The Young Irelanders, followed by most modern historians with the exception of Professor Maurice O'Connell, have seen the latter proposition as a mere pretext for drawing attention from the former.[28]

Contemporaries certainly perceived such a strategy. O'Connell himself mixed the physical force issue with a rambling justification of Dungarvan; when the Young Ireland orator, Meagher, complained of the Whig alliance and the apostasy of a certain Repealer, John O'Connell incautiously interjected that physical-force supporters like Meagher would soon be out of the Association. O'Brien's Limerick friend, Samuel Bindon, was amazed to see 'Mr Meagher, a stripling, pitted against the great O'Connell' and patently holding his own. Distraction was clearly in the Liberator's interest.[29]

The Peace Resolutions against violence contained two parts. The first simply reaffirmed Repeal policy which sought 'the amelioration of political institutions by peaceable and legal means alone.' The second, 'abhorring all attempts to improve and augment constitutional liberty by means of force, violence, or bloodshed', was more controversial. Did it apply to other countries? O'Connell's report, however, specifically endorsed 'the necessary defence against unjust aggression on the part of a domestic government or a foreign enemy'. In fact, 'it leaves the right of self-defence perfectly free to the use of any force sufficient to resist and defeat unjust aggression.' John O'Connell later claimed that the defence loophole made the policy 'more lax' than the original resolution of 1840. This was consistent with the Liberator's oratory, even in 1843. But O'Connell clouded the issue by asserting that 'if I were a Quaker I could not abhor violence more than I do.' *The Pilot*'s dutiful insistence that Quakers supported defensive violence was a travesty of their position, as James Haughton demonstrated when he criticised O'Connell's attitude to war.[30]

John Mitchel immediately perceived the contradiction. Like the other Young Irelanders he concurred in the 'no drop of blood' theory as a rule of the Association, but opposed the sinfulness of force as an abstract principle. When O'Connell accepted Washington's revolution as defensive, Mitchel invited the Liberator to embody the Quaker position of literally turning the other cheek in the resolutions. Mitchel also distinguished between rules for an individual's guidance and the condemnation of others.

Mitchel's challenge was not taken up. It would have destroyed ambiguous threats of defensive violence against the government, while it ignored the Young Ireland sticking point, the condemnation of violence in all places and times. O'Connell, after suggesting other arguments, the need to reassure Orangemen and the possibility that revolution, as in South America, would become habitual, admitting that his intention was 'to draw a line of demarcation between Old and Young Ireland'. Meagher, who, like O'Gorman, objected to the word 'abhor' could not continue in the Association. The Young Irelanders, with the exception of Meagher, did not oppose the resolutions in the Association vote. *The Pilot* rejoiced that O'Connell's surgical knife had separated 'what was tainted from what was sound.' Bindon, however, found such meetings evenly divided and outside gossip 'almost unanimously with Meagher *against the Whigs*.'[31]

In *The Nation*, Duffy developed Mitchel's argument in an editorial, 'Moral Force — Ways and Means'. He incautiously admitted that in 1843 many good men had expected O'Connell to 'right her wrongs in battle line.' Duffy also demonstrated the inconsistency between O'Connell's alleged Quakerism and his doctrine that 'England's weakness is Ireland's opportunity'. 'To Quaker nations there is *no* opportunity in the weakness of their oppressors.' The idea of no force save in self-defence was too abstract. Duffy saw no moral difference between resistance to old wrongs and new acts of aggression. What Duffy implied was openly asserted by the unionist *Warder*, which agreed that the strong language of *The Nation* in 1843 was no stronger than that of

O'Connell. The difference was that, while the Liberator rejected the obvious interpretation of his language, *The Nation* 'fearlessly and frankly' accepted the literal interpretation.[32]

The then little-known Repealer, Fr John Kenyon, advanced a similar argument. At a meeting alongside O'Brien at Kilrush he depicted 'moral force' as 'false and visionary'. Smith O'Brien, still claiming independence of Repeal factions, also rejected the absolute condemnation of physical force in all places, times, and contingencies. He was unwilling to remain in the Association under such a rule. Ironically, while most Young Irelanders tried to evade this issue and remain in the Association, O'Brien, an experienced politician, gave the Old Irelanders a perfect lever with which to prise him out.[33]

Duffy and his close friends were overjoyed by O'Brien's Kilrush speech. But Pigot reminded them that the Limerick MP, possibly because he had too much to lose, did not want an intimate connexion with either the group or its leadership. O'Brien perhaps hoped to pay his debt to *The Nation* by pre-empting the issue, and thus saving the young men from expulsion. Even before Dungarvan, O'Brien had heard that O'Connell intended a rupture with *The Nation* writers. He therefore told the Liberator through Ray that, despite his neutrality, he could not silently acquiesce in their expulsion. The speech at Kilrush was an earnest of his intentions. His assumption that O'Connell was serious when he declared that he would not lead the movement without O'Brien at his side was soon tested. For his part, O'Connell up to 18 July appears to have believed that O'Brien was likely to side with him against the Young Irelanders. On that date the Liberator wrote to O'Brien asking for his help in choosing a candidate for Dundalk as he could not co-operate with the Young Irelanders until they accepted the new peace resolutions. He suggested, however, that the latter could be amended, but if not the Young Irelanders would have to accept them or leave. It is possible, though difficult to accept in the circumstances, that both O'Brien and O'Connell were misled as to each other's positions till it was too late to avoid a rupture.[34]

Duffy's editorial and the Kilrush meeting, far from dampening down controversy, embittered the dispute at the Repeal Association meeting on 20 July. With both O'Connell and O'Brien absent, Mitchel again rebutted the complaints of Repeal correspondents that the Young Irelanders were creating dissension. He agreed that the Association must keep within the law. J. A. O'Neill, a prominent Repeal landholder who was managing the meeting, gladly offered the Young Irelanders friendship, but again the malevolent Reilly demurred. He opposed amity, preferring to cut 'out a cancer at once'. Duffy was attacked for secretly contemplating revolution while ostensibly a member of O'Connell's movement.

Duffy replied in *The Nation*, denying any revolutionary conspiracy in 1843, but accepting the *Warder*'s earlier contention that the Young Irelanders foolishly took O'Connell's 'rhetorical flourishes' seriously and thought that the promises made at monster meetings and Repeal dinners would be valid in a 'great emergency'. Duffy naively believed this confession a 'peace offering' to accommodate O'Connell's resolutions.[35]

The Two-Day Debate

The climax of the dispute came on 27 and 28 July 1846. O'Brien, for the first time in several weeks, attended in person, but O'Connell was represented by his son John. O'Brien opened proceedings breezily, moving, without total agreement with its contents, the minuting of O'Connell's letter. This reiterated the distinction between offensive violence and defence against an unconstitional attack, which the Liberator regarded as necessary to avoid prosecution. O'Brien denied Reilly's right to interrogate him but stood by his Kilrush views. For the first time he explained the inconsistency between the Peace Resolutions' Quakerish insistence on peaceful means and the acceptance of resistance to unjustified aggression. He linked the attack on *The Nation* with the paper's support during his imprisonment and then attacked the Whig alliance in some detail, dismissing the Whigs as little better than the Tories. Their programme failed to provide against a likely second failure of the potato crop. Repealers should fight all constituencies instead of driving out their own members. Doheny had offered to contest Mayo: was he to be expelled? Meagher should also be in parliament. O'Brien concluded in a conciliatory manner, deprecating his own services as less than those of either Daniel or John O'Connell. He had waived many points in the past for the sake of consensus. He did not believe that O'Connell or Association members were deserting Repeal; rather they had adopted different means of attainment. Though despondent, O'Brien did not despair.

John O'Connell, however, took offence at an implied criticism of family patronage. He defended the Whigs and the decision not to fight Dungarvan. More important, he challenged anyone to demonstrate anything but defensive violence in the Liberator's speeches. The American Revolution, really self-defence, was the only example of a justifiable appeal to arms, and even that had resulted in slavery and lynch law. The Liberator was not inconsistent in maintaining Quakerish means alongside a belief in justifiable defence. The context of the 1843 speeches at Mallow, Lismore and Mullaghmast must be considered. The Liberator had insisted that while a rag or plank of the constitution remained, he would not appeal to force. If Irish liberties were attacked, the Association put down, public meetings prohibited, and the Repeal rent stopped, that would be a different matter. Anyway, if O'Brien thought the Peace Proposals self-contradictory, why did he scruple to accept them? John O'Connell finally denied that Young Irelanders were being turned out for 'speculative opinion'. It was a matter of 'instant practicability' to preserve the Association from prosecution. If the rules were modified to accommodate Young Ireland, it would be necessary for the Liberator to withdraw.

After this hard but rational debating, the egregious John Reilly intervened with more personal abuse of several Young Irelanders. O'Brien tried to restore goodwill by denying any imputation on the O'Connell family, but John accepted the olive branch with ill grace. He rejected O'Brien's final plea to forget all that had passed. O'Brien had even offered to withdraw — he would not resign unless expelled — from the

Association to avoid impeding the Liberator. The production of a letter from Duffy secured an adjournment till the following day to allow tempers to cool. O'Brien had originally intended to leave early for the parliamentary session.

Duffy's letter launched the second, adjourned, debate. He justified *The Nation* at length, arguing shrewdly that he had never depicted O'Connell's threatening language as anything but defensive. 'I am not aware of any great popular struggle that was not defensive.' Duffy was one of several Young Irelanders to perceive the elasticity of the defence loophole.[36]

John O'Connell's lengthy refutation of Duffy interpreted his father's more bellicose 1843 speeches at Mallow, Lismore and Mullaghmast defensively. He also maintained that a 'beautiful' article in *The Nation* on moral force was repudiated in the following week by a writer (Davis in fact) who sneered at the 'fat and sensual Quakerism of this age'.[37]

In the adjourned debate, Mitchel made an extremely effective reply to John O'Connell, again showing none of the rashness of judgment later attributed to him. He created consternation by arguing that *The Nation* articles now denounced had mostly been penned by the honoured Davis. For all John O'Connell's examples of the Liberator's defensive speeches, Mitchel counterposed remarks which clearly implied war. What else was the purpose of the constant insistence on Irishmen's physical superiority to the English? Mitchel cited two priests using bellicose language in 1843; John O'Connell contested this; Fr C. P. Meehan, a priest sympathetic to Young Ireland, was shouted down when he tried to speak. Uproar again broke out. Blows were almost struck when an Old Irelander seized Devin Reilly's collar for cheering his friend Mitchel too loudly. Perhaps Mitchel's strongest argument was his contention that the real division was not over violence at all. 'Nobody is in the least afraid of physical force, but there are some of us mortally afraid of Whiggery.' These included bishops like Kennedy of Killaloe and MacHale himself. The latter in late June 1846, fearing that Repeal might be abandoned, looked forward to a meeting with O'Brien. Rejection of violence might divert church criticism. Ironically, Mitchel in later life almost

vindicated O'Connell by declaring that the independent principles of Young Ireland were, in the absence of a European
war, almost certain to lead to an unsuccessful revolt.[38]

Meagher, challenged by Steele to repudiate violence, except
for defence, in 'every possible contingency of O'Connell's
movement', was soon carried away by the flights of his carefully prepared oration, which as usual captivated its audience
by its imagery. After attacking the Whig alliance, Meagher
launched his famous paean on the sword with its standard
endorsement of heroes like Hofer, Tell and Washington.

> Abhor the sword? Stigmatise the sword? No, for in the
> passes of the Tyrol it cut to pieces the banner of the
> Bavarian, and through those cragged passes cut a path to
> fame for the peasant insurrectionist of Innsbruk.
> Abhor the sword? Stigmatise the sword? No, for at its
> blow, and in the quivering of its crimson light a giant
> nation sprang up from the waters of the Atlantic, and
> by its redeeming magic the fettered colony became a
> daring, free Republic.

The climax quickly followed. John O'Connell stopped
Meagher's flow, insisting that he himself would have to
leave if the Association voted against him. O'Brien, declaring
Meagher's views 'fair and legitimate' and no breach of Association policy, walked out. He was followed by most of the
Young Irelanders, including Fr Meehan, and a number of
ladies from the gallery.

Why did O'Brien quit at this point? Ironically, one of the
examples given by Meagher, the American Revolution, had
already been accepted by both the Liberator and his son as a
'defensive' event. The other examples might also have been
interpreted as defence. True, Meagher threw away the debating point by celebrating the sword 'be it for defence, or, be it
for the *assertion* [my italics] of a nation's liberty'. A priest
interjected, 'No, No.' Meagher's words suggest that he was
deliberately negating O'Connell's distinction between violence
defending existing liberty and force to acquire new, or
lost, rights. Daunt, who did not appreciate the distinction,
blamed the walkout on the mutual provocation of Captain
Broderick, then in the chair, and young Meagher. An un-

seemly brawl between these two men did occur in the street after the meeting. However, as Meagher usually prepared his speeches beforehand, it is possible that his gaffe was intended to commit O'Brien finally to the Young Irelanders.

After the previous Association meeting, which O'Brien had addressed by letter only, Gavan Duffy had written him 'brusquely, perhaps rudely', pointing out that the young men were unhappy. 'One and all, they believe that, having got into this battle in your defence, you left them, when a crisis came, to take care of themselves.' After O'Brien's Kilrush speech, however, Duffy assured O'Brien that all feelings of irritation against him had vanished. Indeed, 'no man of us, trust me, desired to implicate you with our, or any other peculiar opinions. We felt the value of your neutral position.' To a man with such a punctilious sense of honour as O'Brien this was indeed a sharp challenge. The arbitrary closure of discussion by John O'Connell was another blow to O'Brien's pride. As O'Brien pointed out in his final Yeats-like speech, 'you are charged with being a people who will never give fair play to an adversary. You are charged with being willing slaves to any despot who may obtain the reins of power at a particular moment.' This was in the same vein as Mitchel's earlier assertion which proudly evoked Davis's doctrine: 'I am one of the Saxon Irishmen of the north, and you want that race of Irishmen in your ranks more than any others: you cannot well afford to drive even one away from you, however humble and uninfluential. And let me tell you, friends, this is our country as well as yours. . . . Drive the Ulster Protestants away from your movement by needless tests, and you perpetuate the degradation both of yourselves and them.' Both Mitchel and O'Brien demonstrated an outspoken Protestantism that the Association, linked increasingly to the Catholic policies of Archbishop MacHale, found too difficult to absorb. *The Pilot* met Mitchel's assertion head on, rejecting his United Irishman father as a member of an anti-Catholic movement, now absorbed into Orangeism. Ironically, Orange papers like *The Warder* were as opposed to Young Ireland on the vital issue of education as *The Pilot* itself.[39]

Significantly, Barrett's paper maintained that 'the brute force question was merely a collateral branch of its [Young

Ireland] destructiveness. The great cementing principle of the party was the College demoralisation scheme, and all connected with its contamination.' Young Ireland, said *The Pilot*, was in alliance with the Whigs on education. Meanwhile John O'Connell attacked infidel education in the July 1846 Association debates. Two of the MacHale bishops, Drs Cantwell and Higgins, were delighted at Young Ireland's departure from the Association. Higgins later specifically referred to mixed education in his condemnation of the group's infidelity. It is thus arguable that education was as important as violence in achieving a split.[40]

Given the Young Ireland devotion to the nationalism of Davis, and total rejection of the Whig alliance, a clash with Old Ireland appears inevitable. But the Young Irelanders, as the reports of the relevant Association meetings demonstrate, did try to remain in the Association as long as possible. The real issue was whether Young or Old Ireland would win the adhesion of O'Brien. The latter, to avoid a decision, remained as far as possible outside Dublin. Even after the split O'Brien told Duffy that he was unwilling to visit the capital as his presence would force him to decide whether or not to attend Association meetings.[41]

Unionist papers, like *The Warder*, took the Young Ireland side, arguing, like *The Nation*, that 'the quarrel was wholly unprovoked.' As usual, *The Warder* waxed poetic on 'The Split in the Camp'.

'Twas a great day, and a display that'll be forgotten ne'er,
The jesuitry and avarice and humbug were laid bare;
All honour to the cellar man, that cut the swindlers there;
His ancient name will be revered in Limerick, Cork and Clare,
As a manly Irish gentleman, one of the present time.

This was indeed how the Young Irelanders wanted the country to react, and it was a hopeful sign that unionists were attracted to their position, thus partly endorsing Mitchel's remarks in the debate. *The Pilot* saw *The Nation* as a mere adjunct to the Tory press.

The Split Widens

Any hope that the division would prove temporary was soon dispelled by Old Ireland action. The next week O'Connell returned to the Association. After reading the two ferocious episcopal letters against *The Nation*'s infidelity, the Liberator shed some tears for O'Brien, whom he refused to link with the Young Irelanders. Their 'filthy partisans' in different parts of the country were traitors to Repeal, frightening away Catholic and Protestant gentry by their talk of violence. Ignoring previous debates, O'Connell again identified with Quakerism. Ironically, one of the gentry, the former Tasmanian landowner, William Bryan, 'a gruff but kindly old gentleman, always in a state of sustained indignation against England and everything English', submitted his resignation. O'Brien wrote to the Association to condemn the unjustifiable exclusion of *The Nation* from Repeal reading rooms. O'Brien had had little communication with its staff since Davis's death, but believed that *The Nation* effectively raised the poor without challenging the rich. The Liberator retorted that the letter was tantamount to a rejection of his invitation to O'Brien to return to the movement.[42]

According to *The Nation*, O'Connell had now ended any hope of healing the breach. The seceders, however, would not fight back, as some demanded, but would concentrate on constructive work. O'Brien could decide for himself. For his part, O'Brien was happy to wait in the country with his family and books, away from 'the turmoil of agitation'. By October he was convinced that O'Connell and his sons did not want the seceders back.[43]

At O'Brien's suggestion, several Young Irelanders tested their rights in the Association by asserting their status as members. Secretary Ray's invariable reply maintained that their failure to support the Peace Proposals automatically excluded them. Fr Kenyon demanded a rebate for his locality of that percentage of the subscription previously purchasing *The Nation*. He was refused. Most dramatic was the action of Mitchel's old friend, John Martin. Martin, in the light of the defence loophole, was unable to perceive any essential difference between the position of O'Connell and the Young Irelanders on physical force. To Martin, O'Connell desired a ban acceptable only to the Society of Friends. Despite his retiring nature, Martin travelled to Dublin to question the Association in person. He was refused a hearing on the ground that his opinions excluded him from the Association. As *The Nation* asked, how could Martin now justify Repeal freedom to Northern Protestants?[44]

The Nation Seeks a Policy

Protests like Martin's which ridiculed O'Connell's 'Quaker' policy, and raised the old issue of Repeal funds, did little for the image of the Repeal Association. Ray's letters of rejection appeared exceptionally arbitrary. He privately told Daunt that most Repealers were glad the Young Irelanders were out and criticised the Liberator's tardiness in expelling them. John Dillon, long absent through illness, returned from Madeira to denounce proceedings reminiscent of the 'degraded senate of the Roman emperors, which used to assemble for no other object than to register and applaud the capricious edicts of a despot'. Free speech, emphasised by O'Brien, became an important Young Ireland issue. The right to differ, said *The Nation* , was the 'essence of liberty'. James Haughton, a genuine pacifist who disliked Young Ireland's warlike tendency, nevertheless resigned from the Association in protest against the refusal to counter Young Ireland principles. Several places, Drogheda, Templederry (Kenyon), Rathkeale (O'Brien), Rosbercon, Ballaghaderin (Dillon), for example, refused to eject *The Nation* and accept *The Pilot*. Duffy asserted indifference to financial losses after the exclusion of *The Nation* from Repeal reading rooms. It meant only a reduction of 1,100 copies from a total circulation of 10,000, but the moral effect was considerable.[45]

Barrett's *Pilot*, speaking for Old Ireland, waxed divisively poetic.

And, oh, may we ne'er live the sad moment to see,
When those silly schoolboys shall rise out again;

Oh! may thou who now struggle their country to free
Rebuke the young puppets with scorn and disdain.[46]

The Pilot anticipated with initial accuracy a considerable
revival in Repeal rent after the Young Ireland departure. It
applauded the *Freeman's Journal*'s new strong line against
Young Ireland. As for free speech, Barrett's paper rejoiced
at the new unanimity of the Association, maintaining that
the right to differ was fatal to any organisation. It also considered the correspondence with Ray indicative of Young
Ireland's mistaken self-expulsion. *The Nation* clique was
'dying soft'. Far from being victimised, the Young Irelanders
had allowed little individual freedom on the Repeal committee, when dominating with their compact block. Now
that *The Nation* depended on the support of the Tory press
and the subscriptions of low Dublin Orangemen its life
would be short. No earlier challenge to O'Connell had been
so serious; only Young Ireland caballed secretly against the
leader and possessed a newspaper to re-fight the battles of
the Association committee.[47]

Against so determined an onslaught, *The Nation* failed to
maintain its original low key post-secession policy. Boasting
that *The Nation* needed the Repeal Association less than the
Association needed it, Duffy's paper deprecated criticism of
O'Connell; to avoid assailing the Association, *The Nation*
claimed to have jettisoned valuable controversial weapons.
Now that public opinion was moving towards the seceders,
O'Connell in return should admit he was wrong. An amnesty
'alone can save our gigantic organisation from speedy ruin'.
O'Connell in the past had yielded to strong public feeling. To
The Pilot, however, the only remedy was the return of
O'Brien without restoring *The Nation*. *The Pilot* denied that
The Nation had kept its promise to avoid division. Nor did
The Nation have the power to prevent open confrontation in
the provinces. When, in mid-September, Old Irelanders met
at Chapel-Lane, Belfast, to resolve in O'Connell's favour,
local Young Irelanders disrupted the demonstration, turned
off the gas, cheered Duffy and *The Nation* and reprobated
the Whig Alliance. As *The Warder* said, 'mutiny, vehement and
undisguised' appeared at all promiscuous Repeal gatherings.[48]

Force became less relevant in a dispute emphasising the Colleges, infidelity and episcopal opinion. *The Nation* gained nothing by demonstrating that Old Irelanders like Dillon Browne now defended past violence in words almost identical to those of Meagher's 'sword speech'. Indeed *The Pilot* shifted from condemnation of force in the past, to insistence on moral force alone in the future, a position suggested by John Mitchel. With force a mere distraction, *The Pilot* regarded war on *The Nation* clique as essential to defeat infidel Colleges. There thus appeared little chance of *The Nation* group being readmitted.[49]

The Nation over-estimated its support in the country. According to John O'Connell only forty members resigned with the Young Irelanders. This seems an underestimation, but probably not by much. Relatively few districts protested against the banning of *The Nation*. Only a handful of other newspapers endorsed it. Duffy, however, claimed that where meetings were held, as in Cork, Belfast and Meath, there was always strong support for the seceders. *The Pilot* later admitted that some good provincial advocates were persuaded to join the Young Irelanders. Despite the efforts of Fr John Kenyon as the Young Ireland clerical hatchet-man, it is also clear that relatively few of his brother clerics were persuaded by his insistence that Young Ireland was not infidel. Duffy calculated that, apart from Kenyon and Meehan, twenty-one Catholic clerics openly supported the secession, while others gave private encouragement. However, only two were parish priests and three lived outside Ireland. Unfortunately, the bishops least estranged from *The Nation*'s education policy were not Repealers and therefore of little help. Young Ireland, said *The Warder*, was exhausting its might in high sounding sentences and making too much of the support of a strong curate or drunken Repeal warden. O'Brien privately warned Duffy in September that neither the clergy nor the middle classes were enamoured of Young Ireland. He disagreed with Duffy that in autumn 1846 there was much immediate prospect of reconciliation, but hoped that O'Connell might seek it by Christmas. *The Nation*'s outward confidence was partly whistling to keep its spirits up, and partly an assertion of strength to exact better terms from Old Ireland.[50]

Enter the Remonstrants

Unexpected and embarrassing allies now appeared in Dublin. A group of thirty to forty workingmen, inspired by Patrick John Barry, who described himself as 'a very humble person', met nightly for two weeks to counter the Association's 'cruel policy'. As Barry told O'Brien, they kept the movement secret, 'until it was completely out of your power to check it if you desire to do so'. Barry may have been an *agent provocateur*. By 1848 the Young Irelanders were certain that Barry was a government spy, and there is evidence that he provided information to Castle informers. As some of the workers' group had Chartist leanings, the young Ireland élite feared an ultra-democratic reaction. D'Arcy McGee was infiltrated into a committee of ten, which organised a public meeting for 27 September. The Old Irelanders, led by the demagogue, Tom Arkins, aided by the coal porters, blocked the entrance to the house on Bolton Street and the committee was forced to withdraw and draft a remonstrance without further recourse to the public. Local tradesmen and 74 of the 120 Dublin Repeal wardens were persuaded to sign. The Old Irelanders' disruption of the meeting parallelled the Young Irelanders' disruption of theirs in Belfast. *The Nation*'s efforts to claim that the protest was spontaneous was denied by *The Pilot* which argued that good Dublin citizens had successfully confronted a motley crowd of Chartists and Orangemen, led by well-dressed members of the clique. That the chairman was William Bryan and the eventual remonstrance drawn up by D'Arcy McGee indicates upper-class control. But Duffy denied that other Young Irelanders had interfered in the movement. After initial misgivings, the Young Ireland leaders adapted the movement for their own use.

The remonstrance opposed the new Association policy, demanded freedom of speech and sought the rehabilitation of *The Nation*. *The Pilot* disparaged the remonstrance, claiming that the signature hunters could only have consulted the police charge-sheets to obtain their names. The Repeal Association on 26 October gave the protest of O'Brien's friend, the Clare landowner and JP, John Shea Lawlor, short shrift and threw the remonstrance out of the window into the gutter outside Conciliation Hall. O'Connell fully endorsed the action. O'Brien, who had been advising Duffy to suspend hostilities, to avoid alienating half-supporters, considered the treatment of the remonstrance sufficiently scandalous to justify verbal retaliation. The Liberator received a similar document from Cork with a dismissive 'Bah!' In the latter incident, the Liberator lost an opportunity to exploit Cork's apparent attempt to by-pass Young Ireland, and divide his opponents.[51]

The Repeal Association thus helped to develop the secession into an opposition movement. Its arbitrary and dictatorial nature was effectively dramatised. The Liberator himself became a target for criticism. Dr I. H. West, an apothecary, chaired an angry meeting on 2 November at the Rotunda, with the dubious P. J. Barry as secretary. The crowded gathering, contrasted with the 'naked benches and languid prose of Conciliation Hall', attacked O'Connell more vigorously than the hostile *Times* or *Standard*. O'Brien appeared the acknowledged leader, while McGee declared O'Connell to be 'crumbling' in intellect and rendered dictatorial by adulation. Fr Kenyon's name evoked loud applause. He had declared the famine, now at its peak, 'a paradoxical Godsend' to the Repeal Association, diverting attention from its misdeeds. The meeting not only condemned the Repeal Association but endorsed the co-option of a committee of twenty-one to organise another meeting. A new remonstrance was to be circulated throughout Ireland to Repealers, especially of the working classes. M. J. Barry's claim, that the Young Ireland epithet, once confined to a few, was now assumed by a great number, was premature, but movement had begun.[52]

The Pilot derided the 250 attending the Rotunda as boys, a few tradesmen, some labourers, and a large sprinkling of law clerks, chaired by an associate of the notorious bigot, the Rev. T. D. Gregg. But the failure of the Association policy was undeniable. Instead of cauterising a small 'clique' and undermining their newspaper, the O'Connells had evoked, in Dublin at least, a standing opposition, certain, whatever its own success, to permanently weaken the Association.

The Nation believed that the Liberator's ability to divide his opponents by 'rash and unfounded charges', 'convenient and impossible promises', and 'ingenious expedients' to evade temporary difficulties had clearly deserted him. The handling of the Young Irelanders on the Colleges and physical-force issues had been characterised by fanatical overkill tactics.[53]

But the errors of the Association did not ensure the success of its opponents. As Daunt, a cool Old Irelander who agreed with much of the Young Ireland assessment of O'Connell, asked, how could the seceders hope to carry Repeal in opposition to the Liberator? The unionist *Warder* meanwhile proved remarkably accurate in its prophecy that the new unpurchaseable anti-Whig party would eventually try physical force, only to be 'crushed in a storm of grape shot'. After a period of calm, it believed that a new generation of lawyers would emerge to play out the game again.[54]

Other Young Ireland Expedients

The moderate John Dillon suggested legal arbitration by a panel of six lawyers (including law officers of the crown), the circulating of no newspapers through the Repeal Association, thus avoiding discrimination against *The Nation*, and, tongue in cheek, the hanging of anyone in correspondence with France in 1843. Though this idiosyncratic letter almost broke rank with the Young Irelanders, it encouraged O'Connell's reconciliation attempt in December 1846. Duffy believed that Dillon's object was to secure legal opinion against O'Connell.[55]

O'Brien, rejecting suggestions for the reactivation of the Eighty-Two Club as a common forum, proposed, as a substitute for work on the Association committees, a *Nation* forum of eight reserved columns to educate Ireland in its history, legislation and resources. The object was to develop beyond mere newspaper articles. Duffy was happy to oblige with a list of twenty-five contributors. O'Brien even wanted to use Thomas Carlyle. Mitchel feared, not without reason, that the series might grow tedious. Signed articles under the heading of 'The Irish Party' appeared in December. The title 'Young Ireland' was considered too sectarian.[56]

The articles, useful in themselves, were only a step towards further organisation. On Wednesday 2 December the Irish Party held a public meeting at the Rotunda, attended by 2,000 according to *The Nation* and *Warder*. This time there was no evasion of responsibility. Most Young Ireland leaders, with the exception of O'Brien, were present. Five priests took part. A lengthy report by Duffy pressed a formidable list of demands on the Association, ranging from a publication of its accounts to the reactivation of a vigorous Repeal policy, independent of the Whigs. Speakers, including Meagher, likewise deprecated any appeal to arms. Haughton, as an absolute pacifist, disagreed with both Young and Old Ireland positions, yet lamented that he had been driven out of Repeal as a physical-force man. He considered the Whig Alliance the real cause of the problem, and the Young Irelanders absolutely correct in opposing sectarian discussion in the Association. The clerics present dismissed the infidelity issue. Fr Meehan and Dr Carroll of Westland Row parish implied that Archbishop Murray favoured Young Ireland and defended him and Archbishop Crolly against the MacHale prelates. According to Meehan, every *Nation* article could be safely read by a nun in her convent. Arrangements were made for a follow-up meeting in January.[57]

The Pilot disparaged the meeting as a gathering of separatists and anti-Repealers whose imputations against O'Connell made reconciliation unlikely. But *The Warder* found it 'remarkable as a barometer of Repeal opinion', attended by a number of respectable middle-class shopkeepers. According to Duffy, 'the effect of the meeting was electric; men talked of nothing else from Kerry to Donegal.' It even destroyed the Liberator's appetite for breakfast the next day. When, according to Young Ireland sources, his cronies demanded that the rebels be crushed, the Liberator demurred: 'we must have them back.' The arrival of John O'Connell, however, forced him to change his mind. O'Connell was now only a shadow of his former self, finding concentration difficult and becoming less audible in public. He was increasingly dependent on his single-minded son. But O'Connell, or his minders, had to act quickly and decisively if his opponents were to be divided and neutralised before they could present a really formidable threat to the Association. Tom Steele and Daunt warned the Liberator that the people were deserting him. Despite *The Pilot*'s initial bravado, the Repeal rent fell from £237.3.0 in January 1846, to a pitiful £54.18.8 in November. *The Warder*, refusing to attribute the decline entirely to the famine, concluded that 'it is quite clear that Young Ireland is taking Conciliation Hall by blockade, having failed to do so by storm.'[58]

O'Connell still had some cards to deal. There were divisions to exploit with a peace offer. O'Brien was still separated from Young Ireland and unresponsive to appeals to come to Dublin. On the other hand, Dillon, whose legal opinion the Liberator professed to trust, and others initially believed that, despite John O'Connell's malign influence, the Liberator himself was sincere. Dillon indeed told O'Brien that Mitchel was 'hopeless' and would have to be fought. Doheny, author of a 'contrite missive' of 3 December retracting previous criticism of O'Connell, thought the Liberator's sincerity should be carefully tested. O'Gorman frankly wanted to return to practical work in the Association, fearing that even the popular success of the seceders would destroy the movement.[59]

At the Association on 7 December, with the Repeal rent rising slightly to £116.3.5, O'Connell ambiguously declared his anxiety to heal the breach. The Liberator, willing to sacrifice his pride, proposed a conference between himself and O'Brien, with the lawyers Dillon, O'Hagan, O'Hea and Colman O'Loghlen acting as advisers. To O'Connell the issue was the legality of Young Ireland's attitude to force.[60]

O'Connell sought a contest on his chosen ground with a hand-picked conference. He encouraged the impression, however, that everything was open to consideration. Duffy, who also had legal training, was pointedly not invited, though *The Pilot* regarded him as the Young Ireland puppet master. The Young Irelanders feared that the Liberator's strategy might make them appear hostile to accommodation. The atmosphere was not conciliatory as attacks in *The Pilot* continued unabated. The Young Ireland leaders begged O'Brien to come to Dublin to advise them, but the latter refused. He dreaded a face-to-face encounter with the wily

Liberator, and wanted the tough Mitchel on any delegation, or Dillon as sole negotiator.[61]

O'Connell sent his own emissary, Fr Miley, to Cahirmoyle, only to discover that O'Brien would not negotiate on force, which he considered a non-issue, and insisted on raising awkward problems like the misuse of Association funds. Furthermore, John O'Hagan blunted the Association strategy by refusing to advise in what was a political, not a legal, issue. Though apparently breaking rank with O'Brien, Young Ireland sent a deputation, led by Haughton, and containing Duffy, Dillon and O'Gorman, to the Liberator on 15 December. Letters from the country indicated a strong demand for negotiation with O'Connell. The latter conceded only that, if legal arbitration favoured them, the Young Irelanders could press for reforms within the Association. The Liberator now denied that the conference had been intended to resolve all differences. Since O'Connell had refused general negotiation, O'Brien's intransigence appeared less mistaken. As Dillon told O'Brien, his presence was no longer needed in Dublin. The deputation sent to force O'Connell to state that only violence would be discussed was 'eminently successful'. Duffy, regretting a verbal misunderstanding with O'Brien, agreed that the Liberator appeared in the wrong, while O'Brien's apparent intransigence was no longer condemned by public opinion.[62]

On 21 December, at the next Association meeting, after lamenting the recently revealed famine horrors at Skibbereen, O'Connell insisted that, despite his own sacrifice of pride, Young Ireland had refused his test. 'I set them at defiance.' He was glad that the Young Ireland effort to dictate in religious matters was ended. J. A. O'Neill, the influential landowner, who regretted the split, cast doubt on the Peace Resolutions and suggested a joint conference of Old and Young Ireland. The Liberator, whose debility had not blunted his tongue, showered him with sarcasm.[63]

Outwardly, *The Nation* accepted the breakdown of the negotiations philosophically: 'so be it.' The paper had proved that it could continue without the Association. Mitchel told O'Brien privately, 'I am heartily glad, as I think most of us are, that the "Reconciliation" is all over.' But

O'Brien's own role in the breakdown was castigated by *The Pilot* as disgraceful. If force had been only a pretext, why did O'Brien have any qualms about discussing it? One Young Irelander, M. J. Barry, had in fact advised O'Brien to accept O'Connell's legal arbitration on the issue. The criticism that O'Brien could have done more to heal the breach, so disastrous during the famine, was not unreasonable.[64]

Now that the divorce appeared absolute, what was Young Ireland to do? Duffy seems to have envisaged a move to the right. *The Nation* claimed that, free from O'Connell, an approach could be made to the gentry who had hitherto stood aloof. This could be done by the aggregate meeting scheduled for January. Without O'Connell the middle-class Young Irelanders, whatever their success with the Dublin trades, had little appeal to the country people. Already *The Pilot* had complained of O'Brien's recent 'letters' that 'his leading idea is the interests of the landlords.'[65]

Duffy, writing to O'Brien on 26 December, after the breakdown of negotiations, emphasised the importance of the latter as leader to win the Protestants and men of property who would never listen to young Catholics 'sprung directly from the trading class'. Duffy wooed O'Brien with language identical to that of O'Connell, eulogising his value to the Association: 'You seem to be providentially gifted with qualities and attributes for the time and place.' The basic plan for a Council and committees was suggested by O'Brien himself, whose presence in January was again tactfully urged. *The Pilot* had some justification for its sneer that O'Brien 'has been the spoiled child of Repeal, and we who have pampered him to petulancy, now that we find it necessary to chide, should not forget the blame to which we ourselves are patent in this affair.'[66]

O'Brien had no ambition to dominate Young Ireland. Preferring to act as a remote elder statesman, O'Brien wanted Duffy as leader, and deliberately publicised the latter in the detailed public reply he now felt constrained to make to his critics, headed by O'Connell's emissary, Dr Miley. The reply expressed a haughty disdain for personal relations with opponents who had failed to behave like gentlemen. But O'Brien would return to the Association if Repeal really demanded it. Rejecting force as a serious issue he outlined proposals for substantive change in the Association. These included political independence of English parties, publication of accounts, the exclusion of salaried Repealers from the committee, the elimination of religious topics, apart from grievances (an elastic category), and notice and formal voting before any expulsion. Several items had been suggested by Dr Griffin of Limerick; a seceders' meeting had pressed for the exclusion of sectarianism and the reformed committee. O'Brien revealed that the old Repeal committee, after checking expenditure, left the surplus funds to O'Connell's discretion.[67]

O'Brien's account was amplified by other seceders. Mitchel and Dillon, leaders of the two sub-factions co-operated on an address on the negotiations 'to sweep away all the rubbish behind us and leave us free to look *forward* for the future.' The Irish Council (or Party) acting committee and the Remonstrant committee now worked together. The Mitchel-Dillon 'Address of the Committee of "The Irish Party" to the People of Ireland' traversed all the old issues from the Whig Alliance to the Colleges and gave a step-by-step account of the negotiations. It related the Colleges issue, and the resultant cry of infidelity, to the demand for the exclusion of sectarianism, pointing out, like Fr Meehan, the absurdity of stigmatising as infidels those who held the views of the archbishop of the diocese in which the Association met. Was an entirely new organisation to prove the answer to Repeal division?[68]

The Irish Confederation United, 1847

The Irish Confederation Established

Criticism of the Association was embodied in the final establishment of the Young Ireland organisation at a Rotunda meeting on 13 January 1847. With John Shea Lawlor in the chair, O'Brien, despite all his doubts, at last appeared in person to make the keynote speech and set out the tactics, objectives and procedures of the new organisation. Duffy had previously made it clear to O'Brien that he must be the official leader. O'Brien explained that, as their original name 'The Irish Party' had recently been pirated by Lord Sligo's organisation of Irish landlords, it was necessary to change 'Party' into 'Confederation'. The new 'Irish Party', which met on the following day, was seen as an ally. O'Brien, in line with Duffy's letter of 26 December, asserted the need to obtain Repeal by a combination of aristocracy and democracy. 'There is no man among you who does not desire to sustain the right of property.' His policy was nothing if not conservative. Meanwhile O'Connell at Conciliation Hall applauded the landlords and rejoiced in the new Irish Party.[1]

The Rotunda turnout was disappointing. If 2,000 had attended the previous meeting, only 1,000 to 1,200 were now claimed. As there were 100 people on the platform, the proportion of leaders appeared excessive. All the Young Ireland notables were present, including Duffy, glad to participate once more in open politics after his long exclusion from the Repeal Association. He and Dillon, also returning from a lengthy absence to the public arena, acted as secretaries. They were soon replaced by Meagher and O'Gorman. No doubt, as the prejudiced *Pilot* jeered, a large section of 'the Little Ireland Gathering' consisted simply of the curious. All the 'puffery and preparations', it claimed, had achieved little accession of strength.

In proposing the new Confederation O'Brien minimised the split. The new organisation was 'not founded in antagonism to the Repeal Association. [*Hear, hear*]. It is founded for the purpose of enabling those who found themselves unable to co-operate with the Repeal Association to aid in furthering the objects which the Repeal Association professes to have in view.' While the Association acted honestly it need fear no opposition from the Confederation. The correspondence of O'Brien and his colleagues indicated their use of the Confederation as a bargaining counter for ultimate reform of the Repeal Association and reunion. As Duffy said later, 'the policy of the Confederation was substantially the policy of the Repeal Association, honestly and vigorously worked out.' But a new organisation was a dangerous experiment as formalised opposition was likely to encourage, rather than diminish, antagonism. Though McGee later asserted that Duffy was the real father of the Confederation, the Young Irelanders had to a great extent been manoeuvred into organisation from below.[2]

The policy spelled out by O'Brien was directed towards ultimate union. Physical force was repudiated. Though peaceful, the Confederates were required to have moral courage. This was close to O'Connell's original moral force. The stipulation that there would be no Catholic ascendancy was also a repetition of O'Connell's original policy, obscured by the bitter squabbles in the last months. The contentious sectarian issues would have no place in the Confederation. The insistence on independence of both English parties was another instance of approving O'Connell's theory while opposing his recent practice.

Many organisational stipulations, especially financial, were levelled at the Association. That the accounts of the Confederation would be regularly published surprised no one. But the new movement went further. Unlike the Association with its 'Volunteers', 'Members' and 'Associates', distinguished by financial contribution, there was 'no money test in the Irish Confederation'. During a terrible famine a fund-raising competition with the Association was unthinkable. The Confederation also hoped to encourage artisan membership. In the event, though Repeal funds soon dropped to almost negligible proportions, the Confederation's finances were even more scanty. The original treasurer, the conscientious James Haughton, provided a meticulous, if tedious, account of ink stands, fire irons, coal boxes, candle snuffers and sweeping brushes purchased. In the seven weeks, 9 January to 26 February, £230.1.3 was contributed. By April if a total membership of 900 had produced only £107.1.10 in funds, expenditure had been a mere £65.10.1. According to the standard of Mr Micawber the Confederation was wealthy indeed. Occasionally Confederation weekly takings exceeded those of the declining Association. Subsequently, Confederate accounting became as chaotic as that of the Association, John Pigot being particularly critical. A paid secretary, J. Hamill, was appointed on an annual basis to avoid the long dominance of T. M. Ray over the Repeal Association.[3]

Such blithe disregard for the sinews of war compelled the Confederates to curtail their activities. This avoided a direct clash with the Association. O'Brien foreshadowed weekly meetings of the Confederate council, but public meetings only monthly, or when required. Pigot later complained that unnecessary meetings, without adequate agenda, were imposed on the leadership, sometimes by working-class enthusiasts like the suspect P. J. Barry. Committee members were expected to organise throughout the country. Local assemblies and societies with reading rooms were recommended. Fraternisation between Old and Young Ireland seemed more likely in the country than the city. Clashes with the Association were not anticipated, especially as the Repeal reading rooms were in decline. Electors were advised to register and vote, not for Young or Old Ireland, but for a good Repealer. O'Connell's rival, the aged Robert Holmes, was declared chief Young Irelander.[4]

The proposed Confederate Council of 39, clergy, MPs and JPs being *ex officio* members, was almost as large and unwieldy as the Repeal general committee. It was allowed to co-opt still more members. All the leading Young Irelanders were included, even D. F. MacCarthy who had recently disclaimed all political interest. Some of the male poets like Mangan and Frazer were, however, left out. There was then no question of female participation. M. J. Barry indeed called on women to use their 'gentle influence' to reinforce man's 'steady resolution'. William Bryan of Raheny, who had made money in Van Diemen's Land and quarrelled bitterly with the colonial administration, John Shea Lawlor, Richard O'Gorman Sr, and Francis Comyn JP of Woodstock, were probably, after O'Brien, the most wealthy and influential. George Smith, T. B. MacManus and Dr P. Murphy represented the powerful Irish community in Liverpool. Born in Monaghan in 1823, and an early friend of Duffy, MacManus was destined to be a potent symbol of revolutionary nationalism. After migrating to Liverpool he became a shipping agent and earned the large income of £1,000 or £1,200 a year. MacManus had been an important Repealer before the secession. He was also regarded as a Chartist. Since many of the nominal members of the Council were unable to attend weekly meetings, the original Young Ireland group, or Clique, had little opposition in controlling the Confederation.[5]

The Irish Confederation was launched with some panache. Barry, O'Gorman, Mitchel, Martin, Comyn, Meagher, Doheny, McGee and Haughton supported O'Brien with an abundance of rhetoric, a characteristic of the Confederation throughout its brief life. Confederates dissolved the famine in purple passages and won Repeal by force of verbal imagery. Differences between radicals and conservatives on the famine were already obvious. The antagonistic *Pilot* conceded only Meagher's oratorical ability. *The Warder* was more impressed by the new 'Irish Party' meeting, believing the Confederation's attempt to inject new life into Repeal would certainly fail. Even Duffy's own *Nation* gave only two cheers for the Irish Confederation. It might succeed or fail but its originators had put their hearts into the project. As for the new 'Irish Party', no similar assembly had been seen since the Volunteers of 1782.[6]

The Drift Towards New Unity Negotiations

In the months before the Liberator's death in Genoa on

17 May the Confederation clumsily sought a famine role. As Duffy said, the Confederation was only one experiment. Its Council met regularly with alternating chairmen, and set up committees on finance, the famine, public instruction, trade, elections and parliament. Membership ranged from ten to nineteen on each. The Confederation soon mirrored the Association. Duffy's *Nation* in support attacked the Whig government's famine relief.[7]

But the vendetta with the Repeal Association continued. In his final appearances in January 1847 the Liberator stressed the dangers of speeches by Young Irelanders like Mitchel and Meagher, and even suggested that the Confederation Council might be in itself illegal. He was accused of felon setting. *The Pilot* poured inexhaustible vitriol on 'the Irish renegade party'. In return *The Pilot* was excluded from the list of newspapers which Duffy persuaded the Confederations to send to popular reading rooms. These included unionist papers like the *Dublin Evening Mail* and *The Warder*, which *The Pilot* suggested was 'a particular pet' of *The Nation*. Indeed, *The Nation* was delighted at the growing nationalism of the conservative press.[8]

The Confederation in February 1847, on Dillon's suggestion, intervened for Repeal at a by-election in Galway against the candidature of the James Monaghan, the solicitor-general. It offered its own candidate if necessary, but withdrew when O'Connell insisted on Anthony O'Flaherty, believed by O'Gorman to be sympathetic to the Confederation. A Confederation delegation, including Barry, Meagher, Doheny, O'Gorman and Mitchel campaigned lustily in Galway and shared a platform with the Old Irelanders. Intoxicated by election fever O'Gorman believed the Confederation popular 'to an amazing extent'. Mitchel reported a reconciliation deal from the Association, asking only for renunciation of revolution without a hope of success. When Monaghan won by 4 votes the Confederation organised a petition, drafted by John Pigot with the help of O'Brien's English Catholic friend, Chisholm Anstey, against personation for Monaghan. It failed and disillusionment set in. The sanguine O'Gorman admitted that the Association still maintained 'a sickly vitality'. *The Nation* suggested committees in all localities to nominate a strong Repealer, undirected by national organisations. Unimpressed by such forbearance, *The Pilot* insisted that Young Ireland's 'baleful influence' played a part in O'Flaherty's narrow defeat.[9]

Tensions had quickly developed in the Confederation. The question of O'Brien's practical leadership was not resolved. He had made it plain to Duffy in late 1846 that, while always available to give advice, he could only visit Dublin for a short time each year. Accordingly, after setting up the new movement O'Brien disappeared again, this time to fight in parliament for adequate famine measures. He was not only removed from Ireland, where the young men urgently required his presence, but was working again with fellow Irish Repeal MPs. Like O'Connell he participated in the sessions of the 'Irish Party' or 'Irish Parliamentary Party'. After the Liberator's withdrawal to begin his fateful expedition to Rome, O'Brien co-operated with John O'Connell at Westminster. In his denunciation of unproductive relief, support for Bentinck's railway bill and general onslaught on the Whig government, O'Brien was praised by John O'Connell and intimated that he would be prepared to work under the latter's leadership. As the Repeal party was disintegrating at Westminster, O'Brien was a more reliable ally of John O'Connell's than some Old Ireland MPs. In Dublin, Mitchel pleaded with O'Brien to return home as action was vitally necessary in Ireland to check what he saw as the deliberate policy of the government in uprooting the Irish from the soil. O'Gorman also asked O'Brien to 'come Home as soon as you can.' Some Young Irelanders wanted to fight elections and establish an obstructive party at Westminster, but O'Gorman believed this impossible and, like Mitchel, a distraction from necessary work in Ireland. 'The Irish Confederation is working badly or rather not working at all.' John O'Connell now wooed Young Ireland with promises of forgiveness. The Confederation committee, despite O'Brien, resolved in favour of the non-attendance of MPs at Westminster.[10]

Another indication of dissatisfaction was John Pigot's proposal in April for a self-denying ordinance by which some of the rash young men, including himself, should be dropped from the Confederation Council and kept busy on committees where they could do less to harm the organisation. Even John Mitchel admitted that a speech of his friend, Devin Reilly, was 'ludicrously violent'. Duffy, who saw the speech only after publication, feared prosecution of the Confederation. To a number of the young enthusiasts the massive death toll of the famine rendered political non-violence absurd. John O'Connell, however, still drew diametrically opposed conclusions from the catastrophe. Pigot, who had been an intimate of Davis and a pallbearer at his funeral, took a high principled stand against any compromise with the Repealers. He was 'utterly sick of the policy of perpetual toleration of what is dishonest, base, and therefore polluting and damnable, for the sake of any temporary expediency.' His father, D. R. Pigot, had just obtained high judicial office under the Whigs, but John asserted pure nationalism.[11]

Another man of undeviating principles was James Haughton, whose adherence to the Confederation was of enormous propagandist value because of his well advertised abhorrence of all physical force. Haughton, born in Carlow in 1795, was brought up as a Quaker and educated at the famous Ballitore school. He became a corn merchant in Dublin in 1817 and threw himself into a variety of liberal causes, including temperance, anti-slavery, the abolition of capital punishment, and land reform. An early member of O'Connell's Repeal Association, Haughton refused to take O'Connell's professed non-violence seriously. In the Confederation Haughton continued to insist that liberty must be universal and that Irish nationalists must strive as vigorously for the freedom of other countries as for their own. Haughton was preoccupied with the ill-treatment of the Rajah of Satara, appealing against his deposition on false evidence, despite an excellent administrative record. *The Nation* accommodated Haughton with an editorial. Slavery proved more difficult. Haughton's views on the subject were identical to those of the Liberator, and, as he continued to urge them in the Confederation, a dispute was inevitable. Before the end of January 1847, Haughton was confronted by the Young Ireland Junius, Fr Kenyon. Refused further space in *The Nation*, Haughton continued the debate in the Confederation, insisting that it should be totally committed not only to anti-slavery, but teetotalism and the abolition of capital punishment as well.[12]

The issue climaxed in early April when Haughton, in Smith O'Brien's presence, chaired a public Confederation meeting. Haughton complained of a denial of free speech, his very reason for seceding from the Repeal Association. To O'Brien, Haughton had expressed one opinion on slavery, the meeting another. Haughton announced his withdrawal from the Council, despite a deputation to beg him to reconsider his decision.[13]

Though Haughton was a crotchety colleague, as Duffy said 'a secession from the secession would lay us open to damaging ridicule'. The Confederation had encouraged him to act as its conscience. Most of the principles on which he stood so firm had long been ventilated in *The Nation*, which had opposed smoking, drinking and capital punishment. Slavery, however, was a perennial bone of contention between O'Connell and Young Ireland; the Confederation's reaction was almost inevitable. But Kenyon's arguments allowed Old Ireland to portray him as 'the slavery-tolerating Catholic clergyman of Tipperary', and cite other Catholic opinion against him. In early 1847, *The Pilot*, ridiculing Young Ireland in action, stressed division in the Confederation between physical force and pacifism, and between slavery and abolitionism. What had become of the forward policy? Where was the Confederate Council of 300 which they had so long criticised O'Connell for not calling? *The Nation* talked only vaguely of a future national convention.[14]

Chartism also embarrassed the Confederation. O'Connell repudiated Chartist violence vigorously. After the secession, Young Ireland tried to attract the Protestant gentry while relying on the Chartist-tinged Remonstrants in Dublin. In his *Morning Star*, Feargus O'Connor, the militant Chartist who had once been a Repeal MP, backed Young Ireland. *The Pilot* meanwhile lambasted the Confederation's Chartist tendencies. William Bryan's decision to chair a Chartist meeting was declared injurious to the organisation by the Confederation Council. Bryan resigned, but returned several weeks later. The Council finally allowed members to chair

meetings for organisations compatible with the Confederation.[15]

John O'Connell's Overture

Though the Confederation's difficulties and divisions were
easily exposed, they did not solve the Association's problems.
The Liberator's rapidly deteriorating physical condition had
long been known to his colleagues and those who observed
him in the House of Commons and the Repeal Association.
The timing of O'Connell's demise was of vital importance to
the Young Irelanders. Even before the split of 1846, O'Brien
was warned that seceders from the Association before
O'Connell's death would be at a huge disadvantage in the orgy
of national lamentation following the hero's demise. By
March 1847 the Young Irelanders had little time left. John
O'Connell, responding to a priest, Fr McHugh, offered Young
Ireland a conference.

When he approached the Confederation leaders, O'Gorman
found McHugh 'almost abject', dismissing the Peace Resolutions as a 'mere humbug' whose annulment was certain. At
the Association on 29 March, John O'Connell apologised for
giving any offence in the past. He suggested that acceptance
by Young Ireland of defensive force only would solve the
legal problem. Were the last remnant of the constitution
trampled on, Old Irelanders in good conscience could assert
their rights in arms. For the first time the Association offered
the defence loophole as conciliation. Earlier, Daunt, the
would-be peacemaker, had asked why the Young Irelanders
had not used it. Several Young Irelanders had certainly taken
the point, but in July 1846 John O'Connell and his father
had preferred silencing and expulsion to debate and analysis.
In March 1847, therefore, John O'Connell, who superficially
appeared to be harping on the old theme, made the important
tacit admission that the Peace Resolution, as a means to
exclude Young Ireland, had been unwise.[16]

How were the Confederates to react? According to Duffy,
he and Dillon, aware of the urgent need for closing ranks,
favoured conciliation. A general election was due, and in-
dividuals like Lord Cloncurry and Anthony O'Flaherty, soon

to be MP for Galway, who had obtained Young and Old Ireland support, were insistent on unity. Duffy, as he subsequently claimed, saw that unity was the only hope of obtaining the support of the priesthood, though he also feared that a restoration of links with Old Ireland would finally alienate Protestant gentry. The unionist *Warder*'s hostility to John O'Connell's initiative was shared by the more militant Young Irelanders. Pigot, for example, was totally unwilling to sit on committee with the Liberator's henchmen. The abuse and the persistent accusations of infidelity could not have been more savage, and it is remarkable that Dillon and Duffy were, the famine nothwithstanding, prepared to reconsider negotiation.[17]

But what of O'Brien? He was again sceptical of the offer, and his response in the Confederation was ambiguous. He expressed kindly feelings to the O'Connell family, and maintained that without a Repeal split the government could have been effectively pressured to alleviate the famine disaster. Nevertheless, O'Brien insisted that force and the Whig alliance were still stumbling blocks. As usual he ignored the 'defence' loophole. *The Pilot*, like Pigot opposed to any overture, claimed that John O'Connell had been 'met with contumely'. The editor, Barrett, shrewdly perceived that Young Ireland's choice lay between the Catholic masses, approachable through O'Connell, and the upper-class Protestants. 'Well, this is their plan. They wait for the Landlords and Tories, and despise the People.' He sarcastically recommended the Confederates to their Orange friends.[18]

The Rise of James Fintan Lalor

Meanwhile, a vital force had emerged from obscurity. Its influence provoked new Confederate divisions. If Pigot and others still looked to the Protestant gentry, Confederates like Mitchel and Martin, while disliking reunion, grew increasingly disillusioned with the landowners. Their catalyst was James Fintan Lalor, born in 1807, the son of a strong farmer and MP. A hunchback enduring poor health, Lalor was educated at Carlow College and studied chemistry for a brief period before travelling to the continent on his mother's money. He became a sardonic recluse, studying social and political relations. On 11 January 1847 Duffy published the first of six letters from Lalor, arguing that the land question was of infinitely greater importance than Repeal and warning the landlords that their last chance of self-reform, before the people took the law into their own hands, had arrived. The letters attracted considerable attention, Mitchel recommending them to O'Brien. Lalor, though previously unknown, was co-opted to the Confederate Council at the meeting (13 April) which received Haughton's resignation. Lalor was so hostile to the Repeal Association that in 1843, while the monster meetings were in full swing, he had written privately to Prime Minister Peel advising him that the concession of tenant right would fatally undermine O'Connell's movement.[19]

Unity Negotiations again Collapse

Though Lalor's accession to the Council did not strengthen the hands of the unity advocates, a Confederate deputation, comprising O'Brien, Duffy, Mitchel, Dillon, Meagher, O'Gorman Jr, McGee and Doheny met eight old Irelanders, led by John O'Connell, on 4 May 1847. John O'Connell as usual saw physical force as the essential issue. He was willing for the application of the Peace Resolutions to be restricted to the British Empire. This would in effect have limited the objection, according to the defence loophole, to advocacy of a rebellion in Ireland before all constitutional remedies were exhausted. Yet O'Brien and the Confederates were not impressed, arguing again that violence had been sufficiently debated. They denied the right of the Association to impose new tests on its members. Instead, O'Brien demanded the dissolution of both organisations and the formation of a new movement which would incorporate the reforms established by the Confederates: no sectarian issues, no English party alliance, open accounts, elimination of salaried officials from committee, electoral support for pledged Repealers only, and the admission of newspaper proprietors.

John O'Connell agreed to ban placehunting, but demurred at the inclusion of journalists, still considering that they could endanger the movement. In his father's absence he refused to consider the dissolution of the Association, though his opponents pointed out that O'Connell had dissolved and reconstituted many organisations in his long career. The Confederates, for their part, had no intention of joining the Association while a question mark hung over its debts and £130,000 of Repeal rent remained unaccounted for. Thus negotiation again came to nothing. Pigot was delighted, declaring that he would have resigned if unity had been achieved. He rejected '*conscious* co-operation with what is rotten'. On the other side, *The Pilot* professed fury at Young Ireland's only novelty, the 'monstrous proposition' that the Association be dissolved. It denounced the renewed demand for the exclusion of sectarian issues as the 'lug-in-religion-by-the-head-and-shoulders' calumny. The paper rejoiced that 'the Orange Confederates' had 'now thrown down the gauntlet'. Let the people decide. 'The Catholic voice can never be heard among the Orange affiliations of Young Ireland.' Fr McHugh, instigator of the negotiations, totally disagreed. Enduring hisses and points of order, McHugh at the Association's next meeting supported nearly every point made by the Young Irelanders. He even raised religion, asking how Protestants could tolerate sectarian topics. John O'Connell was goaded beyond endurance. He would have silenced McHugh had he been a layman. 'What!' expostulated the Liberator's son, 'submit to the Orange oppressors in order that we may conciliate them.' Another priest, the eccentric Fr Thaddeus O'Malley, made a last minute attempt to persuade O'Brien and John O'Connell to sink their differences in the face of the famine, but achieved nothing with either.[20]

The Confederates were encouraged to adopt an equally intransigent tone. O'Brien agreed with *The Pilot* that the country would have to decide between the rival groups. Meagher, opposed to any reunion two weeks earlier, invited the people to take 'vengeance' on one of the rival organisations. He also attributed famine mortality to the division in Repeal.[21]

The latest negotiation had thus widened, rather than closed the gap. The desire for total victory and the absolute crushing of rivals, exhibited on both sides, proved disastrous for the country. Who was to blame? Both factions overestimated their resources. The Repeal Association was certainly moribund, receiving only a trickle of rent, reduced in May 1847 from £300 per week to under £30. The Whig alliance, which John O'Connell was at pains to disclaim, had been totally discredited by the famine. The Young Irelanders were 'not in the habit of parading ourselves as the commissioned agents and plenipotentiaries of the Catholic Hierarchy'. But the Association's most powerful ally, Archbishop MacHale, in his attacks on placehunting appeared almost a Confederation ally. On the other hand, the Confederation, for all its brave talk, was in no position to supersede the Association. As demonstrated, it originated more as a weapon to impose reform on the Old Irelanders than an independent organisation advocating an alternative policy. With his father abroad, John O'Connell was considerably more vulnerable than he would be on the Liberator's return, either as a reinvigorated statesman or a lifeless corpse. Realising this, John, opposed by his own hardliners like Barrett, could not afford to make many concessions. Similarly, O'Brien and Duffy, with potential radicals like Mitchel in the wings, had to avoid any sign of appeasement. But O'Brien, had he been a little less determined to stand on his dignity, probably possessed sufficient authority at the time to draw even Mitchel into a magnanimous accord.[22]

The Death of the Titan

The negotiation wrangles were still in progress when news of O'Connell's death at Genoa filtered back to Ireland. Fed, until almost the last moment, with misleading accounts of the Liberator's likely return to health, the Irish public was stunned. It was particularly unfortunate, if not foolishly short-sighted, that some Confederates had just declared war *à l'outrance* against the Repeal Association. The Young Ireland leaders tried to avoid isolation. Their supporters were ambivalent. A month before the Liberator's death, O'Gorman found the Confederation divided between those who cheered, and those who hissed, his name. The cynical Pigot was surprised how O'Connell's death affected him, but feared that some of his younger colleagues might not be magnanimous.

The Nation decked itself in mourning bands and the Confederate Council expressed deep sorrow, despite its difference on some matters, for the passing of so illustrious a leader. It likewise adopted the emblems of mourning and announced its co-operation in the obsequies. Duffy's valedictory editorial in *The Nation* was appreciative, while asserting the new nationalism which Davis had grafted onto the roots planted by O'Connell. 'There was nothing petty, small, or spiteful' in O'Connell's nature. Nor was he 'exclusively or narrowly attached to his own ideas', allowing Davis to modify the character of the agitation of 1843. While Repeal to O'Connell 'was the angry cry of an injured people for justice', 'Davis added the passionate and imaginative element of historical nationality.' Though the angry words of the split should be blotted out, in its context it became at a certain stage inevitable.[23]

Duffy's equivocal endorsement of O'Connell, and a fulsome piece of 'stilting exaggeration' by Devin Reilly did not satisfy the fiery Fr Kenyon. Protesting to O'Brien against the sympathy voted by the Confederation Council and preaching on O'Connell in his own church, Kenyon wrote deploring *The Nation*'s mourning bands and Reilly's article. O'Connell's death, the priest declared, was 'no loss whatever'. Judged by what he was doing at the time, it was a positive gain. 'He befooled this country before his death, and he died impenitent.' It was sheer hypocrisy of the Confederation to honour him after its previous opposition. O'Connell, *'un grand homme manqué'*, 'failed in his mission, and he deserved to fail in it.' 'He patronised liars, parasites, and bullies. He brooked no greatness that grovelled not at his feet.' The Liberator was, in short, 'a mere time-serving politician – a huckster of expediencies.'[24]

Though Kenyon's diatribe said little more than *The Nation* itself earlier and moderates like Daunt and O'Loghlen, who showed the Liberator hungry for praise, jealous of associates and willing to adopt tortuous expedients, it was politically inopportune. Duffy published it to secure free speech. Mitchel, though he later published Kenyon's follow up letter in his *United Irishman*, apparently rejected it for *The Nation*. *The Nation* repudiated the priest's 'terrible Mosaic law of vengeance' and tried to rehabilitate O'Connell's motives, but *The Pilot* and *Weekly Register* discovered that another Young Ireland priest, Fr Meehan, had privately been 'extremely and offensively vituperative' about O'Connell.[25]

The Pilot had in fact anticipated Kenyon and Meehan by declaring the Young Irelanders responsible for the Liberator's death. '*We* saw the hornets preparing their stings — he did not.' Finally, 'when treason burst out THEN BURST HIS MIGHTY HEART!' The Very Rev. Dr Sinnott of Wexford then referred bluntly to the Young Irelanders as the 'murderers' of O'Connell. This became a perennial Old Ireland catch-cry. *The Pilot* used it both ways. If O'Connell had indeed been in decline since Richmond prison, the conduct of the Young Irelanders appeared more cruel, cowardly, and parricidal.[26]

A Dead Liberator and a Live Election

The Confederate attempt to secure a place at O'Connell's funeral was icily rebuffed. Even worse, the Liberator was not buried till 5 August, thus providing the Association with a considerable political advantage before the autumn election. As Duffy told O'Brien, he was not surprised at the unpopularity of the Confederation while the Liberator lay unburied. John O'Connell, moreover, needed to establish himself firmly as leader of the Association.[27]

The Confederates, who a few weeks previously, had talked blithely of appealing to the people to decide between the two branches of Repeal, now found themselves confronted by a contest in the worst possible conditions. Far from taking the initiative they faced a serious and at times violent backlash. Their very appearance could provoke trouble. O'Brien reverted to his customary tactic of digging himself in at Cahirmoyle. Both publicly and privately, the Young Irelanders acknowledged that their support in the country was small, and John O'Connell gloated at the admission.

In late June, while O'Brien was in the country, the Confederate Council decided on Mitchel's motion to oppose John O'Connell's candidature for the City of Dublin seat. O'Brien disapproved of the action, believing that O'Connell as a Repealer should have the seat. An offer to Meagher from

Sligo was revoked. *The Warder*, however, considered that the Young Irelanders were compelled to make this gesture to prove their consistency. In the event John O'Connell opted to stand for the City of Limerick, adjacent to O'Brien's own constituency. There the redoubtable Fr Kenyon demonstrated foolhardy derring-do when, in the teeth of a furious mob, howling for his blood, he proposed the rival candidature of Richard O'Gorman, against the latter's wishes. Brother clerics extricated Kenyon from the murderous throng, who 'dared to lay violent hands on an anointed Priest of God.' As Gwynn argued, Kenyon's action almost certainly increased John O'Connell's support.[28]

Ultimately no Young Irelander stood for election, though Duffy, Lane, Meagher, and O'Gorman were suggested by Pigot to O'Brien. Meagher decided to contest for Dublin was too provocative; only an extreme emergency would have persuaded Denny Lane to hazard Cork. Even O'Brien, the only Confederate sitting member, under hostile Association pressure refused to nominate. He took a holiday in Scotland and Donegal. During the cellar crisis O'Brien had wanted to resign. He now believed that Irishmen could more profitably work at home, while English Repeal sympathisers could agitate at Westminster. He therefore encouraged an English Catholic lawyer and academic, T. C. Anstey, who like William Bryan had resided in Van Diemen's Land. Anstey chose Youghal and won, apparently with some Association support. He later joined the Confederation, acting as its inspector of English clubs. Anstey disappointed Young Ireland by voting for Irish coercion. John Pigot, who had remonstrated with O'Brien that the election of English Repealers contradicted the policy of Thomas Davis, was thus justified. Dillon, Mitchel and Duffy supported Anstey; Duffy also suggested running the federalist, Torrens McCullough.[29]

O'Brien's evasive tactics were again successful. Without requiring him to lift a finger in his own cause, local Young Irelanders and conservatives secured his return, by fourteen votes, for Co. Limerick. Even the local Catholic bishop, Dr John Ryan, with whom O'Brien was on good terms, signed an address in his favour. This was an unexpected bonus. The Young Irelanders had not attempted the impossible task of electing Confederates; instead they demanded pledges against placehunting from candidates. Though John O'Connell categorically rejected a pledge allowing unionists a monopoly of Irish offices, some candidates complied. When the Whigs were returned to office, with 39 Repealers in Ireland, *The Nation* claimed a victory. It admitted that the Confederate organisation had 'some reason for mortification'. Confederate anti-Whig principles were often accepted but its association with force was unpopular. However, 'we are willing that as a party we should be discredited so the CAUSE be advanced.' *The Nation* interpreted the Irish results as Tories 38, Whigs 16, Whig Repealers (John O'Connell and his close allies) 21, Independent Repealers (including O'Brien and Anstey) 18, and, most interesting, 'nationalists' (O'Brien's brother, Sir Lucius, G. H. Moore, The Marquis of Kildare and others) 12. In reality only four MPs, including O'Brien and Anstey, were elected by Confederate influence. Thus by discreet labelling, a disaster which partly revived John O'Connell's wilting Repeal Association was portrayed as a kind of victory. The election, especially O'Brien's success, indicated some rapport with the gentry.[30]

The Confederation Reorganised

One of the unfortunate features of the election contest was the development of street violence. As Doheny, who endured mob hostility in Tipperary, put it, 'the moral-force disciples, hitherto kept in awe by the mustered strength of the seceders and their followers, determined to give a practical illustration of the sincerity of their pledge by breaking the skulls of their opponents.' In semi-racist terms, Duffy maintained that the Irish as an 'emotional race', subject to 'rapid transitions of popular feeling', were easily stirred by the death of the 'sainted Liberator'. Feeling manifested itself not only in Limerick against Kenyon, but also in Dublin.[31]

The Confederation, unlike the Repeal Association which met in the early afternoon and dispersed at 6 p.m., organised its meetings in the evenings to encourage working-class attendance. It also left members vulnerable to attacks from opponents when they returned home. Thus in July there were two onslaughts on Confederates. Richard O'Gorman Sr was struck by a stick on one occasion, and his son, Mitchel and Meagher were forced to secrete themselves in a grocer's shop for ten minutes to let the crowd disperse. *The Nation* claimed that the police, obviously in league with Conciliation Hall, did little to quell the riot. The Association resolved against such attacks, but they continued. It was the same story in Cork. When the Confederates held a big meeting the 'moral-force' advocates tried to break it up, and *The Nation* again accused the police of standing idly by. Later in the year, the Confederate leaders, O'Brien, McGee, Mitchel and Meagher, undertook a mission to Belfast. There the opposition was overwhelming, not from Orangemen, but from Old Irelanders. Mitchel graphically described the 'shrieking, whistling, stamping, imprecations in the uncouth accentuations of Antrim country'. At the first meeting on 15 November at the Belfast Music Hall the police had to intervene twice to enable the speeches to continue. The authorities prevented the second, and the third was virtually drowned out with rattles. Only Meagher, whose entertainment value as an orator evidently triumphed over political hostility, was allowed to speak for long. In lieu of the second meeting, O'Brien intransigently insisted on proceeding to Hercules Street, in the heart of Belfast's notorious rookeries, to remonstrate personally with his butcher antagonists at home. He was forced back to his hotel. Later the butchers became the bodyguard of a local Confederate, John Rea. O'Brien considered the mission a success. He spent two days with William Sharman Crawford, whom Duffy wanted to entice into the Confederation as a federalist and held a satisfactory meeting in Newry.[32]

Though the actions of O'Brien and his colleagues might be dismissed, like Kenyon's at Limerick, as foolhardy, they also created heroic myths. *The Nation* suggested that Kenyon, with solitary hand raised in Limerick for O'Gorman, was a subject worthy of the great Irish painter of the time, Daniel Maclise. *The Warder*, which believed that Kenyon's sincerity, passion and eloquence would eventually make converts, considered that the Young Irelanders, standing their ground in a smoke filled Belfast Music Hall, while assailed with stones, bludgeons and gunpowder squibs, 'showed no lack of resolution and pluck'. On the other hand, 'the intolerance and rascality' of their opponents was fully exposed. The Young Irelanders believed that they had vindicated free speech. When Fr Kenyon appeared at the next Confederation meeting after his Limerick defiance of John O'Connell, he was cheered continuously for five whole minutes. *The Warder* saw the Confederates as 'unquestionably the chivalry of agitation: they pursue the loved phantom with all the wild romance of Aslanga's knight.' The mobs provided ready-made propaganda for *The Nation* which could declare that 'principles are irrefragable by brickbats'. The absurdity of using violence to maintain moral force was continually emphasised.[33]

The Young Irelanders projected themselves in the image of David versus a Goliath, representing 'the greatest social despotism in modern times'. The emphasis of the Old Irelanders on religion and theoretical non-violence also appeared undermined by the current actions of the new pope, Pius IX, elected in late 1846. In his early liberal and anti-Austrian phase, Pius IX appeared to justify Young against Old.[34]

When Association mobs assaulted Confederates during the 1847 election campaign, the latter considered tighter organisation. At a Confederation meeting on 14 July, Richard O'Gorman Jr, lamenting opposition attacks, proposed systematic Confederate clubs. The first two had just been formed in Dublin. Such clubs had an immediate role in defending Confederation meetings. Their implications, however, went deeper. Duffy, the real instigator, had been impressed with an unrealised suggestion by Thomas Wyse to O'Connell's Catholic Association. Clubs appeared to Duffy the basis of a Council of 300. During the Richmond incarceration Duffy and Davis had worked on a methodic system for the score of Repeal reading rooms established by T. M. Ray. By the end of 1845 the reading rooms, existing only in towns, attracted little interest. The Association was highly centralised and Repeal wardens dependent on the committee. In contemporary France and Germany radical and artisan clubs proliferated.

The Dublin Remonstrance movement contained similar democratic elements which Duffy was determined to control. English Confederates, often associated with Chartism, applied pressure, strengthened by their possession of funds. By September 1847, MacManus reported the Liverpool Irish 'iron hot'. When unity proposals collapsed immediately before O'Connell's death, organisation for London, Scotland, Liverpool and other English cities became essential. In late June, the Davis Confederate Club was established in Thomas Street, Dublin, with D'Arcy McGee, formerly Remonstrant secretary, as president. McGee now replaced Hamill as the Confederate paid secretary and resigned from the Council. McGee, a close associate of Duffy, worked to inhibit democratic excesses likely to frighten the gentry. He and Mitchel's friend, Devin Reilly, were mutually antipathetic.[35]

The Confederate clubs represented a decisive break from the Repeal Association. They became an important factor in subsequent unity negotiations; inevitably they maintained antagonism at a popular level. *The Nation* admitted the Confederation's lack of achievement. It presented the clubs, less rule-bound than the Repeal reading rooms, as a forum for lectures, discussion and meetings. Their basic autonomy was stressed. The Young Ireland leaders assumed club presidencies. Their inaugural addresses stimulated debate on essential aims and objectives. Even the club names were significant. O'Brien, at the inauguration of the Sarsfield Club, Limerick, emphasised Sarsfield's willingness to fight for his country, while depicting the clubs as adult schools of nationality. But John Mitchel, establishing the Swift Club in Dublin, repudiated the idea of clubs as mere reading rooms or mechanics' institutes. The objects of their lectures and study was to discover 'how we should re-conquer this country from England'. McGee and O'Brien were more conservative, preferring the 'golden link' with the crown if possible. The Confederation's new forward policy inevitably accentuated division. Duffy tried to restrain Mitchel, while prodding O'Brien into action.[36]

Despite the Confederation's weakness during the August 1847 election, Duffy confidently briefed O'Brien, who must not resign his seat, on the new organisation. 'Next week the elections will be all over, O'Connell is buried, and our time is come.' *The Warder* was impressed by the Confederation's Napoleonic 'forward' principle when so savagely assailed by its opponents. The government complimented the Confederation by infiltrating more spies into its ranks. John Donnellan Balfe of Sallyford had gained publicity in the Repeal Association by attacking Lord Gormanston's treatment of his tenantry. In late June 1847 he was, on Duffy's motion, co-opted to the Confederate Council and soon chaired a meeting. Balfe was thus well placed to inform the government on the reception of Duffy's reorganisation report. Secretary Halpin appears to have become aware of Balfe's dual role. Shortly before participating in the latter's arrest in July 1848, Balfe indignantly assured O'Brien that he was no spy. Previously Balfe had been given the sensitive task of liaising with English Chartists. Confederation policy accepted any member, Chartist, Orangeman, or opponent of Catholic emancipation, pledged to Repeal.[37]

Published in late August, Duffy's reorganisation report showed that informal organisation had been originally intended. Then 10,000 unsought members enrolled and clubs mushroomed in every town and village. Dublin clubs spread to the suburbs. Suggested rules, incorporating old provisions such as the prohibition of sectarian discussion and expulsions without hearings, were drawn up. A minimum of twenty members could start a club. Provincial inspectors were appointed to oversee old and organise new clubs. O'Brien and Meagher handled Munster; Martin and Mitchel patrolled Ulster, while Duffy and Pigot were responsible for Leinster. The Dublin clubs sought permanent rooms. By late August four clubs were well established in the capital: Swift, president O'Gorman, later sacked for non-attendance (120 members); Grattan, president Meagher, with P. J. Barry advocating extremism (70); Davis, president McGee (110); and St Patrick, president Meehan, just founded. *The Nation* gave regular reports on club growths.[38]

McGee's first general report in late October claimed considerable club progress in Ireland and England. The Dublin clubs had permanent premises with membership varying between 100 and 200. Clubs had formed in Cork (Desmond),

Limerick, Belfast (Drennan), Kilkenny, Ballina and Drogheda. Others were being established in Galway, Sligo, Cappoquin, Waterford and Newry. Across the Irish Sea, London had two clubs and Rochdale, Leeds, Glasgow, Bradford and Stalybridge had one each. In three months twenty clubs (twelve in Ireland) had appeared. Each ordinary member was required to introduce another and each Council member to form a new club. Inevitably, there was much window-dressing. Liverpool, with its huge Irish population initially founded no club because its members were too scattered. In Cork fear of the Old Irelanders created great reluctance, rationalised as the need for a published scheme of organisation. When Duffy finally secured a public meeting, M. J. Barry admitted that some of his fears had been exaggerated. The Drennan club in Belfast failed to obtain a fair hearing for the Confederate delegation later in the year.[39]

In England, the Confederation became increasingly dependent on the Chartists. By mid-1848 Chartists and Confederates there were almost indistinguishable. Spies like Balfe were ideally placed as *agents provocateurs*. Another dubious English leader was Edward Vaughan Keneally, the barrister and future MP. Though the Confederate leadership tried to keep him at arm's length, the pushy Keneally established himself as president of a London Confederate club. An inflated movement gave considerable scope to suspect peripheral members. *The Nation*, in fact, overestimated the importance of clubs outside Dublin.[40]

The 'poor be-stoned and be-Billingsgated' Young Irelanders were partly justified in their opposition by the collapse of John O'Connell's parliamentary party in the winter of 1847. The Russell government introduced not a magnanimous measure of famine relief but a tough coercion bill to deal with increasing violence in the Irish countryside. The Repeal party split. Some MPs, including Henry Grattan Jr and Chisholm Anstey, supported the government. John O'Connell was left with a handful of members battling against the bill alongside the ailing Smith O'Brien. To the disgust of Richard O'Gorman, even Confederates like Duffy and McGee feared that excessive opposition to the coercion bill might alienate the gentry. Tensions were increased by the prominent role of the Chartist, Feargus O'Connor, recently returned to parliament, in opposing coercion and introducing a Repeal motion. O'Gorman feared that O'Connor's action had fostered 'a very violent spirit of Chartism' in the clubs. This would encourage members to think of England rather than Ireland. Mitchel and Meagher repudiated Chartism as such, but the latter asserted his respect for O'Connor. In the Association, John O'Connell argued that the coercion bill might have been worse. Radical Confederates, influenced by Mitchel, now talked of resisting coercion by organisation in the country. Mitchel, opposed by D'Arcy McGee, had failed to persuade an Irish Council public meeting in November to support tenant right. O'Gorman denounced the 'mawkish sentimentality' which reacted against the murder of a gentleman but ignored the starvation of a score of poor people. Violence, justifiable even according to the Liberator's defensive condition, seemed a possible option. Force brought to a head divisions long festering among the Confederates.[41]

The Confederation in 1848: A Road to Fiasco?

Duffy Versus Mitchel

In early 1848, when the Confederation seemed to Doheny 'in full career', a bitter quarrel erupted between Duffy and Mitchel. Mitchel had been much influenced by Lalor's letters to *The Nation* at the beginning of 1847. On 21 June Lalor addressed Mitchel directly, complaining that the latter, like other Young Irelanders, still placed an unrealistic hope in the landlords' 'Irish Party'. Lalor's object, in the oft quoted words, was 'to repeal the Conquest — not any part or portion but the whole and entire conquest of seven hundred years — a thing much more easily done than to repeal the Union.' Lalor and Fr Kenyon saw the famine as a deliberate plot by government and landlords to 'exterminate' the Irish peasantry and turn the country into a stock farm. As the famine persisted Mitchel and Reilly were converted. On the other hand the Confederate moderates, O'Brien, Duffy and McGee in particular, still sought to effect Repeal through a union of classes. O'Brien, a self-conscious landlord, hoped to convince his counterparts of the necessity of moderate tenant right and self-government. Duffy emphasised the co-operation of the middle classes. All were aware of the difficulty of reaching the peasantry and lower orders. As Doheny publicly admitted, once armed the poor would turn their weapons on the Young Irelanders, not the government. Mitchel, however, was finally disillusioned at the end of 1847 by the failure of his motion in the Irish Council, the disarming coercion bill, and the consequent delight of many landlords. His belief in a class war grew. Class war implied violence as opposed to the constitutional class conciliation, favoured by O'Brien and Duffy. Yet Mitchel was slow to move unambiguously beyond the 'defensive' violence of the O'Connells, as indeed was Lalor. The passive resistance of an armed peasantry appeared the first step.[1]

On *The Nation* staff, tension between Duffy and Mitchel mounted towards the end of 1847. Mitchel was often considered by the public as the chief leader writer, if not the paper's editor. Duffy disliked the growing radicalism of Mitchel's views and the latter's desire, partly inspired by Kenyon, to defend negro slavery. Mitchel, for his part, complained that his views were being censored. Duffy's redrafting of O'Brien's summary of moderate Confederate objectives dissatisfied Mitchel and Reilly. The crisis came at a Confederate meeting at the Rotunda in early December. Mitchel spoke forcefully of the effects of the coercion bill, demanding arms and the establishment of local militias, with or without the landlords. According to Duffy's report to O'Brien, Mitchel threatened the government with secret societies and warned the people not to obey the coercion. Duffy still felt that Mitchel was 'one of the most resolute as well as the honestest and most disinterested of men'. Mitchel emphatically denied that the current Confederation had the strength and public support to obtain independence. Duffy remonstrated with Mitchel as they walked home from the meeting and later cut sections of the latter's speech from *The Nation* report. Duffy rejected Mitchel's passive resistance against the poor rate, complaining that this would worsen the effects of the famine. He wanted Mitchel to discuss his views fully in the Confederation before making them public. Mitchel announced his resignation from *The Nation* and the Confederation Council. Personal misunderstanding reinforced policy difference and the quarrel between the two men was to persist long afterwards. Richard O'Gorman Jr, who opposed Mitchel's views, was also hostile to the 'symptoms of intended dictatorship on the part of Duffy and McGee'. O'Brien accordingly remonstrated with McGee.[2]

Duffy hoped to contain the quarrel by seeking Mitchel's permission to publish a generalised account of their breach. As Duffy told O'Brien, he needed publicity himself to dispel criticism and to prevent the Confederation from 'being slowly drawn into Mitchel's views without knowing what they were.' Mitchel published his own powerful apologia, demanding passive resistance and an armed people. Mitchel rejected parliamentary tactics; while disclaiming immediate rebellion he decried 'legality' in favour of studying guerrilla warfare. Reilly published a similar letter.[3]

The division attracted considerable public attention. O'Gorman believed that all the clubs were for Mitchel's 'infant Ireland' and that the Confederation was doomed. McGee feared that Mitchel could swing a public meeting. Mitchel was elected to succeed the retiring Fr Meehan as president of the Dublin St Patrick's Club. Ironically, the latter was phasing himself out of Young Ireland in the hope of a government appointment to a College. Several of Mitchel's colleagues, while opposing his remedies, fully accepted his critical analysis. M. J. Barry of Cork agreed with Mitchel on the hopelessness of conciliating the gentry and the futility of constitutional action but feared, somewhat inconsistently, that abandonment of legality would result in anarchy. Meagher felt that the only hope lay in constitutional methods. He wished Davis alive for a single day to guide them.

There was considerable interest in the Old Ireland camp. John O'Connell, whose Association was in very poor shape financially, and who had seen his parliamentary party disintegrate in the debate on the coercion bill, suggested a renewal of the negotiations which had broken down in July 1847. There was even a hint that the Confederate demand for a new movement and the dissolution of the old might become negotiable. A split in the Confederation, excluding the militants, would clearly make things easier. Barrett's *Pilot*, which had never wanted reconciliation, at first condemned Duffy's 'weak and cowardly' refusal to follow the 'inevitable tendency' of the principles he had long advocated. A few weeks later, however, it argued that there was less difference between the Duffy group and the Conciliation Hall than between Duffy and Mitchel.[4]

The decision of Duffy and O'Brien to bring matters to a head in the Confederation was partly motivated by hopes of Repeal unity. Dillon, even more moderate, was prepared to accept a reorganisation of the Association if place-hunting were abandoned. The trouble with Mitchel and Reilly made reunion imperative. In late 1847 both O'Neill Daunt and Sir Colman O'Loghlen approached O'Brien with suggestions for reunion. Sir Colman pointed out that Mitchel and Reilly justified John O'Connell's denunciation of Young Ireland's revolutionary tendencies. Once again, O'Brien refused to yield to Duffy's plea to come up to Dublin in early January 1848, though the latter claimed that with O'Brien present more work was done in a week than in a month without him. On the publication of Mitchel's letter, O'Brien wrote unsuccessfully to the Confederation suggesting that Mitchel and Reilly should not be re-elected to its Council and seeking legal opinion on the effect of their views. O'Brien came in person for the Confederation meeting on 31 January.[5]

Duffy's report on Confederate objectives was first brought to the Council. Mitchel and Reilly presented their own document, which Dillon thought 'drawn with great ability'. The dissidents wanted to present both documents to the clubs but Dillon managed to stall on a tactic likely to achieve victory for the radicals. When Duffy's report was considered by Council, the amendments of Mitchel and Reilly were defeated six to one in a total of thirty. Mitchel, however, secured the acceptance of a moderate preliminary section in the document, while Duffy's objection to education in arms gained little support. Pigot found Mitchel in a conciliatory mood.[6]

The Confederation Split, January-February 1848

The contested report, however, was shelved when O'Brien attended the general Confederation meeting in person. He presented ten propositions, suspiciously like O'Connell's Peace Proposals. Though subsequently cited to show Duffy's moderation, Doheny claimed that the propositions were designed to replace the contentious sections of his report. Specifically, they insisted on a combination of classes, ruled out non-payment of rents and rates, asserted the right to bear arms while deploring agrarian crime, and adopted 'force of opinion' constitutionally expressed as the means of the organisation. In contrast to the earlier Peace Proposals,

O'Brien's resolutions placed no restriction on personal beliefs. Mitchel's amendment to allow total freedom of expression failed. The resolutions were adopted by 318 votes to 188. Though *The Pilot* marvelled at the 'closeness of the parallel' with the Association debate of July 1846, it was at least even tempered, concentrating on issues rather than personalities. Martin, a supporter of Mitchel, was in the chair. O'Brien defended the usefulness of the poor rate and rents representing industry like that of his grandfather. He rejected talk of guerrilla warfare and armed revolt before its justification and success were certain. O'Brien, like Doheny and P. J. Smyth later in the debate, warned that the people were not with them.[7]

Mitchel in reply denied that he was advocating the shooting of opponents from behind hedges and reiterated that his policy was passive resistance, based on the poor rate, with the peasantry armed to resist an attack on them. He would give his right hand if class unity were possible. The real issue was constitutionalism versus passive resistance. 'There is no opinion in Ireland worth a farthing that is not illegal.' Meagher, however, saw the issue as constitutionalism versus dependence on French help. Several speakers believed that Mitchel's opinions should not be penalised. Duffy, backed by McGee who had resigned his secretaryship to participate in the debate, disagreed. It was impossible to have two parties in the same organisation relying on different means and teaching different principles. Rifle clubs were hardly 'social and moral influence', while guerrilla war was scarcely synonymous with 'force of opinion'.[8]

The 'United Irishman'

Mitchel chronicled the end of the lengthy debate, which like its July 1846 predecessor, could not be concluded in a single day, in his new paper, the *United Irishman*. From this power base Mitchel, Martin and Reilly made ambiguous retirement statements. While leaving the Council they did not relinquish the clubs. Martin, like Mitchel no longer a club inspector for Ulster, promised to continue his visitations as an individual. The door was left open for their return and there was no equivalent of the witch-hunt organised through Ray in the Repeal Association. If Duffy and O'Brien hoped for a clean break with Mitchel's small group, the *United Irishman* became as great a threat on the flank of the Confederation as *The Nation* had been to the Repeal Association.[9]

Mitchel, who needed an income after his break with Duffy, originally attempted to start a newspaper in Cork. However, in late January Mitchel issued his Dublin prospectus. Though rejecting English law, and the conciliation of classes, while asserting the right to bear arms, the prospectus did not, however, spell out any form of violent resistance. Despite an aggressive tone most of the demands were susceptible of a moderate, or even a conservative, interpretation. On 12 February the first issue of the *United Irishman*, edited by himself and Reilly with Martin and Kenyon contributing regular letters, and Mangan, 'Eva' and 'Mary' from *The Nation* submitting poetry, created a sensation comparable to that of the original *Nation* in October 1842. According to Doheny, who opposed Mitchel in the great debate, 'every word struck with the force and terror of lightning.' Once again the first edition was swept away and the office so besieged with demands for additional copies that the police had to keep order. 'In every corner of the island the influence of the *United Irishman* was instant and simultaneous.' Circulation, according to *The Warder*, which probably underestimated, was 5,000, and twice the copies could have been sold. It lamented that *The Nation* would be partly superseded and the whole country 'saturated with its bloody principles.'[10]

Why did a new weekly, edited by a man then little known in the country, create such a stir? The swashbuckling defiance of the authorities affected by Mitchel from his first number was one reason. Unlike *The Nation* , whose format he generally copied, Mitchel scorned the slightest hint of ambiguity. His opening editorial was a signed diatribe addressed to Lord Clarendon, 'Englishman; calling himself Her Majesty's Lord Lieutenant General and General Governor of Ireland'. Mitchel promised 'the naked truth' and a 'public conspiracy' to overthrow the British government, as opposed to the 'secret conspiracy' of the United Irishmen, whose name and general principles were adopted by the new paper. Tone's apostrophe to the 'men of no property', heading the leader column, was reaffirmed in the initial Clarendon letter, as it had been in the prospectus. A move to the left was clearly popular with many Confederates, and not only the Dublin Remonstrants. Denny Lane, complaining that Cork Confederates were captivated by Mitchel, feared the encouragement of ultra-democratic attitudes.[11]

Reading between the lines, however, Mitchel still remained within the defensive parameters laid down by Daniel O'Connell. His tactics, like those of modern revolutionaries, were clearly to provoke the government into repressive action which would turn the masses against it by demonstrating that constitutionalism and legality were empty forms: 'You will resort to courts-martial, and triangles, and free quarters? Well, *that*, at last, will be the end of "constitutional agitation", and Irishmen will then find themselves front to front with their enemies. . . .' Even the Old Irelanders would be drawn into national resistance.

Mitchel's tactics were more subtle than Duffy, who dismissed them as the naive theory of spontaneous unplanned insurgency embedded in Carlyle's *French Revolution*, was prepared to admit. Duffy, moreover, had shown himself opposed to training in arms. In the short life of the *United Irishman* before its suppression in May, Mitchel continued his letters to Clarendon, 'butcher' and 'high commissioner of spies', with the occasional assistance of Devin Reilly. A challenge to prosecute was maintained: 'pack away, then, *if you dare*.' As Mitchel declared on 8 April, 'The idea of men preparing in broad daylight to overthrow a powerful government by *force*, and giving them a programme of their plans beforehand, seemed to you wholly absurd.' So absurd that Clarendon assumed that Mitchel must speak for an extremely powerful and well organised insurrectionary force.

The viceroy was eager to over-react as required. The Tory *Warder*, after the first letter to Clarendon, demanded action, not only against Mitchel's paper, but the whole Repeal movement, including Conciliation Hall. Such a response would have played into Mitchel's hands and united Repealers behind the radical Confederates. In London the Whig government seemed aware of the trap that Mitchel was springing. While the Prime Minister, Lord John Russell, oscillated between indifference and alarm at Mitchel's tone, the Home Secretary, Sir George Grey, advised against prosecution before success was certain. The Chancellor of the Exchequer, Sir Charles Wood, told Clarendon on 27 March 'to be forbearing to excess', as prosecution was precisely what the Young Irelanders wanted. The Irish Tories were left to fume in impotent rage, exactly as they had been by the Peel government in 1843.[12]

How Duffy's *Nation*, threatened by a periodical whose vehemence attracted the attention even of those opposing its policy, would have fared in a long antagonistic rivalry can only be surmised. Duffy's elaborate plan for constitutional action provided the basis for future nationalist movements. Beside Mitchel's heroic fulminations it appeared insipid. The first step in its implementation, when the most charismatic Confederate, T. F. Meagher, contested a by-election in his home territory of Waterford, was a failure. Dillon and O'Brien believed that Meagher's victory would force Old Ireland to submit. Though the populace apparently supported the Confederates (by six to one, according to the *United Irishman* of 26 February), thus indirectly justifying Mitchel's policy, the fact that Meagher polled weakly amongst middle-class voters succeeded only in splitting the Repealers to give the seat to a Tory. The Colleges were used against Young Ireland by a hysterical local priest, Fr Cuddihy. Mitchel opposed Meagher's candidature on the ground that his success would give greater publicity to Westminster.[13]

The French Revolution of February 1848

Confederates had no time to lament Meagher's defeat when on 24 February the government of Louis Philippe suddenly collapsed after a not quite bloodless revolution accompanied by the now celebrated Parisian barricades. Though important in European history as the first major uprising of 1848, the French Revolution encapsulated the Young Ireland aspirations since the establishment of *The Nation* and raised hopes that Europe would be forced into war. Most leaders of the French provisional government were intellectuals associated with radical newspapers which had sometimes quoted *The Nation* with approval. *The Nation* suggested a number of parallels. Thus the poet Alfonse de Lamartine, who headed the provisional government, was equated with Thomas Davis who had translated one of his poems, Ledru-Rollin with Smith O'Brien, the journalist Armand Marrast with John Dillon, the veteran French republican Dupont de l'Eure with Robert Holmes, and Carnot, son of the first Revolution organiser of victory, with Duffy. The token working-class representative in the French revolutionary government, 'Ouvrier' Albert [Martin], gave colour to Mitchel's claim that 'the men of no property' had triumphed. The *United Irishman* accordingly ran a series of articles on Tone's movement which ventilated his quest for French help.[14]

The *volte face* of conservative Confederates was more apparent than real. Smith O'Brien was impressed by the discipline of the French Revolution which left the social order intact. His first thought was the need for Repeal unity which, he believed, would make Ireland arbiter of the Empire. O'Brien angered Pigot by his talk of resisting French aggression. Chisholm Anstey later claimed that O'Brien had opposed emphasis on the French Revolution, but the latter denied this. Even Pigot was himself wary of talk that Ireland's time had come. The landowner, David Ross of Bladensberg, abandoned the Confederation in anger at its apparent abandonment of self-reliance. O'Gorman, fearing a premature crisis more than a lost opportunity, begged O'Brien to come to Dublin.[15]

Though Duffy assured O'Brien that he attempted, despite Mitchel's wrath, to preserve rational discussion in the Confederation, he took the radical initiative there. Amidst loud and tumultuous cheers, Duffy proclaimed what Pigot denied, that the 'time is at hand'. 'Ireland will be free before the coming summer fades into winter. All over the world – from the frozen swamps of Canada, to the rich corn fields of Sicily – in Italy, in Denmark, in Prussia, and in glorious France, men are up for their rights.' His means were still the union of classes and creeds which he expected to follow the French success, but this was lost in the general assumption that the 'no drop of blood' theory had finally been exploded. When John Dillon expressed some reservation about immediate plans for a national guard, a lady in the gallery interjected, 'You're a moral force man!' Pigot, who feared the effects of rhetoric like Duffy's on an excitable people, commended the realism of Dillon and Barry of Cork.[16]

Duffy, concerned for *Nation* circulation in competition with Mitchel, seems to have been forced to escalate his rhetoric. A Duffy editorial, 'Ireland's Opportunity', declared that French action 'warms our blood like wine'. It hoped for success without bloodshed if possible. 'But if no other way is left us out of famine, bankruptcy, and disgrace, than such a struggle, then, may God give us the "vantage ground and the victory."' As Duffy later summed up the situation, all the omens seemed favourable. The Catholic clergy 'began to thrill' as Pius IX appeared in the vanguard of nations striving for freedom; the Chartists, much praised in the *United Irishman*, eroded England's power; half the British Army was Irish and ready to fraternise with a local uprising.[17]

Excitement in Ireland intensified. O'Brien publicly demanded peace between the Repeal factions. He found Duffy ambivalent: 'Why do you write articles in *The Nation* against John O'Connell and Old Ireland at the same time that you suggest *Union*. You cannot expect to produce co-operation as long as this is done.' Old and Young Irelanders fraternised in places like Kilkenny and Limerick, asserting that France had destroyed all distinctions. The belief that inevitable war between England and revolutionary France would enable Ireland to make her own terms, as in 1782, seemed plausible. John O'Connell accepted this assumption, arguing that Ireland needed no bloodshed, and interpreted the French Revolution as a result of disciplined, defensive action. His attitude approximated that of O'Brien and Duffy.

But Mitchel appeared totally vindicated by events in France. As the man of the hour he returned triumphantly to the Confederation. Duffy sourly remarked that 'never was a man so metamorphosed; he used to be a modest and courteous gentleman, now he demeaned himself as if the French Revolution and the new opportunities it furnished were his personal achievements.' Duffy and Dillon did not find Mitchel's apparent notion of a spontaneous peasant uprising any more attractive. To the Tories, however, *The Nation* and *United Irishman* were now following a parallel course in treason, with the latter some distance ahead. Both papers had sections on arms and drilling, the sceptical Pigot compiling those for *The Nation*. As early as 11 March, when arguing for an Irish militia and Council of 300, *The Nation* praised pikes above the over-valued firearms, likely to require 600 shots before killing a single man. The Dublin clubs now marched to Confederation meetings as impressive bodies sometimes 500 strong. Arms were collected enthusiastically and pikes multiplied.[18]

For St Patrick's Day, 17 March, the Confederates planned a demonstration to redeem the anticlimax of Clontarf in 1843 and achieve Repeal unity. Clarendon was genuinely concerned, not just pretending as Mitchel later claimed. O'Brien offered to take the chair if the meeting was proclaimed. At the Confederation on 15 March O'Brien admitted that 'the state of affairs was totally different' from a few days previously when he had denounced force. He now advocated a national guard.[19]

Clarendon's position was difficult. He reinforced the troops. His law officers, however, saw nothing illegal in a national guard. Though members of the cabinet had misgivings, Clarendon decided, if violence broke out at the demonstration, to prosecute the editors Duffy and Mitchel as accessories before the fact; if there was no disorder, Mitchel, O'Brien and Meagher were to be indicted for sedition.

The demonstration, delayed till the 21st to persuade Old Irelanders to take part, was held at the North Wall in Dublin. In the form of a meeting of the Dublin trades, attended by 10,000 to 20,000 people, it was addressed by O'Brien, Duffy, Mitchel and other Confederate leaders. A permanent body was formed and due sympathy declared for France. There was no outbreak of violence, but after the meeting a thousand people marched up the quays and were met by numbers of sympathisers who poured out of the weekly Conciliation Hall gathering to demonstrate solidarity.

Mitchel had expected more, announcing in the preceding *United Irishman*: 'We await attack. We shall not provoke the shedding of blood; but if blood is shed, we will see the end of it.' The Liberator himself could not have put it better. When Clarendon after the meeting followed his intention and charged Mitchel, O'Brien and Meagher with sedition, Mitchel told the Confederation, 'sedition was a small matter, but he intended to commit high treason.' Bail was easily obtained. John and Maurice O'Connell demonstrated solidarity by offering to go bail for O'Brien and Meagher. Even the pacifist Haughton contributed to the defence fund to indicate his opposition to coercion. *The Nation* declared that war had begun. Such sedition was overturning thrones throughout Europe. While O'Brien and Meagher were prosecuted for speeches, Mitchel was indicted for three articles, including the 'butcher' Clarendon letter, and one, in fact by Reilly, drawing lessons from French revolutionary experience to suggest, *inter alia*, that vitriol could be thrown from windows on advancing government troops. The vitriol article raised a storm amongst conservatives, but Mitchel remained unrepentant. It was finally suggested that vitriol was more useful in the making of gunpowder than burning holes in cavalrymen's coats. O'Brien believed that by prosecuting him with Mitchel the government skilfully identified O'Brien with the advocates of immediate insurrection. To O'Brien, the Irish, dependent on foreign corn, required training in arms to achieve independence by the threat of force.[20]

The momentum was now too rapid for realistic reflection. There was an increasing tendency to mistake profession for fact, heroic intransigence for concrete victory, and symbolic success for socio-economic achievement. The intoxicating effects of Meagher's spellbinding rhetoric and Mitchel's crackling prose turned real setbacks into apparent success. A type of revolution by analogy appeared to have already taken place in Ireland. It became conventional to assert that the time for words had passed before launching into yet another four column diatribe.

By the end of March there was much amiss with the Confederate movement. John O'Connell still dragged his feet over union. The divisions between *The Nation* and *United Irishman* factions remained unreconciled. Both the Confederates themselves and the British government realised that outside Dublin there was little mobilisation of the country. Even in Dublin the clubs were not as strong as they appeared. The Chartist diversionary allies in England were about to have their own bluff called by an intransigent government.

The first clear setback to the unrealistic optimism of the Confederates came at the end of March with the French response to a Confederate delegation. It comprised Smith O'Brien, Meagher and Edward Hollywood, a Dublin silk weaver intended as a token counterweight to Albert Ouvrier. O'Brien denied that the delegation was attempting to achieve French material assistance, but later admitted he sought Franco-Irish volunteers if war broke out with England. French help was certainly not forthcoming and Lamartine, 'a mere Anglo-Frenchman' as Mitchel later dismissed him, implied in his address in reply to the delegation that Ireland was an internal British problem. The British government, which had pressured him, was delighted. It was clear that there was to be no war of revolutionary France against Britain and thus no 'opportunity'.[21]

Confederate Difficulties Increase

On 10 April, after his return from France, O'Brien courageously confronted a furious House of Commons. It was debating a new treason-felony act designed to provide a more flexible antidote to the Confederates, without requiring strict proof of overt treason. In his last Westminster speech, after ten minutes of abusive yelling had died down, O'Brien distinguished between loyalty to the queen and loyalty to the House of Commons. He denied that he had sought troops from France, accepted responsibility for encouraging the Irish to arm and welcomed aid from the Chartists. Back in Ireland O'Brien, on 29 April, was stoned, sufficiently seriously to require two months recuperation, by an inflamed crowd in his home territory of Limerick.

The rage of the populace was directed, not against O'Brien, but against Mitchel, who, despite an agreement not to identify

O'Brien with his principles, had been invited to a common meeting. As in 1847, the lower classes were infuriated by criticism of O'Connell, a stock-in-trade of the *United Irishman*. A recent article by Reilly had, in anticipation of subsequent socialists, depicted the Liberator as 'the mortal enemy of the Irish working man, tiller and artificer'. The upshot of the incident was that O'Brien's resignation from the Confederation could only be averted by the resignation of Mitchel and Reilly. This cleared the air to some extent, but the fact that the *United Irishman* enjoyed the largest circulation in Ireland and a particular influence over the Confederate clubs, demonstrated the instability of the situation.[22]

Though the target of the Limerick mob had not been O'Brien himself, the incident showed how precarious was the hold of Confederate views on opinion outside Dublin and how essential it was to link Young Ireland with the faltering movement of the Liberator's son. As Duffy stated publicly in early June, the Repeal Association still ruled the rural districts and had the ear of the clergy. A Catholic priest, Dr O'Brien, had organised the opposition to Mitchel in Limerick. An Old Ireland deputation, including John O'Connell, waited on Smith O'Brien shortly after the Limerick episode. Organised meetings working seriously for unity between the groups began. Bishops like Cantwell and Browne, previously very hostile to Young Ireland, now favoured reconciliation. Even *The Pilot* was partly converted to the same position. John O'Connell, still reluctant to abandon the Association, continued to prove difficult. He did, however, hold powerful cards, and the Confederate position on force was extremely ambiguous. The *United Irishman*, moreover, sniped at these negotiations as an attempt to substitute unity for action. Though all were now agreed on arming, Mitchel still considered O'Brien's policy of class conciliation 'a very bad one.' The national movement must become a class movement or stand still.[23]

The Conviction of Mitchel

But Mitchel's challenge to the government now bore fruit. Clarendon with dubious legality issued a proclamation, answered by a counter-proclamation signed by O'Brien, against both the Council of 300 and the National Guard. The sedition trials of Meagher and O'Brien failed as in both cases at least one juryman refused to convict. Mitchel, hoping to gain time till November, pleaded a dilatory abatement to the sedition charge, but was immediately indicted according to the new treason-felony act.

This time the authorities took his advice and packed the jury with extreme care. Defended by the octogenarian Robert Holmes in a sensational trial which ended by the defence counsel inviting his own indictment and Mitchel calling for and receiving the shouted endorsement of his supporters in court, the editor of the *United Irishman* was convicted and hurried off to penal exile and the composition of his classic *Jail Journal*. 'Eva' gave poetic form to Mitchel's rhetorical appeal for one who shared his principles:

> For one — for two — for three —
> Aye! hundreds, thousands, see!
> For vengeance and for thee
> To the last!

But Mitchel had intended no mere demonstration. Intoxicated by the success of the *United Irishman*, he believed that his conviction by a packed jury would trigger a massive rescue by the Dublin clubs whose action would ignite spontaneous revolution throughout the country. Meagher had originally endorsed this strategy, spreading the notion that Mitchel could only be transported in a sea of blood. However, after an investigation of the state of the Dublin clubs, and their lack of provisions, Duffy, Meagher and the other leaders agreed that any such premature outbreak would be disastrous to the Irish cause. Mitchel was furious at the decision, and never forgave Duffy.

Despite the collapse of the rescue plan, Mitchel became an instant hero-martyr, and a name with which to conjure. Even *The Warder*, which had long demanded action against him, could not forbear to cheer. Rejecting the efforts of English publications like *Punch* to portray Mitchel as a coward or 'monkey', *The Warder* saw something 'unmistakeably noble and heroic' in his trial demeanour, and granted him 'a certain grandeur'. He was the 'victim of Whig duplicity and procrastination', deserving less than his excessive sentence of fourteen years transportation.[24]

The 'Irish Felon' *and the* 'Irish Tribune'

Mitchel's now suppressed *United Irishman* was succeeded by two papers in adjoining offices, the *Irish Felon*, edited by John Martin, and the *Irish Tribune* of two young medical students, Kevin Izod O'Doherty (b. 1824), and the poet Richard D'Alton Williams (b. 1822). Martin and Devin Reilly obtained the services of James Fintan Lalor, who had refused to co-operate with Mitchel because, it was said, he was offered insufficient remuneration and was aggrieved by Mitchel's pirating of his ideas without acknowledgment. The *Tribune* openly admitted that it hoped the issue would come to blows as only freedom achieved by the sword could raise the degraded Irish population. This was to introduce a new attitude to violence, moving unequivocally beyond the 'defensive' notions still found in Mitchel. The *Felon* and the *Tribune* continued to act as gadflies to the Confederation. Like the *United Irishman* they were highly sceptical of union between the Confederation and Conciliation Hall. Joseph Brenan (b. 1828) a poet recruited from Cork by Mitchel earlier in the year, argued that the negotiations with Conciliation Hall sapped the spirit of the clubs. Despite their numerous members they were neither well armed nor interested in becoming so. Such warnings were timely, but what Mitchel called 'King Talk' still reigned over the Confederates. The clubs were riddled with government agents, sometimes reporting the exact location of arms caches. Doheny, who wrote for the *Tribune*, also believed negotiation with Conciliation Hall a great mistake.[25]

Both the *Felon* and the *Tribune* were well supplied with poets who intensified patriotic fervour. Apart from Williams ('Shamrock') and Brenan, they had contributions from Frazer, Mangan, John Savage and 'Eva' (Mary Kelly). The *Tribune* obtained a story from William Carleton, but the latter eventually renounced his connection with the paper. Much of the poetry spread a warlike message. 'Mary' (Ellen

Downing), who had already answered criticism in *The Nation* that women should encourage a softer spirit, had written rousing poems for the *United Irishman*:

> But fling back your fearless defiance,
> And up for the Irish Brigade![26]

She published, moreover, an address to the women of Ireland, admonishing them that a little blood-letting caused small pain compared with the misery of the famine. 'Eva' fully agreed. Her poems in the *Felon* taught the message 'arm yourselves'. Such ladies were not immune to Cupid's darts. 'Mary' had an unhappy little romance with Joseph Brenan, while 'Eva' ultimately became Mrs Kevin Izod O'Doherty.[27]

Secret Conspiracy or National Union: The Confederate Dilemma

The departure of Mitchel left the way open for two totally incompatible developments, both opposed to his views. In public the reunion of Repealers was finally brought to an ambiguous conclusion with the formation of the Irish League, which held a public meeting on 11 July. On the other hand, a small group of Confederates formed a secret junta to prepare for insurrection. It was assumed that an open constitutional movement would work in co-operation with an underground conspiracy, as Provisional Sinn Fein now works with the IRA. The difficulty lay in the fact that many potential members of the open movement were still basically constitutionalists who regarded force as very much a last resort. Conspiracy backed by a rhetoric which, like that of the *Tribune*, approached the idea of purifying violence as good in itself, was incompatible with constitutionalism. This issue was never resolved.

1.   The Irish League

The negotiations between the Old and Young Ireland factions lasted for fourteen days at the *Freeman's Journal* office, ending on Tuesday 23 June; Dr Gray, relatively impartial between the factions, acted with O'Loghlen and others as facilitators. Doheny later questioned whether the negotiators of compromise had ever been properly authorised. It was the Old Irelander, A. R. Sticht, once a fellow student of Thomas Davis, who proposed what John O'Connell long resisted, the dissolution of both organisations. O'Loghlen, aided by Dr Miley who hoped for episcopal control through John O'Connell, drew up eight principles for a new organisation. John O'Connell was eventually induced to accept the exclusion of placehunting and discussion of religious issues. The original compromise had excluded any mention of force, but stipulated against encouragement to arm. As John O'Connell told the Repeal Association, if the government initially allowed arming it had power to act decisively before the potential insurgents were ready. Ultimately, O'Brien agreed with John O'Connell, but now both O'Brien and Duffy unwisely anticipated the completion of negotiations by announcing that Confederation principles had prevailed. In the final meeting, John O'Connell therefore resurrected the Peace Propositions, fearing that Meagher could commit him to a violent policy. As a compromise, Dillon suggested that while neither organisation abandoned its beliefs, no individual or newspaper be authorised to interpret the principles of the League. Moral and physical force were therefore not mentioned in the agreement. But John O'Connell also disliked the Confederate clubs, long associated with arms. He twice demanded an additional fortnight to consult country branches. Though radical Confederates complained of the delay, O'Brien himself considered it useful. Finally reunification, initially without the clubs, was resolved. Clubs could arm, but arming was not to be preached in the League. The Council of the Confederation decided to dissolve on 21 June to place the onus for rejecting terms on the Association. At the Dublin Music Hall on 11 July the Irish League met for the first time. Four thousand attended with only one day's notice. The winding up of the Association remained in doubt. None of its hardliners attended the Irish League or sought positions on its committee. John O'Connell decided against the new organisation and withdrew to concentrate on his parliamentary duties. On 22 July, publicly denouncing both League and clubs, he announced the continuation of the Association.[28]

The situation could not have been more confused. At the meeting of 19 July the League's policy was declared as 'constitutional but decided'. McGee pointed out that 'constitutional' meant the right to bear arms. Was this the interpretation of Dr Maginn, bishop of Derry who joined with eighty of his priests when assured of constitutionality? Duffy's claim that Maginn later wrote privately to endorse violent resistance if delayed till after the harvest has been discounted. The correspondence of Maginn, previously very hostile to Young Ireland and the Colleges, shows an understanding of the importance of church control of the League, and regret that he had not participated earlier. The pro-Young Ireland Fr Thaddeus O'Malley talked ambiguously at the Irish League meeting of using the organisation, like Wellington's lines at Torres Vedras in Portugal, as a resting-place from which to launch an attack. Clearly, there were as many different interpretations as members of the League. Without the magic name of O'Connell, the League was of little use in mobilising the country areas. According to Halpin, the Confederation secretary, clubs were forming rapidly throughout the country with hardly a thought for the League. Ominously, on the day of John O'Connell's withdrawal, news arrived that the archbishop of Paris had been shot dead by working class rebels against the new bourgeois regime. The notion that the Irish clubs were riddled with infidelity was assiduously propagated at this time.[29]

2.   Secret Preparations

After Mitchel's departure the Confederation Council, on Fr Kenyon's suggestion and against Duffy's wishes, was reduced from an increasingly unwieldy body to an elected committee of twenty-one. Fr Kenyon and Meagher headed the list with 31 votes each, followed by O'Brien, Duffy, Dillon and O'Gorman, all with 30. Meanwhile, representatives of the conservative wing, Duffy and Dillon, joined three radicals, Kenyon, Martin and Reilly, to plan for a revolution. They sought arms, money and officers from America, began training local men for the struggle, and tried to organise the Irish in England to create a diversion. O'Brien, considered too slow in deliberation and too favourable to his own class, was not invited to join. Duffy later demonstrated that the secret caucus totally abandoned Mitchel's open, spontaneous and leaderless revolution. Duffy and Dillon played a double game as revolutionary conspirators, while negotiating a compromise reunion with Old Ireland. John O'Connell was right to be suspicious. However, conservatives like Dillon thought of a show of force rather than actual violence.[30]

The Road to Widow McCormack's Cabbage Patch

The secret conspiracy was no more successful than the botched reunion in achieving Irish self-government. The fire-eating Fr Kenyon, and another radical priest, Fr James Birmingham of Borrisokane, were compelled to submit to their bishop, Dr Kennedy of Killaloe. Birmingham's attempt to anticipate modern liberation theology in his declaration that 'in this country politics and the very existence of the people are almost indissolubly united' proved premature. Agents were sent to the United States, but could achieve nothing in time. The Chartist threat evaporated after parliament's rejection of their monster petition on 10 April. French intervention was out of the question. On 20 July, a meeting of club delegates decided by a small majority to offer passive resistance to disarmament. O'Brien declined to sit on the special executive then established.[31]

The executive comprised Dillon, Meagher, McGee, Reilly and O'Gorman. Fintan Lalor originally tied with Reilly, but Frs Kenyon and Thaddeus O'Malley received few votes. A spy attended to report to Dublin Castle. Duffy had already been arrested on 9 July; Martin, O'Doherty and Williams of the other journals were also taken into custody. They edited their papers from Newgate. The club executive never met. The government rushed through parliament a suspension of the Habeus Corpus Act. A warrant was taken out for the arrest of Smith O'Brien, currently inspecting clubs in the south. What John O'Connell feared had come to pass. The ministry, now thoroughly alarmed, declined to await the insurrection, long promised by the Young Ireland papers after the harvest. A great meeting was organised by Meagher and Doheny, on Slievenamon mountain in Co. Tipperary.

According to Doheny 50,000 men 'clambered that steep mountain side, under a scorching July sun'. This probably, as he suggests, persuaded the cabinet to suspend Habeus Corpus. Lord Clarendon feared that once the insurgents began operations in the Kilkenny, Cashel and Waterford triangle, of which Slievenamon lay on the south-west base, rebellion might spread dangerously.[32]

Why did an outbreak not occur in Dublin where the clubs were most reliable? According to Meagher the strength of government forces ensured bloody defeat there. Elsewhere there was some chance of success. In fact, the strategy of the Young Irelanders was as chaotic as their organisation. Meagher and Dillon hastened to Ballinkeele to alert O'Brien. The latter considered three options, accept arrest, escape, or initiate insurrection. O'Brien, an extremely reluctant revolutionary, had objected to Duffy's recent inflammatory articles in *The Nation* and had been pointedly excluded from the conspiratorial caucus. He had never desired the leadership which the Young Irelanders had thrust upon him. In a retrospect intended for his trial, O'Brien emphasised personal honour in his decision to opt for resistance. 'So much had been said by the Party with which I was associated and by myself, about the necessity of preparation for conflict, that we should have been exposed to ridicule and reproach if we had fled at the moment when all the contingencies which we had contemplated as justifying the use of force were realised.' O'Brien and his colleagues thus appear prisoners of their own rhetoric. But O'Brien still believed that there was a sporting chance of success. He reflected that people from all classes now favoured Repeal, that the government forces of 40,000, some doubtful in their allegiance, could not suppress eight million, that the Catholic clergy were supportive, and that help would come from other countries like the United States. A leading Confederate, Michael O'Farrell, maintained that O'Brien, against his better judgment, had been forced into revolt by Dillon and Meagher. O'Brien's subsequent disillusionment indicates a modicum of truth in this claim.[33]

Years later, O'Brien was outspoken about his experience in July 1848. He then believed that the right course was the first option of accepting arrest and embarrassing a government which could prove nothing against him. But his decision to resist was conditional on a demonstration of mass support for rebellion. At first this appeared forthcoming. Large bodies at Enniscorthy, Craigue and Kilkenny told O'Brien to resist arrest. At Carrick-on-Suir the feeling was 'so intense that I hesitated no longer'.[34]

O'Brien soon found that he had grossly overestimated his chance of success. Despite earlier encouragement, local Kilkenny Confederates now assured him and his entourage, eventually including MacManus from Liverpool, Patrick O'Donohoe from Dublin, and James Stephens and John O'Mahony, the future Fenian leaders, that no stand could be made without reinforcements. For a week O'Brien led his fluctuating force to towns and villages like Carrick, Mullinahone, Callan, Killenaule, and Ballingary. For a time he had several thousand in his train, but these melted away after clerical discouragement, often from priests who had hitherto appeared Confederate supporters. Fr Kenyon's refusal, despite all his bombast, to give any support whatever to a hopeless cause was a cruel blow. His agreement with his bishop precluded him from any revolutionary initiative, and he had always stressed a reasonable chance of success as a vital condition for rebellion. His Confederate colleagues, however, felt misled and angry. A minor success against a handful of policemen and a contingent of dragoons, who baulked at encountering the insurgents, was achieved at Killenaule, but provided overt proof of high treason.

Despite pressure from Reilly and Doheny and others, O'Brien rejected decisive action which they believed would spark the necessary national conflagration. He forbade the comandeering of private property before he had been in arms for a week. On 29 July came his final anticlimax near Ballingary. Forty retreating police barricaded themselves inside Widow McCormack's house at Boulah, using her children as hostages against O'Brien's diminishing and dispirited forces. Gallantly attempting a parley, O'Brien nearly achieved martyrdom when undisciplined stoning of the cottage provoked police fire which killed at least one bystander. Unable to permit the burning out of the police,

O'Brien withdrew before police reinforcements arrived; according to one account he accepted the advice of a local priest.[35]

Leading participants like John O'Mahony and Patrick O'Donohoe agreed that O'Brien himself was one of the chief causes of the failure of the Rising. O'Mahony considered that resolute leadership could have overcome the hostility of the clergy; O'Donohoe, while accepting that a man of O'Brien's ideals could never succeed in a revolution, nevertheless considered his efforts to preserve property against the mob a triumph of virtue over vice. Others were less tolerant. Reilly reportedly said O'Brien should be shot. Chisholm Anstey heard that O'Brien was nearly assassinated by his followers. Though this appears unlikely, only Dillon really endorsed O'Brien's actions in July 1848. Ironically, O'Brien's most treasonable action was his letter to the Boulah Collieries management, threatening nationalisation unless wages were raised and prices lowered. Little has been made of this quasi-socialistic gesture by a conservative landowner.[36]

Pockets of resistance remained after Ballingarry. John O'Mahony, subsequently a founder of the Fenian Brotherhood, won an instant reputation as a guerrilla leader and terrified local conservatives before escaping to France. Outbreaks continued into September at Carrick-on-Suir, Carrickbeg, Lowry Bridge, Curraghmore Wood, Kilmacthomas and Glenbower, where a man was killed when a group, some in 82 Club uniforms, attacked the police station. Rebel camps were maintained for a time near Slievenamon and elsewhere. The emphasis appeared to be poverty rather than politics; some guerrilla war was waged against distraining landlords. According to D'Arcy McGee, from his exile in America, the 500 clubs, containing 30,000 men, ceased to meet, but their ten-man sections remained a revolutionary nucleus. McGee had attempted unsuccessfully to liaise with a Ribbon organisation, hitherto anathema to Young Ireland. There was certainly an undercurrent of club activity in 1849, culminating at Cappoquin in September, and the sections provided a basis for Fenianism some years later. If O'Brien was an inadequate leader, his successors proved no more effective or realistic.[37]

The Post-Mortem Begins

The original Young Ireland movement and rebellion effectively ended when Smith O'Brien, finding the peasantry neither willing to protect nor betray him, was arrested at Thurles attempting to take a train home to Cahirmoyle. Other leaders were either arrested or escaped abroad. So disastrous did O'Brien's failure appear at the time that rumours circulated that he was a government agent. Contemporaries and subsequent historians have ransacked the dictionary for contemptuous epithets to depict Smith O'Brien's revolt. As he himself said: 'our escapade — it does not deserve the name of an insurrection — was in a supreme degree contemptible as the result of a great national movement in which many an idle boast and many a futile menace had been employed.' Late in life, however, he saw it as 'a forlorn hope' not deserving of ridicule, and challenged an MP to a duel for repeating the canard that he had grovelled in the widow's cabbage patch. O'Brien considered the Irish peasant ready to fight, so long as he had the support of his priest. He blamed himself, 'a fatal mistake', for not ensuring such support. O'Brien's awe of clerical authority may have contributed to failure, as when he agreed with the Tipperary priests to suspend aggressive operations for a fortnight and remain on the defensive. But other Young Irelanders, with the possible exception of O'Mahony, agreed with O'Brien on need for church endorsement. None had more convincing plans to offer. O'Brien, moreover, had had an unwelcome leadership forced upon him. To a considerable extent, therefore, he emerges as a convenient whipping boy for the errors of others.[38]

The Triumph of Failure?

If uninspiring as a military leader, Smith O'Brien was superbly equipped as a patriotic martyr. The 'escapade' of July 1848 became an interlude in an essentially literary rebellion already in full bloom. On his arrest, a 'poetic effusion' was found in O'Brien's pocket. Poets, male and female, abounded. Mitchel's *Jail Journal* and Doheny's minor masterpiece describing his escape to the United States were in the making. McGee, MacManus, Meagher, O'Donohoe, O'Mahony and O'Brien left personal accounts of the Rising. Gavan Duffy's magisterial account of the period appeared in the 1880s. Though Duffy became premier of a self-governing colony, Lucy O'Brien's opinion that he was 'altogether intellectual and not at all a man of action' seems accurate. Other participating revolutionary men of letters like the subsequent Fenians, John O'Leary and Charles Kickham, also described the period. The latter's great novel, *Knocknagow*, is a compendium of Young Ireland thought though it fails to mention the Rising.[39]

The Clonmel trials for high treason in October 1848 provided an appropriate denouement for literary rebellion. The journalist defenders of treason-felony charges were disposed of with less publicity, Martin and O'Doherty being sentenced to transportation, Williams acquitted, and the ailing Lalor released after a short imprisonment. Duffy's trial stalled. O'Brien, Meagher, O'Donohoe and MacManus were tried for their lives. They were duly convicted. After ten days of up to nine hours each standing in the dock before a hostile audience, which nevertheless included most of his family, an almost disoriented O'Brien was first to receive 'the awful sentence of the law, with all the ghastly details of its feudal accessories'. Opting simply to state that he had done his duty, O'Brien, sustained as he said later only 'by some of our old Irish pride', appeared 'cool and collected'. He left the dock with 'a steady step and smiling countenance'. His formidable mother Charlotte, wife Lucy and sister Grace attended him in prison and were won over by Meagher's charm. *The Warder* complained that O'Brien savoured his 'delicious immortality' with 'the irrepressible complacency of a gratified coxcomb'. It admitted, however, that the Young Irelanders were now 'divested of their farcicality'. Earlier it had tempered ridicule — 'widdy M'Cormack's cabbages shelthrin' poor O'Brien, an' he skelpin away on all fours' — with respect. 'In the midst of the guilt and farcicality of Smith O'Brien's "life and adventures", there is a mixture of good, and even chivalric feeling.' Meagher, O'Donohoe and MacManus were no less stoical. Meagher sent Grace O'Brien into fits of laughter 'with descriptions of their folly and the scenes through which they passed'. When condemned to death Meagher told O'Brien of his hope 'that in our very failure — in the contemplation of it hereafter, there will be instruments found to a purer, better system of political action in this country.' MacManus was also proud that they had acted their parts. Even in his 'dismal cell' his hopes for Irish nationhood were stronger than ever. Across the Atlantic the *Boston Pilot* quoted O'Brien's pre-Rising poem:

> Whether on the gallows high,
>   Or in the battle's van,
> The fittest place for man to die
>   Is where he dies for man.[40]

There was, however, to be no 'terrible beauty' in 1848. All classes, even Orangemen, united in demanding the reprieve of the Young Irelanders; special legislation was passed to enable them to be transported, eleven months later, to Van Diemen's Land. There O'Brien, Mitchel, Meagher, O'Donoghoe, Martin, O'Doherty and MacManus for a time experienced a common exile in what Mitchel described as 'the most beautiful country in all the world: magnificent forests, precipitous forests, and grand lakes, lying in crystalline beauty amidst umbrageous hills.'[41]

What of the others? Dillon, McGee, Reilly, and P. J. Smyth escaped to America. Several used clerical disguise, and O'Gorman female dress. The government particularly wished to convict Gavan Duffy, considered the brains behind Young Ireland. The discovery in O'Brien's portmanteau of a Duffy letter demanding that O'Brien assume revolutionary leadership, suggested indictment for high treason, not treasonfelony. Despite the abandonment of this charge, Duffy was tried five times. His counsel, Isaac Butt, not yet a Home Ruler, in a superb defence used every legal artifice to abort prosecution. Duffy's friends meanwhile clamoured against jury packing. In April 1849, after nine months in prison, *The Nation* editor finally emerged a free man. A final jury could not agree. Court tactics, including the use of character witnesses like Fr Mathew, earned Duffy the nickname 'Give-in' Duffy from his enemies. He re-established *The Nation* in time to catch the last flicker of rebellion in September 1849. A Young Ireland group, including John O'Leary, John Savage, Joseph Brenan, now editing the new *Irishman*, and Fintan Lalor, organised an attack on Cappoquin police station. Seven police beat off and killed two of the seventy assailants who were armed mainly with pikes. *The Warder* blamed the revived *Nation* and the *Freeman's Journal* for incitement by their criticism of the landlords. Brenan escaped to America, while Lalor, whose constitution had always been weak, died of bronchitis in December. Brenan's former fiancée, 'Mary', or Ellen Downing, entered a convent in October of the same year. Her fellow poet, James Clarence Mangan had concluded an eccentric existence in June.

The End of Young Ireland or the Beginning?

Little appeared to remain of Young Ireland. Defeated in 1848 the movement burned brightly in the writings and subsequent deeds of its members. Gavan Duffy played a leading role in a new Irish tenant-right movement, sitting in the Westminster parliament, before emigrating to Australia in 1855, leaving Ireland a 'corpse on the dissecting table'. Smith O'Brien advised him to take up politics and Duffy in 1871 duly obtained the premiership of the new colony of Victoria. He accepted a knighthood before returning to Europe to reinterpret Young Ireland for a new generation. Mitchel, after escaping from Van Diemen's Land in 1853, settled in America where he published a series of journals, the *Citizen*, the *Southern Citizen* and the *Irish Citizen*. He clashed with Archbishop Hughes of New York and the opponents of slavery. His latter views were put to the test on the outbreak of the American Civil War, when he became editor of the Richmond *Examiner* and a major propagandist for the South. He assisted the new Fenian movement but became disillusioned with its attacks on Canada and attempts at rebellion while England was at peace. He quarrelled with the Fenian leader James Stephens. Mitchel refused the American Fenian presidency in 1867. Returning to Ireland as an undischarged felon in 1875, he was elected unopposed, and when disqualified re-elected, for Tipperary which had failed Smith

O'Brien in 1848. Mitchel died in his moment of glory. His friend, John Martin, released from Van Diemen's Land, returned home to participate in establishing the Home Rule movement, led by the advocate, Isaac Butt. He sat for Meath at Westminster, dying within hours of his brother-in-law, Mitchel. D'Arcy McGee, after establishing a new *Nation* in New York and engaging in other journalism, moved north to Canada where he helped to achieve the 1867 Confederation of Canada. McGee sat in the Canadian cabinet before his assassination by a Fenian who considered him a traitor to Irish nationality. Smith O'Brien, after a long publicity battle with the Van Diemen's Land authorities to gain attention for his cause, was released from Van Diemen's Land in 1854 and allowed in 1856 to return home to Ireland, where apart from visits to Europe and North America, he lived quietly till his death in 1864. Meagher, like Mitchel, escaped from Van Diemen's Land and moved to the United States. He also dabbled in journalism. During the American Civil War he led Irish brigades as a brigadier-general and, in some of the bloodiest battles ever fought — Bull Run, Antietam, Chancellorsville, Fredricksburg — saw his men decimated in a manner he never imagined when he composed his 'sword speech'. In 1867 Meagher was drowned mysteriously in the Missouri while temporary governor of Montana. Kevin Izod O'Doherty practised medicine in Australia and, happily married to 'Eva', sat in the Queensland legislature before returning home to Ireland to obtain election for an Irish constituency to Westminster. John Pigot, unable to participate in the 1848 rising because of illness requiring recuperation outside the country, not pressure from his Whig family, eventually made a fortune at the Bombay bar but refused an Indian judgeship while Ireland was denied her rights. Richard O'Gorman, however, accepted judicial office in the United States. John Dillon, after practising law with O'Gorman, returned to Ireland 1855. Ten years later he was elected to parliament. His son became the last leader of the Home Rule party.

Thus the leading Young Irelanders whose rebellion had egregiously failed demonstrated remarkable ability and resource abroad. Their fitness for government was amply proved. Some, like M. J. Barry and D'Arcy McGee, turned away from the politics of their youth. Most remained staunch. Few of the older generation agreed with the new Fenian politics of the younger men of 1848, O'Leary, Stephens, Kickham and T. C. Luby, but they created a fund of national ideas and debate from which all subsequent Irish nationalist generations have been obliged to draw, often without acknowledgment.

PART TWO

Analysis

Religion, Education and Secularism

The Infidelity of Young Ireland

The pluralist nationalism of Davis and his colleagues was long resisted by *The Pilot* and Old Ireland faction. The Colleges issue turned a bitter dispute into a veritable witch-hunt. Accusations of Young Ireland 'infidelity' preceded the introduction of Peel's celebrated bill. Davis's casual equation in an early *Nation* of Muslim and Christian 'crusaders' led to an accusation of rationalism.[1] The issue became pressing in October 1844 when a Davis leader provoked a full-scale onslaught by 'An Irish priest' in the *Weekly Register* against the 'un-Catholic and infidel spirit which has been exhibited in *The Nation* newspaper, from time to time'. The priest criticised the previous issue in which a leader, in fact by Davis, separated religion and politics, asked whether the Irish leader's motives were patriotism or 'superstition', asserted the right of Catholics like D. O. Madden to convert to Protestantism, and lamented the 'Roman censorship'. The provocative allusion to 'superstition', referred to Dr Miley's sermon of 8 September, in which he declared that the release of the Liberator by the House of Lords was not the action of Whig partisan law lords, but a Providential miracle through the intercession of the Virgin Mary. Davis, moreover, claimed that 'superstition' applied to Catholics and Protestants.[2]

Duffy, defending Davis's unsigned articles, admitted their Protestant authorship; he would not himself have used the same phrasing. O'Brien privately told Davis that the 'Irish Priest's' article was fair comment, and warned of the need for unity in a Catholic majority country. Davis, however, was encouraged by others. The Catholic Doheny believed

O'Connell himself by subtle hints had instigated such attacks and considered resistance essential. Hely Hutchinson, a Protestant aristocrat, endorsed Davis's objection to the criticism and reported that the Liberator's son Maurice was shocked when shown the extent of antagonism to *The Nation*. The Catholic poet, J. D. Frazer, considered the 'Irish Priest's' letter 'contained some of the most illiberal sentiments, unjust insinuations and indecent assumptions of authority it was ever my lot to see.' Later the judicious John Dillon opined that the 'infidelity howl' and the hypocrisy of its authors should have been boldly met as soon as it arose. In 1847 Dillon had a frank interview with the 'Irish Priest' himself. Fr Murray, a Maynooth professor, now spoke of the O'Connells as 'reptiles' and their Conciliation Hall as an 'abomination' harmful to the Catholic faith. He had written his letter under the mistaken conviction that *The Nation* was deliberately established to undermine Catholicism. He subsequently apologised to Duffy and undertook to repair any damage he had done.[3]

Attributing this episode, as the Liberator did when replying to Davis's demand for restraint on *The Nation*'s critics, to Davis's 'Protestant monomania' is simplistic. Davis did not hide his Protestantism. In early 1845, for example, supporting at the Association the admission of religious orders to Ireland, Davis criticised the monastic ideal. Smith O'Brien was more tactful. Yet Davis was in fact testing the Liberator's contention that an Orangeman who supported Repeal was welcome in the Association. To avoid such dispute in an interdenominational Association, sectarian discussion would have to be excluded, as the Young Irelanders wished.[4]

The Liberator's claim that he had no control over Repeal newspapers is unconvincing: 'Personal interests are involved in them. As long as I have been an agitator I have observed much acrimony amongst public writers. They *use* every topic to annoy one another and to *transfer* circulation.' This certainly encapsulated the relationship between *The Nation* and *The Pilot*, but it strains credulity to depict the Liberator as a disinterested bystander. Though Barrett was only indirectly involved in the 'Irish Priest' furore, there is little doubt that he would have muted *The Pilot*'s attacks on

The Nation if required to do so by the O'Connell family. The subsequent anger of the 'Irish Priest' indicates resentment at direct manipulation by the Old Ireland faction.[5]

Infidelity charges against *The Nation* thus preceded the battle over the Colleges and mixed education which so greatly intensified it. Yet Davis, when O'Connell was still in Richmond Prison, worried about the development of 'excessive ecclesiasticism', apparently extracted a promise from the Liberator 'that the insolence of *The Pilot* about education and *The Nation* shall not be repeated'. In November 1844 Davis categorised the furore over the 'Irish Priest' letters as 'part of a system for stopping the growth of secular education and free discussion'. The concurrent controversies over the Charitable Bequests Act and federalism were also related to education. Davis was furious when Dillon Browne in August attacked both the Charitable Bequests, over which both the Repeal Association and the Catholic hierarchy were divided, and the federalists who tended to endorse the legislation. As Davis indicated to O'Brien in November the federalists, supportive on the infidelity charge, would back them against an attack on secular education. Federalists, Davis demonstrated, placed control of all ecclesiastical matters under the imperial parliament. Ironically, Duffy had just brutally rejected the Liberator's move towards federalism. With a little reluctance, Davis followed suit.[6]

The Colleges: Mixed versus Separate Education

While the infidelity charges and the Charitable Bequests provided the prelude, Peel's Colleges Bill inaugurated the real battle. Though official Catholic opinion later hardened on the subject, the outcome in the 1840s was not inevitable. With the Catholic hierarchy divided, Peel's ministry was not shaken in its determination to provide undenominational institutions by Archbishop MacHale's categorical assertion that 'nothing but separate grants for separate education will ever give satisfaction to the Catholics of Ireland.' Significantly, MacHale, writing to Peel in July 1844, cited the £2,000 per week subscription to the Repeal Association as an excellent reason for meeting 'our just wishes'. Yet MacHale and his

episcopal friends were currently in bad odour at Rome for
their excessive opposition to the Bequests Act. While Primate
Crolly and Murray co-operated with the government, Bishop
Cantwell of Meath — to the annoyance of both Davis and the
Vatican — threatened to excommunicate anyone who did so.
As already indicated, John O'Connell had good reason for
backing the MacHale faction.

The Liberator and the Integrationists

Not only vital to the Young Ireland/Old Ireland split, the
mixed education debate raised issues of perennial relevance.
Though O'Brien had long advocated mixed education at all
levels, Davis provided the most coherent educational philosophy, spelt out in articles and speeches at the Association.
Mixed education was a natural corollary of the undenominational nationalism he had advocated from the inception of
The Nation. Wolfe Tone, though not so explicit, had criticised the bigotry of Catholic prelates who refused to countenance mixed schools. But what of the Liberator? Until
1844 O'Connell had likewise been known as a friend of
mixed education. The Liberator was surprisingly tolerant
of bias in the National School System. When told of children
excluded for wearing Repeal buttons, O'Connell counselled
their removal in the interests of educational progress. Even
the demonstration of anti-Catholic passages in the school
books failed to ruffle the Liberator; such remarks, he suggested, could easily be glossed over and ignored. Davis, on
the other hand, while applauding its non-sectarianism,
lamented the anti-national bias of the 'National System' and
praised the Christian Brothers for their efforts to instil
patriotism into their pupils.

Though the initial differences between O'Connell and the
Young Irelanders on education appeared minimal, the Liber-
ator in his correspondence with ecclesiastics demonstrated an
emphasis very different from his Repeal orations. Shortly
before the publication of *The Nation* and long before Peel's
Colleges were mooted, O'Connell assured the future Cardinal
Paul Cullen, then head of the Irish College in Rome, that
Repeal would achieve a University, based on strict Catholic

principles, and parish schools 'subject to ecclesiastical control and revision of the Catholic children'. He expected, moreover, the erosion of Protestantism after ten years of self-government. When circularising the Irish bishops on the projected Colleges, the Liberator told the fiery Bishop Cantwell that the National System was only tolerable because Protestants were opposed and left Catholics with a free hand. No chances could be taken with the Catholic upper and middle classes in undenominational Colleges. Less amenable to clerical direction, these could easily be seduced into 'immorality, irreligion and infidelity'. The only mixed education he was willing to endorse was when Protestants attended institutions where 'all the professors were nominated by the canonical authorities of the Catholic Church'. Davis might well have felt that such opinions were hardly compatible with the Liberator's assurance to him that 'if I did not believe that the Catholic religion could compete upon free and equal terms with any other religion I would not continue a Catholic for one hour.'[7]

The Liberator frequently shifted position on mixed education. In mid-1845, after backing his son John's diatribes against 'godlessness' and 'infidelity', O'Connell temporarily acknowledged that mixed education might still be acceptable in literary and scientific subjects. *The Pilot*, in a desperate effort to defend O'Connell's fluctuations, maintained that his earlier advocacy of mixed education had preceded its association with division, demoralisation and infidelity. John O'Connell may have had some such distinction in mind when, after so many tirades implying the contrary, he admitted in 1849 that advocacy of undenominational education was not in itself proof of godlessness or infidelity.[8]

Educational separatists in the 1840s not only criticised integrationism as a mistaken policy, but blackened the characters of its advocates as enemies of Christianity itself. With the Catholic hierarchy divided this led to great anomalies, duly exposed by the Young Irelanders and the unionist press. Could anyone, it was asked, be fairly stigmatised as an infidel for adhering to a policy supported by the Primates, Drs Crolly and Murray? In the 1850s, these prelates were succeeded at the head of the Irish Catholic

Church by the determined separationist, Archbishop Cullen, and undeniable repudiation of the Colleges by the Vatican could no longer be explained away; educational integrationists were then more convincingly portrayed as anti-Catholic. This was not, however, the position in the Young Ireland era.

The Teachings of Davis

Did the Young Ireland teachings on education contain an anti-Catholic element, or were they simply designed to increase social cohesion? Does 'secular', as used by Davis, mean religious neutrality, or is it a synonym for dogmatic anti-Christianity? Young Irelanders certainly argued the former, while their opponents insisted on the latter interpretation. MacNevin, for example, defending *The Nation* against the 'Irish Priest', insisted that the paper avoided religion for religion's own good. Secularism in the first sense can be associated with the idea of religious voluntaryism, a notion urged by O'Connell, without entire consistency, against the Anglican Church establishment.

Davis's famous article on 'Academical Education', published in *The Nation* immediately before the confrontation with O'Connell, is a useful starting point. The Irish, said Davis, remained for centuries paupers and serfs because they were ignorant and divided. While 400,000 of the poor were now educated at National Schools, nothing had so far been done to secure adequate institutions for the middle and upper classes. Peel's proposals therefore required calm and close study.[9]

Davis did not like the external system, preferring residential colleges where students would be isolated from 'the stupefying influences of common society'. Residence required deans, representing the different churches, and halls for religious services. In a non-residential system the onus should be on the churches, not the Colleges, to appoint deans. The parents could be relied on to place their children under religious instruction. Thus Davis was moving from interdenominationalism in a residential system towards religious voluntaryism. O'Connell, however, had earlier accused him of preferring to link church and state. In the Colleges quarrel at the Repeal Association, O'Connell attempted to trap Davis on this issue, by complaining that the latter had ignored the bill's rejection of student compulsion. This was a shrewd argument as the Catholic bishops certainly desired institutional authority over student religion, while Davis appeared to be moving away from it. Davis did not reply to this insinuation and the crying scene distracted attention from the matter.

Immediately after the May debate, both Davis and O'Brien were accused of advocating compulsory religion by the Rev. James Godkin, a Congregationalist minister who had just won third prize in the Repeal essay competition. They preferred, said Godkin, 'the debasing stipendiarism of France to the freedom and independence of America'. Godkin opposed state payment for religious teaching. 'It is vain to scoff at Catholic fears of ascendancy so long as such an attempt to control the secular education of the country is received as this has been.'[10]

Though *The Nation* dismissed Godkin's letter as 'altogether ill-judged and ill-timed', Davis was in a quandary. As he told O'Brien, he did not favour rejection of the Colleges for want of religious teaching: 'I asked and petitioned for such teaching chiefly to conciliate, for I was only part of the opinion.' O'Brien warned him of the necessity for keeping his compact with the separatists. Davis did so by voting in the Association against the control by College presidents, rather than the churches, over student accommodation. His open admission that he felt no personal concern on the issue evoked an hysterical reaction from a Waterford priest in *The Pilot*. With such a 'faithless and heartless' attitude Davis should not have been born in Ireland, but was properly categorised with the French infidels or Tsar Nicholas's barbarians who tore children from their mothers' breasts. Another correspondent claimed that Davis only 'insolently' tolerated Catholics. Thus Davis's frank avowal of opinion and readiness to compromise for the general good evoked bitter opposition.[11]

'Rags and Chains'

While Davis's mild voluntaryism, vigorously attacked on

both left and right, has been little noted by posterity, his paean to undenominational classes is well-remembered by modern integrationists. Mixed education, said Davis, was consistent with piety and 'favourable to that union of Irishmen of different sects, for want of which Ireland is in rags and chains'. This was the logical development of 'The Letters of a Protestant on Repeal'. But Davis endeavoured to take the argument into the enemy's camp. If indeed the attendance of children of different sects at common literary and scientific education would 'taint their faith and endanger their souls', it followed that contacts outside the classrooms would be equally disastrous. Logically, complete segregation into ghettoes, controlled by theological police, became necessary. The arguments for separate education were thus arguments for 'separate life, for mutual animosity, for penal laws, for religious wars', Davis allowed that some subjects, such as history and moral philosophy, were so mixed with theology as to make common instruction difficult. He advised caution in extending this principle unreasonably; to separate medical schools on the ground that Catholics and Protestants disagreed over miraculous cures seemed to Davis absurd. In this he was backed by Smith O'Brien who ridiculed the call for separate instruction in geology. According to Fr Thaddeus O'Malley, the Catholic bishops' demand in May 1845 for a number of separate chairs was an inconsistent sop by the majority to MacHaleite opinion. Ironically, another Protestant Young Irelander, John Mitchel, little involved in the 1845 dispute, later pointed out that Catholic clergy would not be appeased by the removal of all teaching references to Protestantism and Catholicism. 'For we all know that all subjects of human knowledge and speculation (except abstract science) — and history most of all — are necessarily regarded *either* from a Catholic or a Protestant point of view, and cannot be understood or conceived at all if looked at from either, or from both, especially by children.'[12]

This approximated the later separationist case, that *all* education should be *pervaded* by a religious or Catholic spirit, and not simply controversial subjects. Davis had certainly not anticipated this demand, which was scarcely formulated in the 1840s. The supposedly 'infidel' *Nation* in 1847, like

Davis praising the Christian Brothers, admired 'a pervading Catholic and Irish tone' in their school books.[13]

The Integrationists Answered

There was no shortage of opponents of mixed education, ranging from Barrett's *Pilot* and *Old Ireland*, deliberately published in the separatist cause, to John O'Connell's lengthy orations. Basically they argued that integration was bad for both religion and social relations. Occasionally, separatists like Dillon Browne admitted that dangers to religion outweighed social benefits from the mixture of sects. *Old Ireland* encapsulated its philosophy in verse:

Wanted — Mixed Education, to make us all even
All careless alike of religion and Heaven!
Or else set us fighting 'bout doctrines and creeds,
While the Saxon exults and poor Ireland bleeds.[14]

The Old Irelanders thus contested Davis's 'rags and chains', denying the temporal advantages of mixed education. Davis's separatist *reductio ad absurdum* which culminated in ghettoes and theological police was offset by *The Pilot*'s ridicule of secular education at the mother's knee. Old Irelanders claimed that perceived differences in mixed institutions would lead inevitably to abuse and bitterness, instead of subduing the animosities of manhood as Smith O'Brien maintained. *The Pilot* argued against Davis that in the north of Ireland, where a more balanced population produced the most mixed education, bigotry and ill-feeling were most intense. The liberalism of the Catholic priesthood was cited to disprove the notion that separate education led to bigotry. Though the social cohesion argument was difficult to prove, the separationist claim that mixed education caused both denominational hostility and religious indifference appears inconsistent; but John O'Connell maintained that students would laugh at each other's religious practices, 'and the mutual laugh would destroy all religious feelings in their minds'. Even outwardly neutral professors would shrug and sneer. To such arguments *The Nation* answered, 'we have no faith in bringing up young laymen up in a bandbox, and then tumbling them on the rough, fallible, seductive world.' This anticipated the results of some modern surveys demonstrating that Catholics brought up in undenominational schools often retain their religion longer than those initially protected in Catholic institutions. *The Nation*, moreover, argued that bigotry was more likely in Ireland than religious indifference. The chief contention of the separationists was lack of religious authority over instructors, 'uncontrolled in their teaching, when it even affects and directly bears upon doctrinal points, and points of moral regulation'.[15]

Such were the main arguments advanced on the two sides in the mixed education debate of the 1840s. Nearly 150 years later the issues are still under discussion and agreement appears no closer. The Old Irelanders endorsed the MacHale faction in the episcopate, while Young Ireland that of Archbishops Crolly and Murray. The latter did not believe in mixed education as an absolute ideal, but denied that it inevitably led to infidelity, accepting that in current Irish conditions it could prove a social emollient. Priests sympathising with Young Ireland — Frs C. P. Meehan, John Kenyon and Thaddeus O'Malley — had little difficulty defending the mixed educationists during the lifetimes of Archbishops Crolly and Murray. Meehan and O'Malley, however, agitated for posts in the Colleges, the former ironically severing his ties with Young Ireland to make himself more acceptable to the government. The voluntaryist, the Rev. James Godkin, was another candidate, thus partly justifying the Old Ireland contention that their opponents were self-interested careerists.

Other Young Ireland Opinion

Davis, the chief Young Ireland spokesman on education, was in his cautious approach to voluntaryism somewhat unrepresentative. Moreover, he died too young to change his position. The development of his leading colleagues, once considered members of a dangerously sceptical movement, is instructive. Duffy, Dillon, Pigot, O'Brien, Mitchel, and O'Hagan — Protestants as well as Catholics — eventually advocated official Catholic positions on mixed education.

Duffy and Davis both published editorials on 'Academical Education' in *The Nation* on 17 May 1845. Duffy deprecated any clamour against the Colleges as likely to lose an essential benefit to the Catholic middle class. He agreed with Davis in totally opposing government nomination of professors; he believed, however, that a levy on students should pay for chaplains instead of leaving them to the churches' expense. He was more positive than Davis in demanding, before the bishops had officially spoken, separate professors of history. Duffy had no thought of voluntaryism and did not deviate from strictly Catholic objectives. In the next years *The Nation* remained faithful to the mixed education ideal, despite the infidelity charges of the Old Irelanders. When Duffy entered Australian politics after 1855, he was constrained to seek the suffrage of Catholics campaigning for educational separation. In the Victorian Assembly Duffy ultimately admitted that earlier in life he had advocated mixed education 'to see the children of different religions reared up together so that a nationality might be fostered'. But 'political purpose' then blinded him to all other considerations. Now, having seen the effects of secular education in other countries he realised his mistake. Denominational schools were clearly the answer. The colony of Victoria however rejected Duffy's arguments and maintained a purely secular primary education system for a hundred years.[16]

Duffy's *volte face* was very similar to the Liberator's in 1845. Both moved from national to more distinctly religious considerations. Duffy's discovery of the evils of secular education in other countries is ironical in view of his long resistance to John O'Connell's diatribes on this subject. Admittedly by 1869, after the 1864 *Syllabus of Errors*, it was more difficult to deny papal opposition to the principle of mixed education. In 1848 Duffy's *Nation* still clung to the argument that Vatican condemnation of the Colleges did not necessarily rule out undenominational institutions.

But Duffy had not finished his educational Odyssey. When, after his retirement from Victorian politics, he wrote *Young Ireland* in 1880, Duffy described sympathetically Davis's battle for education and denounced John O'Connell. Excessive opposition, leading to episcopal and papal condemnation instead of profitable negotiation with the government, had, Duffy maintained, deprived Catholics of tertiary education for two generations. He contrasted Australian universities, with Catholic Archbishops sitting on councils, but with no separate professors or control over student lodging. Nevertheless, when Duffy wrote his autobiography in 1898, he took a strong line on his Victorian advocacy of educational separation, emphasising the injustice of taxing Catholics for unacceptable state schools, while forcing them to maintain their own schools without public assistance. He also rejected the notion that religious education could be given separately, quoting an American: 'you might as well give children the salt that ought to flavour their daily meals to eat by itself at a separate hour, as give them the religious teaching which ought to flavour their daily lessons in the same fashion.' This is a classic statement for the 'permeation' argument, little appreciated on either side in the 1840s. Duffy had moved a long way from the ideals of Davis.[17]

Was Young Ireland Separatist?

If Duffy showed all the vagaries of the Liberator on mixed education, Smith O'Brien proved extremely consistent. From the 1830s, before he became a Repealer, to his last years, O'Brien believed that young men should be educated together to form friendly associations 'calculated to subdue the animosities of manhood', but always with the proviso that conscientious objectors like Archbishop MacHale should receive public funding for their institutions outside the system. This made him an early advocate of the 'double taxation' argument, so effectively expressed by Duffy in his final memoirs. At the end of his life, O'Brien endorsed the objectives of the National Association, sponsored by a number of Catholic bishops, including Cardinal Cullen, which aimed at 'free' education, secular or denominational according to choice. John Mitchel, in his candidacy for Tipperary in 1875, also advocated such 'free' education.

In the disputes over secular versus denominational education, prevalent in the second half of the nineteenth century throughout the English-speaking world, O'Brien, Duffy and Mitchel can be classified with the denominationalists. But what of Davis? Davis never seems to have addressed this problem directly. He certainly feared a Catholic ascendancy established by prelates such as MacHale. On the other hand he was full of praise for the Christian Brothers as patriotic educators and would hardly have insisted on depriving them of government aid. Moreover in the Colleges dispute Davis showed himself willing to make compromises against his better judgment in the interests of national unity. If confronted by the double taxation issue, Davis might have reluctantly accepted the right of objectors to withdraw, without financial loss, from a mixed state system, while campaigning vigorously for the latter.

Davis's intimate friends John Pigot and John Dillon were far from being educational secularists. Pigot wanted the religious segregation of students in the classroom, but fraternising in sport and other external activities. This was diametrically opposed to Davis's argument in 'Academical Education' that there was no logical distinction between mixing in the classroom and mixing everywhere else. Pigot's fellow law-student, John O'Hagan, later strongly, if ambiguously, distanced himself from the controversy by asserting that the bishops were 'entirely in the right' to reject the Colleges.[18]

In 1845 John Dillon warmly supported Davis, publicly challenging the Liberator's insistence that the Colleges were godless. He approved of Davis's petition with its endorsement of mixed education, but warned against provoking O'Connell further on the issue. In the 1860s, however, Dillon became a leader of the National Association with its denominational education objectives. He strongly attacked the National Education System, and quoted Mill's *Essay on Liberty* against it.[19]

Conclusion

Of the leading Young Irelanders only Davis appears to have been moving towards real educational secularism. Even he was, despite some exasperated private correspondence and tactless speeches, more than ready to compromise in practice.

Several of his colleagues showed a Liberator-like inconsistency and confusion. Few were prepared to go further than the Crolly-Murray bishops; when the latter were succeeded by ardent separationists, Irish nationalists dropped mixed education with alacrity, despite its important implications for the pluralist nationalism which Davis had struggled to develop. The issue has not been extinguished and still smoulders in Irish political life. The infidelity charge against Young Ireland, based especially on their attitude to mixed education, was to a large extent contrived. Resistance to John O'Connell's heated rhetoric, which nearly led to O'Brien's secession in 1845, obscured the fact that there was little difference between Old and Young Ireland. Both sides toyed with the same ideas at different times. Nevertheless, the bugbear of infidelity, which a Young Ireland mission, led by Fr Kenyon, to the Irish hierarchy failed to dissipate, played an important part in ensuring the failure of the 1848 Rising.

The Economics of Young Ireland

The Break from Utilitarianism

The preoccupation of both Young and Old Ireland with violence and denominational education distracted some attention from the economic disasters of the 1840s. Nevertheless, *The Nation* after 1845 persistently denounced the starvation and 'extermination' of the people. Economics separated Old and Young Ireland less than secular nationalism and physical force. Significant division appeared within, as well as between, *The Nation* and O'Connell factions.

Such lack of differentiation was partly due to the common intellectual development of Daniel O'Connell and leading Young Irelanders like Davis, Dillon and Duffy. The Liberator, a correspondent of Jeremy Bentham who regarded him as an essential liberal voice in parliament, was long associated with the English philosophical radicals. Characteristically, O'Connell often voiced opinions incompatible with free trade while asserting an unwavering adherence to the dogma. The leading Young Irelanders, partly under Carlyle's influence, contemptuously discarded the panaceas of the Manchester school. In so doing they anticipated the economic nationalism of C. S. Parnell and other leaders. In the essays 'Udalism and Feudalism' which Davis wrote for *The Citizen* in 1841, Carlyle's opinions are discernible, but the general assault on the Manchester school is specifically supported by reference to the leading French historians, Jean Charles Sismondi and Augustin Thierry, both later condemned by Old Ireland for their infidelity, if not their economics.[1]

Davis prepares the Way

'Udalism and Feudalism' provides a blueprint, not only for Young Ireland before Ballingary, but for Arthur Griffith's *Sinn Fein Policy* of 1905. Davis contrasted unfavourably the 'feudalism' of English landlord ownership and primogeniture with the 'udalism' of peasant usehold under community surveillance, characteristic of most traditional societies. Rent Davis rejected as robbery; he maintained that a society of small yeoman farmers were more productive than the large farms which the Anglicised squirearchy was attempting to establish in Ireland by 'exterminating' the tenantry and shipping them off to the colonies. Manufacturing required protection; Davis cited Germany's impressive industrialisation, excluding English manufactures by state tariffs. In his 'infant industry' argument, accepted by J. S. Mill, if not modern economists, Davis was ambivalent on the desirability of heavy industry, preferring small-scale domestic industry. But Ireland had, he claimed on [Maxwell?] Blacker's authority, the resources to maintain a population of 35 million under correct management by a native legislature. Davis reinforced this argument in *The Nation* by citing Dr (later Sir) Robert Kane's *The Industrial Resources of Ireland*. Kane maintained that Ireland's minerals, which included adequate coal seams, water-power, and peat were sufficient to enable the country to become a manufacturing state if industrial education were improved. Davis reluctantly agreed that the archaic dream, partly influenced by William Cobbett, of a peasant society of small domestic producers might have to give way to full industrialisation. Industrialisation was preferred by Griffith and subsequent economic nationalists.[2]

Davis's modernised dream, as R. D. C. Black demonstrated, though unable to maintain a population of even 8 million, might nevertheless have supported considerably more people than could live tolerably in the late 1840s. Davis in fact epitomised the basic Young Ireland response to Irish poverty. Even the great famine which followed Davis's death in 1845 required no substantial rethinking. Davis had presented the problem as essentially political. The enemy was Anglicisation which sought to 'exterminate' the Irish people and turn the country into a stock farm to supply an industrialised

England. The obvious remedy to both Young and Old Ireland was self-government. The potato blight appeared a mere phase in the extermination movement. *The Nation*, following Davis who had complained of the degradation of a population forced to live on inedible lumpers, rejected the potato as a hateful root which had enabled landlords to steal from their tenants the fruits of their toil. An article, probably by Mitchel, portrayed an armed peasant, enjoying the flesh of his own pig, instead of using it to pay the rent. Such arguments were not quickly forgotten. C. J. Kickham, setting his celebrated novel *Knocknagow* in the late 1840s, depicted extermination in a Tipperary village without reference to a potato famine. The book, which quoted Davis on its fly-leaf, transcribed the spirit of 'Udalism and Feudalism' into fiction.³

Davis followed a long Irish tradition. Swift, who advised the burning of everything English except their coal, and Berkeley, whose *Querist* proposed a wall of brass around Ireland, were frequently contrasted with the 'political economists' Adam Smith, Ricardo and Malthus. The latter was sometimes quoted, by Davis and others, against his own reputed theory of inevitable over-population by utilising favourable comments on the value of national industry and peasant proprietary. In an early *Nation* article, Davis's friend John Pigot attacked 'the Malthusian bugbear' represented by the Scottish economist, J. R. McCullough, who, like Edmund Burke, took the wrong side in the debate. 'It is cant and absurdity to talk of the country being "over-populated" when owing to the criminal neglect of every duty by the landlord class the food and wealth of the people are yearly exported from their shores, while they look on and starve.' This was to remain Young Ireland orthodoxy throughout the years of great famine, still three years away when Pigot wrote.⁴

Tenant Right Ambivalence

Such views were not peculiar to the Young Ireland section of Repeal. The Liberator's speeches in 1843 referred repeatedly to the need for Irish manufactures and fixity of tenure, an idea which *The Nation* claimed to have developed around the time of its own inception. Dillon then had advocated valuation and perpetual tenure as an antidote to socialism and aristocracy, both of which he regarded as inimical to true property rights. Tenant right thus became a half-way house to peasant proprietorship in that it gave the farmer security and compensation for improvements. O'Brien as a landlord was very cautious. He rejected the compulsory valuation principle of Duffy's later tenant right movement as robbery of the legitimate owner, and accepted compensation, but not the full cost of improvements, for an outgoing tenant. *The Nation* supported the 'Ulster custom' where such rights were informally recognised, demanding, with O'Connell, its strengthening by legislation and extension to the whole country. Given the Repeal efforts to create a union of classes, tenant right was a compromise allowing the liberal landlord to retain his authority buttressed by the goodwill and co-operation of the tenants. Though conciliation was still attempted, almost to July 1848, the Irish landlord class was unconvinced. Any tenant right infringed absolute property rights. Though early argued by Duffy, Dillon and Davis that there could be no absolute property rights in land, a gift from God not the result of human labour, such arguments failed to move the governments of Peel and Russell. While the Devon Report, published in early 1845, praised the 'Ulster custom', it did not recommend incorporation into legislation. On the contrary, the land bills of the next years were vigorously attacked by the Young Irelanders and other Repealers as the strangling of existing tenant right in red tape. Politically, Repealers used the erosion of tenant right to campaign for sectarian unity by demonstrating their precarious position to Ulster Protestant farmers.[5]

Ambivalence towards landlords confused the tenures issue. Those Young and Old Irelanders like O'Connell, O'Brien and a number of their allies who owned land were naturally concerned for their class. In late 1845 O'Connell wasted much Association time defending himself from *The Times*'s attacks on the condition of his Kerry estate. O'Brien, a good, if conventional, landlord, was a shade smug about his cottiers' whitewashed cottages, fifteen feet by twenty. The middle-class Duffy, who wanted O'Brien to use his personal influence to draw members of his class into the Confederation to counteract democratic tendencies, was not always aware of landlord attitudes.

Repeal inconsistency is demonstrated by the maverick landlord, William Conner of Inch, who seriously embarrassed the Association in September 1843 by proposing a rent strike to obtain agrarian 'perpetuity' and 'valuation'. John O'Connell, applauded by Doheny in *The Nation*, silenced Conner, as he later suppressed Meagher before the 1846 split, and had Conner expelled from the Association. The Liberator regretted only that Conner had not been forcibly handed from the room. Yet Conner claimed that his method was sufficiently non-violent to appeal to any Quaker. His objects, security and fair rent, were shared by the Repeal Association and agitated for till implemented in Gladstone's 1881 Land Act. In 1847 Conner re-emerged to harass James Fintan Lalor at the latter's tenant right meeting at Holy Cross, Tipperary. The dispute grew so heated that, to unionist amusement, the platform physically collapsed. Conner complained that Lalor had obscured his tenant right objectives in vague and ambiguous language. John Mitchel, when partly estranged from Lalor, allowed Conner to publish in his *United Irishman*. A swing to the left, requiring co-operation with the Chartists, to whom Conner was linked, made the landlord of Inch an acceptable ally. Modern analysts have demonstrated that neither Mitchel, Lalor, nor Conner were real revolutionaries. None wished to displace the landlords, seeking rather landlord-tenant dual ownership. The rent strike, originally suggested by Conner and subsequently taken up by Lalor, was pressure to achieve reform rather than a prelude to dispossession. Mitchel's rate strike even shrank from a direct attack on landlord interests and relieved them of responsibility for the starving poor.[6]

Chartism and Repeal

Chartism indicates Young Ireland's basic conservatism and confused social ideology. O'Connell persistently denounced

Chartism for its violence and intolerance, while professing to support most of the six points of the People's Charter. Fear of the movement's social radicalism was undoubtedly a powerful motive for the Liberator. The Young Irelanders did not normally criticise O'Connell's anti-working-class attitudes till Devin Reilly's outburst in the *United Irishman* during the Chartist entente of 1848. In the early *Nation*, however, Davis consistently advocated a politic alliance with the Chartists. Davis was no socialist. He strongly upheld property rights. Dillon and Duffy also expressed strong disapprobation of socialism, maintaining that social grades would never be abolished. Dillon, like contemporary economists, anticipated Marx and Engels in declaring labour the source of all wealth. After Davis's death *The Nation* admitted that it was opposed to Chartism, not because of its violence, but because some of its then five points were 'an abomination'. The secret ballot and universal suffrage in particular were rejected, the former by later Chartists too. Smith O'Brien also repudiated the five points in 1848 but ten years later came to believe the ballot and universal suffrage necessary in Ireland. Anti-Chartism was inevitable while the Confederation wooed the gentry.

According to Duffy, after their breach in 1854, most of *The Nation*'s anti-Chartist articles of 1847 were written by Mitchel. D'Arcy McGee's insistence that the Confederation was not a democratic body approximates to Mitchel's earlier opinions. Later, in 1847, McGee disgusted Mitchel by opposing tenant right as likely to interfere with landlord interests. McGee, however, despaired of the landlords in 1848. Earlier disclaimers did not prevent the Old Irelanders and hostile bishops like Dr Higgins from branding Confederates as Chartists. As demonstrated, the Remonstrants, who helped to propel the Young Irelanders into establishing the Confederation, did contain Chartists. The latter emphasised their assistance at the time of the split. Duffy complained that the Dublin Grattan Club comprised mainly Chartists, and O'Gorman lamented the violent Chartist spirit in some clubs. But sometimes Duffy's *Nation* adopted a semi-Marxist analysis, denouncing the 'tyranny of accumulation', and the conversion of the poor into 'rent making machines'.[7]

By the end of 1847 Young Ireland opinion on Chartism shifted abruptly. When Feargus O'Connor, newly restored to parliament, vigorously supported Repeal, and English Chartists proved themselves Repealers to a man, it was impossible to keep them at arm's length, though O'Brien attempted to avoid identification. Mitchel, elected to a Chartist convention as representative for Manchester, politely declined to serve. Though still denying belief in Chartism he defended the Charter itself from detractors. His *United Irishman* contained almost as much news of Chartist as Confederate activities. Doheny, sent to England to liaise with Chartists and Confederates, was happy to declare himself a Chartist. William Conner, once scornfully repudiated by Doheny, had no difficulty in swallowing all six points of the Charter.[8]

This marriage of convenience followed the earlier pragmatic prescription of Davis, but greatly weakened the already flimsy chance of a successful appeal to the gentry, frightened by Chartist influence in Confederate clubs. Ideologically, the chief Confederates remained closer to the thought of the O'Connell family on social issues. Both groups worked for a paternalistic society. They were, however, apparently divided by contentious issues such as manufacturing and free trade, and the poor law.

Free Trade and Protection — Young and Old Ireland

Though O'Connell nominally remained a philosophical radical while *The Nation* ridiculed their philosophy, the Liberator demonstrated in 1843 that he was a free trader in a Pickwickian sense only. O'Connell accepted free trade, certainly, but not 'bastard freedom'. Thus free trade was excellent, when other countries adopted it too and no other discrepancies, as in Ireland's case, necessitated protective duties. Here O'Connell, like Smith O'Brien, approached the 'Colonial Reformer' school of E. G. Wakefield and the 'fair trade' of Joseph Chamberlain fifty years later. *The Nation* likewise required only moderate tariffs to stimulate new industries. Nevertheless, O'Connell, with characteristic confusion, insisted that he was unequivocally in favour of free trade — but not if it brought famine and pestilence. John

O'Connell as usual was more straightforward than his father. A report on tariffs for the Repeal Association, which suggested their beneficial effects on trades like linen, received the 'unbounded approbation' of Dillon and Doheny. Probably the only Repealer who accepted free trade in its entirety was the former Quaker, James Haughton.[9]

Protection of Irish industry was an uncontroversial idea in the 1840s. The Tory *Warder*, though it repudiated *The Nation*'s fixity of tenure policy as the transfer of property from the Protestant owner to the Catholic occupier, agreed on protection. It was also enthusiastic about Kane's *The Industrial Resources of Ireland*. Isaac Butt, then a conservative opponent of Repeal, but an original thinker on economics, recurred to the Berkeley tradition of a brazen wall round Ireland. A Dublin meeting on manufactures in early 1845 attracted the bitterly anti-Catholic parson, T. D. Gregg, organiser of Protestant operatives, who endorsed every statement by O'Connell and himself spoke like a sentimental Repealer. The Young Ireland industrial platform thus appeared to have greater potential for creating urban middle- and working-class unity than the agrarian. The rise in north-east Ulster after 1850 of shipbuilding, dependent on British markets and raw materials, made protection unpopular with unionists.[10]

Manufactures without Protection?

The encouragement of specific Irish manufactures was a constant preoccupation of all Repealers, before and after the famine. Much emphasis was placed on the return of absentees. The latter by their expenditure at home, were considered likely to provide a market and incentive for domestic crafts. As even the encumbered landowner Daunt pointed out in 1842, Ireland could not develop as a purely agricultural nation. English encouragement of such specialisation was firmly rebuffed. Though the mixed education of the National schools might be applauded by Young Ireland, *The Nation* was disgusted that the school books treated Ireland as a British stock-farm. Repeal, by recreating the 1782 parliament, which deterred absenteeism and encouraged Irish industry of all sorts, appeared the ultimate answer. Could anything be done in the meantime? There were various suggestions. Duffy tackled the question of Irish initiative, arguing that there were already numerous opportunities for industrial development, requiring little capital but much energy, education and determination. A fishing industry was a case in point. Davis had also emphasised industrial education in Prussia. The Repeal reading rooms were suggested as a remedy for industrial ignorance. The subsequent Confederate clubs were initially expected to fulfil a similar role.[11]

As with Arthur Griffith sixty years later, the hopes of encouraging manufactures led to a clash with labour interests. Thomas Davis in 'Udalism and Feudalism' had accepted that cheap Irish labour was an attraction to industrial development; *The Nation* followed this up with an insistence that the Irish must learn to work harder for less money to negate the higher price of raw materials. It condemned the Dublin tradesmen for destroying a local shipbuilding industry by their insistence on high wages. In 1847 *The Nation* rejected an Irish Ten Hours bill on the ground that it would add one-fifth to the price of Irish goods. There was, in fact, little difference between such opinions and O'Connell's opposition to unionisation, later castigated by Devin Reilly in the *United Irishman*. Like John Mitchel's parallel endorsement of the rights of labour combination, Reilly's attack was a transparent bid for Chartist support in 1848.[12]

The onset of famine in late 1845 forced the Young Irelanders to intensify their efforts to encourage manufacturing as an antidote to starvation. There had already been some gestures towards voluntary consumer preference; O'Brien in 1844 suggested that Repealers use Irish textiles where possible. The buy Irish campaign was formalised in the Irish Confederation. D'Arcy McGee and P. J. Smyth presented a series of reports on Irish manufactures. Efforts were made to form women's auxiliary organisations whose chief work would be to create a climate favourable to the use of Irish cloth; Berkeley's aphorism on ladies who robbed local artisans by dressing in foreign silks was well ventilated. The Confederation published a pamphlet, applauded even by Old Irelanders, consisting of Mitchel's compilation of relevant texts from Swift and Berkeley. *The Nation* itself admitted in late 1847 that voluntary consumer preference would not work. Other expedients were suggested. Industries were sought where production was as cheap as in England; again the possibility of low wages was relevant. The new system of joint-stock companies seemed a possible solution to the apparent lack of Irish capital. Of greater interest was the proposal to use Poor Law Unions and other organs of local government which might fall under patriotic control as patrons of Irish production. Though little was achieved in the 1840s, the idea formed the basis of Griffith's *Sinn Fein Policy* of 1905 and was partially implemented by Dail Eireann during the Anglo-Irish War, 1919-21.[13]

Young Ireland and the Famine — Rival Preconceptions

As the foregoing has indicated, the famine marked no watershed in Young Ireland economic thought. It was not portrayed as a tragic natural disaster, but rather as the logical development of government policies to replace Irish people with livestock. Indeed, the famine was welcomed as a final, incontestable proof of the disastrous nature of the Union. Richard O'Gorman told O'Brien, 'something must grow out of this famine'. The gentry in particular were warned that they had no other option but to accept their own destruction as a class or to throw their lot in with the people.[14]

In their attacks on the famine relief measures of the Peel and Russell governments there appeared a curious dualism in Young Ireland thought, often complicated by internal disagreement. The heartless, cold-blooded 'political economy' of the government on whose altar the Irish were brutally sacrificed, to the tune of an alleged two million dead, was denounced by John O'Connell as much as the Young Irelanders. The very words 'political economy' evoked hisses at Confederate meetings. On the other hand, the Young Irelanders were not only prisoners of their own preconceptions, but shared some of the fixed ideas of their rulers, in particular the dangers of pauperising the Irish lower classes by indiscriminate charity. When the Liberator was reduced to the agonised cry of 'food, food, food', the Young Irelanders were scornful.[15]

1. Closing the ports?

The initial Repeal response, which the Young Irelanders accused O'Connell of playing down, was closure of the ports against the export of Irish grain and measures to force absentee landlords to return to the country. Some confusion resulted from O'Connell's demand, apparently endorsed by Smith O'Brien, for the ports to be simultaneously open to foreign corn. Retention of Irish foodstuffs was an old demand. Repeal, conceding power to close the ports, appeared the immediate answer. The Irish people would then be able to consume the food that they had themselves produced. As there were no outside markets, food, it was believed, must be sold cheaply to the people. The creation of paper money was suggested to provide more credit. The absence of imports, bought with sales of Irish produce, would encourage local substitution industry, which itself would regenerate the economy. Landlords, unable to live on rents derived from the sale of exported produce, would be compelled to return to their estates.[16]

2. Government Relief or Reversal of Injustice?

The Nation therefore denied that any relief, apart from the concession of Ireland's natural rights, was required. Young Irelanders refused to be 'beggars to the bounty of a people enriched by our slavery'. Government had, it declared, no duty to feed the population, but no duty to starve it either. When Peel purchased maize for distribution in Ireland at cost price, *The Nation* was suspicious, believing that the relevant government functionaries were part of a centralising scheme to increase government control of the island. 'Thank you for nothing.'[17]

Peel was marginally more paternalistic than his Whig successor, Russell. Peel's ministry provided a treasury subsidy of half the cost of relief works, thus enabling the purchase of maize. *The Nation* rejected treasury aid, but not the repatriation of moneys extorted from Ireland. This was later calculated, in a Confederation report compiled by John Mitchel, at £208 million. Thus it simultaneously repudiated Irish mendicancy and denounced the government denial of funds as mass murder. Evocative descriptions of the starving

Irish impotently watching the departure of ships bursting with their produce have long been a staple of nationalist invective.

3. Repeal of the Corn Laws

Peel's repeal of the corn laws, an action which split his party and enabled the Whigs to return to office, received no credit from Young Ireland in the weeks preceding the split with O'Connell's Old Irelanders. Tension existed between Smith O'Brien, the only Young Irelander in parliament, and the O'Connell family which, despite doubts about its efficacy, supported corn law abolition in parliament and expected O'Brien to do likewise. The latter, however, favoured moderate duties, fearing that the elimination of the corn laws would sweep away the landed classes. He eventually achieved intellectual stasis on the issue, arguing that as the town wanted abolition and the country retention, it was better to leave the question to the English parties. O'Brien agreed with Mitchel that while free trade was good for England it was not suitable for Ireland. *The Nation* followed up this theme, arguing for free trade in general, but, like O'Connell, pointing out that Ireland needed special protection. Doheny, on the other hand, disagreed with O'Brien, maintaining that corn law abolition would not harm Ireland. Sharman Crawford, moreover, warned that northerners preferred free trade. O'Brien eventually adapted *The Nation*'s Machiavellian argument when suggesting that removal of the corn laws would help Repeal by alienating the gentry from the government.[18]

4. Productive Employment

The Old Irelanders at first hoped that a Whig alliance, when the latter party succeeded Peel in mid-1846, would obtain adequate anti-famine measures. They were soon disillusioned. Russell continued Peel's public works policy till the spring of 1847, but also passed the Labour Rate Act which replaced the treasury grant with a loan, repayable with interest by the landed property of Ireland; Board of Works supervision was established. This amended scheme failed to alleviate the hunger and resulted in widespread jobbery. *The Nation* denounced the system for encouraging the poor to leave their own land and work for the government. Another demand voiced by Smith O'Brien to Russell, was that works, especially when financed by Irish property, be productive. The insistence of Charles Trevelyan, the influential under-secretary at the treasury, that there be no interference in normal trade, was vigorously repudiated. Bentinck's bill, providing a loan to build Irish railways and strongly supported by O'Brien, was rejected by the Commons on similar grounds. Even the ailing Liberator seemed in two minds on the issue. For a period, the Lord Lieutenant, Bessborough, did enable productive work to be done. In his 'Letters to Irish Landlords', published originally in *The Nation* in late 1846 and early 1847, O'Brien outlined a comprehensive programme of land reclamation, railways, fisheries, and emigration, based on government grants equivalent to the sums paid for recent military adventures in places like Afghanistan. Despite a preference for private enterprise railways, he realised that only government action would suffice. *The Nation* fully backed O'Brien's programme, with the important exception of emigration. Here O'Brien was following interests from the 1830s when he had been a close associate of the Wakefield school of colonial reformers. While the Young Irelanders considered emigration the 'last expedient of despair', O'Brien insisted that 'to lay the foundation of an Irish colony in another hemisphere is surely no ignoble task even for an Irish patriot.' Acceptance of the need for emigration, however, was totally incompatible with the position, asserted even by O'Connell, that Ireland's claim to self-government derived from its population of eight million and capacity to maintain a far greater number. *The Nation*, however, minimised its disagreement with O'Brien, maintaining that he was less culpable than John Godley, progenitor of a Canadian emigration scheme. J. S. Mill's *Political Economy* of 1848, like *The Nation*, emphasised the importance of colonising Irish waste lands.[19]

Despite a lack of unanimity, the Young Irelanders, led by O'Brien, did achieve some telling hits against the first phase of Russell's policy, wound up abruptly in spring 1847 and followed by a brief period of temporary relief through soup kitchens. *The Nation* exposed the lack of nutrition in the Soyer cheap food formula. In the autumn, Russell threw relief entirely onto the Irish poor law, extended to enable outdoor relief at the expense of the local ratepayers. Accompanying efforts to provide for some items of the programme suggested by O'Brien were unsuccessful, though the 1849 Incumbered Estates Act facilitated the extermination of insolvent landlords, who thus appeared to pay the penalty for holding aloof from Repeal.[20]

5. Poor Laws — Young and Old Ireland

From 1830 to the end of his life O'Brien was particularly concerned with the establishment and administration of adequate poor laws. His ideas were those of a humane conservative. He saw the workhouses as gaols, insisted that poverty was not a crime, and maintained that voluntary benevolence was insufficient to relieve indigence. He also believed that some workhouse test should be maintained for the undeserving poor, that outdoor relief could pauperise, and that the central government should leave it to parishes to strike rates, paid by landowners and occupiers equally. He was radical in suggesting a compulsory insurance scheme based on existing practice amongst Belgian railway workers. The Young Irelanders, before O'Brien's accession to Repeal, shared something of the latter's pragmatism. Led by Dillon, they clashed with O'Connell in 1842 on the legitimacy of a poor law. The Liberator, despite some inconsistencies in the 1830s, now came out in total opposition to any poor law, for, it has been said, all the conventional moral and economic reasons. He believed that general economic development would eliminate any poverty not amenable to private charity. Dillon, while agreeing that poor laws tended to pauperise, was not prepared to see them completely rejected. Even after industrial development, some cushion, apart from private charity, was required for the economic system's rejects. During the famine, the Young Irelanders hoped that the English demand that Irish property relieve Irish poverty would unite all classes in indignation. O'Brien continued to tread a middle course. On the one hand he defended his class by maintaining that the English howl against Irish landlords was a smokescreen for the misgovernment of Ireland. On the other, O'Brien was congratulated by men like the English MP, Poulett Scrope and Fr Thaddeus O'Malley, for breaking rank with many Irish landlords and accepting the need for poor law extension. As chairman of his local poor law union, O'Brien, despite his conventional views on the dangers of pauperisation, was not as terrified of the expense of outdoor relief as his brother gentry. He remained consistent with his position in the 1830s. He was, however, reluctant to respond to Duffy's insistence that he directly proselytise his own class.[21]

By 1848, when Mitchel, Lalor, Reilly and their allies grew disillusioned with class conciliation and emphasised Tone's 'men of no property', O'Brien, in the weeks before Ballingary, still hoped to lead the gentry into the Repeal ranks. He believed that landlords were entitled to their rent and totally rejected Mitchel's idea of a rate strike as likely to increase famine mortality. Duffy was in general agreement with him. O'Brien's pragmatic common sense in working for an absentee tax at Westminster contrasts favourably with Meagher's initial rejection of the idea as an infringement on liberty, followed by his petulant dismissal of class conciliation in March 1848.[22]

Was there in fact a characteristically Young Ireland position on social and economic issues? Davis's 'Udalism and Feudalism' with its rejection of 'political economy' and aspiration towards industrial protection and peasant proprietary was probably the nearest the movement came to an articulated manifesto. As in other areas, clear-cut differences between Old and Young Ireland are often difficult to lay down with precision. O'Connell tried to appear a laissez-faire liberal while using antithetical arguments; the Young Irelanders paraded opposition to utilitarianism while unconsciously advocating its tenets. Both groups resembled contemporary English politicians, few of whom were ever consistent believers in the full gospel of Cobden and Bright, to which they sometimes paid lip service. It has been suggested that Davis's economic ideas were in line with the distributism laid down by papal encyclicals like *Rerum Novarum* (1891). Insofar as the Young Irelanders steered a wavering course between the extremes of laissez-faire capitalism and the doctrinaire socialism of the day, this is a reasonable conclusion. The economic suggestions of Young Irelanders, generally impotent in their own day, nevertheless helped to inspire other nationalist generations.[23]

Young Ireland and British Imperialism

The Context

Eighteen forty-two to 1848 was a lively period in the history of the British Empire. Under 'the imperialism of free trade', momentous events occurred in India, New Zealand, South Africa, China and Canada. There were good reasons for persistent Repeal criticism of imperial advance. First, the case for self-government was strengthened by rapport with all oppressed people. Repealers needed to dissociate themselves from British imperialism, or lay down conditions for their participation. Second, ruthless British action elsewhere enabled consciousness raising at home. Third, the reaction of others to British imperialism provided examples for emulation or rejection. If colonial resisters made common cause with Ireland and asserted a belief in Repeal, so much the better. Finally, according to O'Connell's 'England's difficulty is Ireland's opportunity' principle, any unrest in a British colony became invaluable to Repeal. Differences of emphasis between Old and Young Ireland on British 'imperialism', a popular contemporary term, need careful analysis.

In October 1842, on *The Nation*'s establishment, imperialism was already vigorously debated in the existing Repeal press. An Irish tradition, critical of imperialism, had long existed. Edmund Burke's dictum that the East India Company never made a treaty which it did not break was quoted ad nauseam in *The Nation*. O'Connell, an inspiration to Indian reformers, had offered to take the Indian natives as his clients. O'Connell, moreover, was renowned as an opponent of slavery. Smith O'Brien, as already demonstrated, in his pre-Repeal days immersed himself in colonial immigration schemes. In the early 1840s, moreover, a British-Indian Association patronised by James Haughton, who was highly critical of East India Company policies, met in Dublin.

The Davis Anti-Imperialist Thesis

Following such precedents, Davis in early 1840 contributed a series of articles to the Dublin *Citizen*, 'India — her own and another's'. Using memoirs and standard sources Davis examined British progress and its impact on Indian society. His detailed research, assisted by his Trinity friend, Thomas Wallis, made Davis an authority on the East. 'India — her own and another's' reads in places like a modern radical polemic. With Molyneux, Davis rejected an unjust invader's acquisition, by effluxion of time, of moral authority over a subjected people. British occupation through the East India Company was lambasted. Davis rejected Britain's alleged mission to civilise barbarous peoples. He denounced the contention that the 'ancient Indian systems were irredeemable and unmixed despotisms'. On the contrary, Davis argued that rulers like Ahalya Baee, Queen of Holkar, were morally superior to their eighteenth-century European contemporaries. The traditional land systems, moreover, were closer to 'udalism' than 'feudalism'. Expressing some preference for Muslim culture, Davis maintained that Hinduism and Islam were drawing together when the East India Company renewed dissension. He denied that Hindu religious customs were mere superstition and bitterly attacked the hypocrisy of missionaries and the 'hideous' use of 'words of love, and self-denial and beneficence, and infinite compassion', to mask 'lust of unnatural, unjust, and unholy gain'. Davis later defended the Hindu caste system as a form of apprenticeship close to the ancient Irish model.[1]

In this treatment of Indian history, never republished in any anthology of his writings, Davis, despite his use of James Mill's Anglo-centred *History of the East India Company*, rejected both the missionary and utilitarian attitudes to native cultures. The implications for an Irish nationalism totally divorced from emotional links with Britain were clear. Davis supplemented his Indian exposition with a

Citizen article on 'The Foreign Policy of Ireland', demanding a total break from 'that atrocious system of aggression and spoilation, which has determined the foreign policy of England in every clime – from Canada to Hindustan.' In fact, 'the interests of Ireland and her uprising people are kindred with those of all the countries, whose freedom is either won, or is struggling into life'. Only the English aristocracy benefited from imperial conquest. To highlight England's recent invasion of Afghanistan, her ignominious expulsion by the forces of Dost Mahommed, and subsequent British reprisals, Davis published detailed articles on Afghan life and culture, concluding that the Afghan people shared many characteristics of the Irish. Critics like Alf MacLochlainn have argued that Davis was racist in his preference for certain apparently Aryan peoples but Davis's criterion for superiority was courage in resistance, not skin pigmentation. Thus the Afghans against Britain, the Circassians against Russia, and even Maori cannibals against English settlers, were commended. The Chinese, who appeared to have provided only feeble resistance in the Opium Wars, and the Hindus, who lacked the 'soul' for effective resistance, were dismissed with some contempt. The former Davis considered to be victims of the Quakerish religion of Confucianism. After Davis's death *The Nation* carried this reasoning to the sad conclusion that the Irish people, who had spinelessly submitted to famine, had no parallel save the Hindus.[2]

Davis's early writings on India and Afghanistan, which he privately regarded as 'very treasonable', demonstrated the value of overseas examples. There was an assertion of universal liberty, the warning of perennial English brutality, the emulative example of Dost Mahommed, in reality not quite so heroic as Davis implied in his 'A Ballad of Freedom':

> Long live the Dost!
> Who Britain crost,
> Hurrah for Dost Mohammed.

Finally, the diversionary advantages of such British problems as Afghanistan was spelled out during Davis's period on the *Morning Register*.[3]

When *The Nation* appeared, it deepened, rather than initiated discussion on imperialism. In early 1842 Duffy's *Vindicator* had complained that 'the plunderers of India were as like the plunderers of Ireland as one horse-leech is like another, and Clive and Cromwell are brothers in every crime.' Yet Davis specialised on colonial and imperial issues in the early *Nation*. Preoccupied as he was with the concept of secular nationalism, Davis's interest is significant. Until 1848, India and Canada provided the main focus for Young Ireland imperial discussion. The first Maori resistance in New Zealand and in the Caffre Wars in South Africa also attracted interest. Natives were supported against land-hungry settlers; it was hoped that Britain's resources were becoming dangerously overstrained. The destruction of the Aboriginal people in Van Diemen's Land, compared with Cromwell's Drogheda massacre, reinforced the case against British iniquity. *The Nation* accepted reports of Australian Aboriginal barbarity, but denied that these justified invasion. Later the *Irish Exile*, published by Patrick O'Donohoe in penal exile, endorsed the rights of Tasmanian Aborigines. The principle, that 'the English calumniate India that they may not be disgraced for robbing her', helped to prevent Young Irelanders from descending into current ethnocentrism.[4]

Repeal and British Advance in India

While India exhibited successful British aggression at its most dangerous, Canada, eventually one repository for famine victims, provided, in its progress towards responsible government, considerable encouragement to Repealers. First, the grim oriental picture. The Afghanistan affair, which in its final punitive phase provided evidence of rape and other atrocities by British troops, was succeeded by the conquest of Sind after the battle of Miani in 1843, when O'Connell's monster meetings dominated. Davis in *The Nation* was vociferously opposed. 'Certainly a more bloody and rapacious power than England never existed.' 'England's latest crime' had involved the usual broken treaties and duplicity. It was particularly galling to find that a large proportion of the 400 European soldiers in General Charles Napier's army were from the 22nd Tipperary Regiment. Opposition to Irish recruitment in the British Army was a constant *Nation* theme. Duffy's successor as *Vindicator* editor, Kevin Buggy, summed it up in his poem, 'The Saxon Shilling':[5]

> Go — to leave on Indian soil
> Your bones to bleach, accused, unburied
> Go — to crush the just and brave,
> Worse wrongs with wrath the world are filling!
> Go — to slay each brother slave —
> Or spurn the blood-stained Saxon Shilling!

Some tension appeared within Repeal. The Liberator never blamed, but rather praised, the heroism of Irish soldiers in the British Army. Tactically, if, as many Repealers hoped, the Irish soldiers were to refuse to fire on their own people in a revolutionary confrontation, it was wise to win their support. This confused Repeal attitudes towards the British Empire. Was empire evil in itself and irrelevant to Ireland's needs, or would a self-governing Ireland demand her share in a justifiable institution?

The problem was exacerbated with the Sikh Wars which followed Napier's success in Sind. Again Irish troops were prominent in the campaign which destroyed Sikh power and secured the East India Company in the Punjab. Even the commander, General Gough, was Irish. Davis had already praised Sikh valour in the *Morning Register* and his successor, John Mitchel, in *The Nation* vigorously supported the Sikhs as the Poles of the East, and denounced Britain's 'blood-stained dominion'. It hoped, however, that the removal of the Sikh buffer would bring Britain into confrontation with Russia. Then those two 'mighty powers of evil' might destroy each other. The 'wicked invasion' of Gwalior and the ill-treatment of the Rajah of Satara were similarly denounced. Yet numerous Irish people related to participating soldiers felt natural pride in what conservatives claimed as a glorious expansion.[6]

Under Young Ireland influence, the Repeal Association took such issues seriously. Sind was accorded a lengthy report by M. J. Barry and a full discussion. After a detailed historical examination to substantiate accusations of British treachery and divide and rule, Barry justified his expenditure of energy on the grounds that 'feelings of humanity' required a protest, and that Sind demonstrated Ireland's need for legislative independence as protection against both English parties. Smith O'Brien fully agreed. A similar report by Mitchel on the Punjab was, however, refused publication by the Association. Mitchel accepted the decision philosophically, but complained to O'Brien against the argument that criticism of imperialism would make the English less receptive to Repeal. After the 1846 split the Old Irelanders dropped such investigations as too expensive.[7]

Should Ireland Support the Empire?

Basing the claim to self-government on the evils of British government appeared incompatible with participation in the imperial system. Here Repealers were far from consistent. In February 1843 a *Nation* editorial declared Ireland under Repeal 'willing — cheerfully willing — as we should be at all times to contribute our just share to the common exigencies of the empire'. In 1844 *The Nation* complained that 'we are excluded from the Colonies, which are kept with all their numerous branches of employment, for Englishmen.' The trend of *Nation* articles, however, was against participation. Had not Grattan declared, 'perish Empire, live Ireland!' But Grey Porter, associated briefly with Repeal, talked of the 'Hiberno-British Empire' in his federal plan. The institutionalised link with empire was one of Gavan Duffy's reasons for repudiating O'Connell's brief endorsement of federalism. Compulsory Irish contributions to costly imperial adventures were a long-standing grievance. *The Nation* totally repudiated Grey Porter: 'A share in the British Empire would be an insecure, mercenary, passionless and wicked partnership.' It rejoiced that Irish 'secession from the policy and feelings of the empire is beginning to be felt'. Mitchel complained that Ireland paid more than her share to what he later depicted as 'the Empire of Hell'.[8]

Many Old Irelanders and some Young Irelanders disagreed. John Martin, strangely for an ally of Mitchel, desired, as late as November 1847, no dismemberment of the British Empire.

O'Brien, two years previously, had agreed, apostrophising the glorious contribution of the Irish to empire. He could not lightly cast off many years of work in the Commons.[9]

Acceptance of empire meant colonies and war. An Irish colonial link balanced additional job opportunity against greater expense. English writers like Adam Smith, William Cobbett and Richard Cobden rejected colonies as advantageous only to what Cobbett and Dillon called the 'tax-eaters' of the upper classes. Cobden and John Bright's 'Manchester School' believed free trade without political entanglement beneficial to national economic interests. The issue was more complicated. Not only did the 'Colonial Reformer' group rehabilitate the imperial idea, but very considerable overseas advance continued at a period when colonies were apparently unfashionable. O'Connell, true to his links with 'Manchester', argued that trade should be Ireland's only link with the colonies. O'Brien, already shown to have differed from most other Young Irelanders on the subject, considered emigration as Ireland's main connexion with the overseas empire. By 1848, however, he was prepared to countenance, albeit reluctantly, Ireland's total separation and consequently the destruction of the imperial bond. After his return from penal exile, however, O'Brien's *Principles of Government* continued to advocate Wakefield's views with no hint of Irish republicanism. *The Pilot* clerical-ised O'Brien's opinion, maintaining that British maladminis-tration providentially dispersed the Irish as missionaries for Catholicism to the outside world. The moderate Daunt later condemned the 'silly fanaticism' of those opposed to Home Rule because it would check the emigration of apostles of Catholicity. Arthur Griffith's Sinn Fein, which borrowed so much from Young Ireland, criticised Irish emigration, but seemed to share O'Brien's view that Ireland was entitled to a share in the British Empire which it had done much to create.[10]

Creation of empire implies military involvement. Buggy's rejection of 'the Saxon shilling' was applicable to a dis-contented Ireland, but might a Repeal Ireland accept military involvement? The O'Connells added the carrot of total support after Repeal to the stick of non-co-operation during

England's difficulty. Thus John O'Connell offered the last drop of blood to defend the empire if justice were done to Ireland, and his father disconcerted Young Irelanders by promising to assist Britain to pluck down the American Eagle. 'Buy us at your price', the Liberator told the government. This was too much for the Quaker, E. Shackleton, who complained that all wars were unjust. But a *Nation* editorial soon promised an imperial contribution from a Repeal parliament. After the split *Nation* opinion hardened; John O'Connell complained in 1848 that Young Ireland refused to assist England in war. This generalisation did not cover Smith O'Brien. As Mitchel put it, O'Brien would not fight for England unless Ireland had its own parliament, while Mitchel himself would not fight for England in any circumstances. Britain's intransigence rendered such distinctions academic, but they illustrated very clearly the confusion within the Irish Confederation.[11]

Slavery and Human Freedom

The possibility of war with America and France was a stumbling-block to Repeal unity as these countries were persistently depicted by *The Nation* as Ireland's long-term allies. United States' slavery not only divided Repealers, but gauged Young Ireland's commitment to universal human freedom.

The Liberator and his son were as passionate opponents of slavery as they later became of mixed education. In his previous work for the abolitionist cause and his speeches in the 1840s, O'Connell was uncompromising. He rejected 'the filthy aristocracy of the skin', arguing that all colours shared a 'common humanity' and a common redemption. Very occasionally O'Connell lapsed into unconscious racism; the Irish, he suggested, might as well be blackened if they failed to assert their rights. He was particularly conscious of bitterly anti-Celtic racist talk emanating from England, which frequently compared the Irish to barbarous natives in the distant empire. As O'Connell's devoted 'Head Pacificator', Tom Steele, put it, the Irish, often equated with slaves, must assert 'the sublime principle of universal liberty', both religious and civil. O'Connell, moreover, pointed to the self-validation of British oppression, in Ireland and elsewhere, which brutalised its victims and then justified itself on the grounds of their savagery.[12]

Most Young Irelanders agreed entirely with such sentiments. Davis had denounced slavery before *The Nation*'s inception in *The Citizen*. Davis exposed Britain's hypocritical connivance at 5 million Indian slaves, and talked of 'our common humanity' in asserting the rights of North American Indians. He desired the unity of all slave nations. 'We are battling for Ireland; if we conquer, 'twill be for mankind.' In his poems, 'A Ballad of Freedom' and 'Oh for a Steed', Davis admirably asserted the universality of his concern.[13]

> Oh! for a steed, a rushing steed, and any good cause at all,
> Or else, if you will, a field on foot, or guarding a leaguered
>   wall
> For freedom's right;
> In flushing fight
>   To conquer if then to fall.

Smith O'Brien was equally outspoken in declaring that 'our sympathies ought never to be withheld from nations suffering under oppression.' Ireland had in fact a mission to teach the principles of nationality. But O'Brien qualified his views. Opposed to the principle of slavery, he was convinced after a visit in 1858 that brutality in the American South was rare, while the activities of Northern abolitionists worsened the situation. Similarly, while deploring injustice to native peoples, O'Brien could not concede the right of uncivilised races to monopolise vast tracts of valuable land. Naively, O'Brien expected kind treatment to reclaim savage races. Davis, with less experience of the world, had a greater appreciation of cultural relativity.[14]

The only Young Irelander unequivocally to reject Irish freedom in the context of universal liberty was John Mitchel, who insisted that Ireland's rights had nothing to do with the rights of other countries. Endorsed by Arthur Griffith this opinion, which helped to estrange Mitchel from Duffy, appears to connect Irish nationalism with a prototype of fascism. Yet Mitchel's opinion was partly a by-product of the contest between Young Ireland and O'Connell on slavery. Even Davis accepted a free society based on helots.

Though both Old and Young Irelanders began from the same moral standpoint, divergence occurred on practical policies. Davis's belief in human liberty is obviously coloured by hopes of a military diversion from other insurgent areas. What if American slaveholders offered sympathy and financial support to Repeal? Though the O'Connells finally appeared to oppose it absolutely, the Liberator was initially challenged by the moral gadfly, James Haughton, when he congratulated the American president John Tyler and his son, both of whom were long-time friends of Repeal. To Haughton, there could be no friendship with slaveholding America. On this occasion, O'Connell dismissed the Tylers' opinions on slavery as irrelevant to Repeal. But during his trial in 1844, O'Connell cited a rebuff to American slaveholders as a proof that he had entered no foreign conspiracies against England. Slaveholding was thus related to other contentious problems like physical-force rebellion. Soon the O'Connells satisfied Haughton who turned on *The Nation*, which insisted that there be no interference with American Repealers. In 1845, Haughton applauded John O'Connell when he abruptly silenced a Repealer who considered that the Association was taking opposition to slavery too far; Haughton, however, demanded free speech when the Confederation rejected his views in 1847. *The Nation* comfortably attributed negro slavery to original British oppression. Davis had argued that Britain's destruction of Muslim power in India had increased slavery. In his subsequent *Jail Journal*, Mitchel extended this argument, suggesting that Britain intensified at the slave trade which it had ostensibly abolished.[15]

In 1845 Davis confronted O'Connell himself at a Repeal Association meeting on the latter's opposition to President Polk's annexation of Texas as a new slave state. Though absolutely opposed to slavery and anxious for its abolition in the USA, Davis refused to endorse passively the Liberator's unmitigated censure of Americans. The latter's reply was, however, even more uncompromising. In what may have been one of Davis's last contributions, *The Nation* pointed out that, as the Association was committed to Repeal only, it was proper to receive contributions from American sympathisers who might support slavery. Reference was also made to the rule that non-Repeal issues should be first raised in committee before being broached at public meetings. On the main point, the article suggested that slavery was more likely to die out in the United States if foreigners kept out of the debate. The Young Ireland attitude on slavery and the American alliance was greatly appreciated by many American Repealers.[16]

Disputes over other issues, the split, and Fr Kenyon's intervention on behalf of slavery, which helped to drive Haughton from the Irish Confederation, made the Association under John O'Connell appear more liberal than its rival. However, the issue was partly tactical; the O'Connells' post-1844 opposition to a militant policy seeking an American backed confrontation with the government played an important part in an apparent ideological difference.

The Canadian Example

The issues, India, participation in empire, and slavery demonstrate the four facets of the imperial question: human freedom, British brutality, heroic precedents, and the possibility of diversion. Canada provided the most apposite precedent. At once a source of inspiration and dismay, Canada (then consisting of modern Quebec and Ontario only) and other North American colonies moved forward to self-government between 1842 and 1849, while Ireland, after the heady optimism of 1843, descended to catastrophic famine and futile rebellion.

On the inception of *The Nation* in 1842, Canada was poised on the threshold of an exciting new era. After years of strife between executive governors appointed by Westminster and locally elected legislative councils, rebellions broke out in French majority Lower Canada, and predominantly English-speaking Upper Canada. Lord Durham, a member of the Wakefield school, in a celebrated Report (1839) recommended uniting the two Canadas to swamp French culture, while according the joint legislature responsible government with control over its executive. This was an improvement on the Irish parliament of 1782, which Repeal would restore. *The Nation* condemned the divide and rule section of the Durham Report, soon implemented by merging the provinces. The

Irish were impressed, however, when in 1842 the Peel government instructed the governor, Sir John Bagot, to implement responsible government by selecting ministers supported by the elected assembly. Even men implicated in the 1837 rebellions were accepted. Robert Baldwin, a Canadian of Irish background, allied with Louis Lafontaine, a French-Canadian of equivalent standing, made self-government a reality.[17]

The effect on Irish politics was electric. As Davis said in an early *Nation*, Canada, like Ireland in 1782, had taken advantage of England's weakness 'to extort from her *almost* independence.' He envisaged Canada calling to Ireland from across the Atlantic, 'sister Ireland, my chains are breaking. Why sleepest thou, oh! my sister?' The Liberator also discussed the issue at length, like *The Nation* denouncing the attempt to undermine French-Catholic culture in a population twice as numerous as Upper Canada. He was delighted at the determination of French Lower Canada and their alliance with English-speaking liberals. However, he dissociated himself from the 1837 rebellion.[18]

On the other side, conservatives deplored the Canadian development. Both Repealers and anti-Repealers emphasised the £500 reward for Lafontaine in 1837. According to *The Warder*, however, Lafontaine was a lesser traitor than O'Connell. In reply to *The Standard*, which complained that the appointment of Lafontaine was as logical as a ministry for Wolfe Tone in 1793, Davis declared, 'a better ruler for Ireland than Theobald Wolfe Tone never lived.'[19]

Nor was the ostensible leader of the Lower Canadian revolt of 1837, Papineau, forgotten. To Davis, the only difference between Papineau and an Irishman was that the former had an 'O' at the end, instead of the beginning, of his name. His idea for arbitration courts was taken up by the Repeal Association. Papineau remained in politics, even visiting Ireland and associating his case for a Canadian republic with that of the one million Irish in Canada. By 1848, there were considerable hopes that Papineau might initiate a new rebellion in Canada and give Ireland the 'opportunity' to achieve freedom.[20]

Meanwhile, the more moderate Baldwin and Lafontaine, who duly identified with Repeal in Ireland, faced setbacks of their own when, as *The Nation* pointed out, the new governor, Sir Charles Metcalfe, dropped responsible government and acted as his own prime minister. Divisions like those of Ireland were exploited. *The Nation* hoped for intervention by US President Polk after his annexation of Texas, suggesting that Canada should accede to the United States. During the famine Canada became a graveyard for many exterminated Irish peasants. J. R. Godley's plan for Irish emigration to Canada was denounced as 'nefarious'. The tough conditions of Canada and the Maritimes were well advertised and the crowded Lazar houses at places like Gross Isle in the St Lawrence and Boston vividly depicted. Smith O'Brien, however, still favoured emigration to Canada, maintaining after his visit to North America in 1858, that Canada offered as favourable prospects as the United States.[21]

In February 1848, with Lord Elgin as governor-general, the Baldwin-Lafontaine team was again victorious and moved steadily towards full responsible government under the crown without further need for insurrection. Baldwin finally persuaded the sceptical Lord John Russell that a self-governing Canada would prove a reliable British ally in time of war. In Ireland, however, Smith O'Brien, who would have given a similar assurance, was moving towards the opposite pole of a protest in arms. The Young Ireland movement finally provided positive feedback for Canada when D'Arcy McGee played an important role in the establishment of Confederation in 1867. In turn the Dominion of Canada provided the model for the Irish Free State of 1922. When it broke new ground by writing the convention of responsible government into positive law, the Irish Constitution of 1922 followed a demand of Smith O'Brien, based on earlier Canadian experience.[22]

Conclusion

In the unhappy 1840s, Canada, an apposite precedent for resurgent Ireland in 1842, diverged from the famine-infested country of 1848. None of the four principles enunciated earlier in the chapter ultimately proved effective in mobilising support for Young Ireland. No diversion occurred. There was some conflict with Old Irelanders over universal freedom, leaving the latter more apparently liberal on slavery, though, like O'Brien, they were reluctant to give up some participation in the empire. Evidence of British brutality elsewhere was insignificant compared with the Irish famine. Finally, overseas resisters like Dost Mahommed, the Sikhs and the Maoris proved impossible to emulate in 1848. Even worse, the grand constitutional alliance between French and English in Canada was not paralleled by Orange and Green fraternity in Ireland. Young Ireland's efforts to bring this about were not, as we shall now see, half-hearted.

Orange and Green will Carry the Day?

The hope of attracting Orangemen and unionists to the Repeal cause antedated the establishment of *The Nation* by many years. O'Connell loudly asserted the need for sectarian unity and lauded individual converts. The Liberator's efforts to campaign in the north, especially in 1841 when assisted by Duffy, had been totally unsuccessful. O'Connell learned his lesson. During the Repeal Year he renounced any intention of provoking the Orangemen by holding a demonstration in their area, thus incurring unionist sneers that he dared not set foot in the north.[1]

Facing the Problem

The Nation determined to do better. It realised that O'Connell's name was anathema to most of the 1.5 million Protestants (half Presbyterian) estimated to live in Ireland, mostly in the north. By the 1840s sectarianism intensified in the growing city of Belfast. Not till after the famine did division, following Catholic migration to the city from country districts, solidify into a perennial tradition of periodic riot and mayhem. There had, however, been sectarian rioting in the 1830s and the days when the erection of a Catholic church was an interesting novelty, to be patronised and financed by liberal Protestants, were long since departed. O'Connell's Catholic Emancipation movement had stimulated the Rev. Henry Cooke's 'banns of marriage' between Presbyterians, hitherto less interested in Orangeism, and the Church of Ireland. Similarly, O'Connell's Repeal campaign of the 1840s helped to revive Orangeism after the stern discouragement received from Under-Secretary Thomas Drummond in the 1830s. Repealers who assembled 'monster meetings' were unable to support with consistency the continued prohibition of Orange demonstrations. The Liberator and his colleagues could but hope that Orange attitudes were on the decline. [2]

Davis Addresses the Protestants

The Young Irelanders appeared well-qualified to win Protestants to their all-embracing nationalism. Davis and Smith O'Brien had been brought up in a strong Protestant ascendancy atmosphere. If Davis and O'Brien had less direct knowledge of the all-important north, they were reinforced by two Ulster Presbyterians, John Mitchel and John Martin. Gavan Duffy, a Catholic reared under Orange repression, could temper the enthusiasm of his Protestant colleagues with a dash of reality.

Davis's 'Letters of a Protestant on Repeal' again established the framework for subsequent policies. First, unity was no optional extra but an essential ingredient of true nationalism. You must have Protestant help. This could be obtained only by appealing to Protestant self-interest. But Davis ultimately accepted that self-government was achievable without such unity. Later in the 'Letters' he warns Protestants of their potential danger if self-government was secured without their active support. 'Cut off from England, and weakened and divided by an unprosperous strife, Roman Catholic justice would remain their chief security.' Though not very explicit, he clearly feared Protestant subordination to Catholic nationalism. But this appears inconsistent with his powerful assertion, ostensibly supported by the O'Connells as well as Young Irelanders, that the Protestant minority was too strong to be persecuted in an independent Ireland.[3]

Protestants able to take care of Themselves?

What precisely was this Protestant strength? Davis's apostrophe to Protestant courage, intelligence and economic know-how was nothing if not élitist and self-confident. It was offset, however, by the apparently cringing belief, at total variance with Davis's proud self-reliance and demand for de-Anglicisation, that Britain would monitor the treatment of Irish Protestants. On the other hand, some British opinion, notably Sir Walter Scott, considered Protestants sufficiently strong to conquer the rest of Ireland. Both the Liberator and the Young Irelander, Thomas MacNevin, who reproduced Davis's arguments, rejected Scott. This was crucial; while even John O'Connell maintained that the numbers, intelligence and military strength of Protestants guaranteed them against persecution, his father insisted that Protestant numbers in the north were exaggerated. Even in Down and Antrim they had a majority of only 50,000 over local Catholics and could hardly hope to achieve victory by their own efforts. It was but a step to the open disparagement, by Old Irelanders and *The Pilot*, of the northern Protestant community. To *The Pilot*, 'the Protestant party in Ireland, as it is called, is not half so numerous or powerful as represented.' Even in the north, not only were the numbers grossly exaggerated but 'their morale is as deteriorated as their physical condition. You would look in vain – in any gathering at present, of these squalid and broken-down weavers – for the "*stalwart* yeomanry" of the North, as *The Nation* lately described them.' There was nothing to 'respect' or 'envy' in the community. Belfast, the Young Irelanders' 'pet town', was in reality the 'only rotten town in Ireland'. Tom Steele, after efforts to negotiate with Orangemen, dismissed them as an 'ignorant rabble', impervious to argument.[4]

The Old Irelanders' contemptuous attitude was partly a by-product of the strife over the Colleges bill. Increasingly the Young Irelanders were portrayed as being soft on unionists and in alliance with their newspapers. The ambivalence of Irish nationalists to unionists and Orangemen was to persist until the present day. Even within Young Ireland itself there was inconsistency between portrayal of Orangemen as potentially fine nationalists, requiring but little re-education, and as a pernicious obstacle to national development.

The Good Orangeman

Many excellent qualities were attributed to extreme

Protestants. Davis praised the Rev. Henry Cooke's 'manly' support of the Scottish Free Kirk against the British government. Presbyterians were credited with firm adherence to the principle of tenant right. Their courage and shoulder-to-shoulder spirit of co-operation was a model to the country. When Orangemen demonstrated at Enniskillen in 1845, *The Nation* depicted them as 'brave, blind men', who marched 'large, stern and erect' like soldiers. Their courage and power would make them invaluable on the right wing of an Irish militia battling against religious tyranny. On a personal level they were excellent sons, husbands and neighbours to each other. Smith O'Brien was sure that their bigoted prejudices would not in the long run prevent Orangemen from standing by their country. Nor was the northern Presbyterian image of 'Scotch thrift, dogged rectitude, implacable integrity' forgotten by *The Nation*. Even the Liberator was happy to declare Orange as good a colour as green. John O'Connell accepted that there was 'much that is valuable in the Orange body', but considered it offset by 'much that is contemptible and intrinsically worthless.' The Head Pacificator could on occasion refer to some Orangemen as 'noble-hearted fellows'. Sometimes praise of Orangemen was almost insulting to Catholics. For example, *The Nation* suggested in 1847 that Catholics needed more conversion to religious liberty and individual rights than Protestants to Repeal.[5]

The Not so Good Orangemen

The optimistic stereotype of Orangemen and northern Protestants presented by many Repealers was balanced by a very different assessment of their activities. *Old Ireland* in its institutionalised hostility to *The Nation* complained that its rival forgot that Ireland was a Catholic country and placed its destinies in the hands of Orangemen whom it depicted as chivalrous and brave. Even amongst *The Nation* élite there were misgivings about lavishing praise on the Orangemen. In 1843 an Orange demonstration at Clones, growing 'riotous and disorderly', ended in a Catholic being stabbed to death. Referring to a later incident, *The Pilot* asked how *The Nation* could make pets of Orangemen who beat a bed-ridden woman and her children. The Protestant practice of attacking funerals at the Catholic Friar's Bush cemetery in the heart of Protestant Belfast, was also noted; so was the provocative Orange march in 1846 through Belfast's Hercules Street, home of the rough butchers whom Smith O'Brien later failed to impress. In 1848, *The Nation* dismissed as 'insolent bravado' the *Banner of Ulster*'s threat that Orangemen might one morning exterminate Repealers.[6]

Duffy, whose childhood convinced him that Orangemen only respected force, abandoned conciliation in several *Nation* articles. Some months after the Clones murder, he warned Catholics not to respond to the provocation of the 'poor, deluded devils' who beat their big drums like superstitious Indians trying to frighten away an eclipse. He followed the Liberator in denying the strength of the Orange community, maintaining that any gathering of Orangemen could be outnumbered by Catholics at an hour's notice. Duffy rejected Belfast as 'the Athens of Ireland'. Its architecture was 'a mass of brick with a mask of stone'; its only theatre was closed and its Mechanics Institute was on its last legs. As for its solitary library, it was filled with nothing but Scottish metaphysics. The Orangemen, an 1844 editorial declared, were dupes to blind prejudice and devoid of human dignity apart from the stubborn courage to defend 'an empty superiority' at any cost. The Ulsterman 'maintained an isolation in his fatherland, infamous in everything but the obstinacy he pledges to its defence'. The theme of the Orangeman as a foolish dupe to English interests was frequently developed. According to Daunt, the Orange Order, like the Ribbon Societies, was created by the 'foul monster' of English influence. A *Nation* editorial saw the Orangeman as a pawn in a game to secure Irish land by dividing English settlers and native Irish, played since the fourteenth-century Statutes of Kilkenny. Davis lamented that Catholics and Protestants could not live peacefully together as in other countries. He believed that the 'sensual aristocrats of Ulster' deliberately fostered sectarian feeling to preserve their high rents when the rest of the country was united for Repeal. Variations on this argument were to prove long-lived in Irish controversy.[7]

Methods of Converting Orangemen

The Young Irelanders tried hard to relate to northern Protestants. Mitchel and Martin, as inspectors of Confederate clubs in Ulster, felt a particular responsibility to their coreligionists, and O'Brien's unhappy delegation of late 1847, which failed even to confront Orangemen, was a serious attempt to show the Confederate flag. Young Ireland remained generally true to Davis's dictum: 'If you would liberate Ireland, and keep it free, you must have Protestant help — if you would win the Protestants, you must address their reason, their interest, their hopes, and their pride.' The alternative was violence. Thus Davis himself, when confident of revolution with foreign aid or diversion in 1843, absorbed himself in military stratagems and neglected unity till after the Clontarf fiasco. This partly explains the apparently inconsistent view that Protestants would be too strong to coerce in a self-governing Ireland, except if they remained aloof from the independence movement. After a violent revolution, assisted by France and the United States, a hostile Protestant community would indeed be likely to face severe repression. M. J. Barry also warned Protestants to ensure their support for the national movement before the first shot was fired.[8]

But the reason, interest, hopes and pride of Orangemen were extremely difficult to tap. The initial problem was contact. The Protestant upper classes might be approached directly through the press, public meetings on the state of the country or forums like the Irish Council. Though the Remonstrant Edward Hollywood of Dublin suggested a drive for *Nation* readership, this was difficult in a community whose horror of popish ascendancy had to be experienced to be believed. Young Ireland gave this difficulty relatively little thought, presuming that its ideas would filter down through upper class converts to Repeal or be acquired by osmosis in unlikely contacts with working-class Repealers. Reason, interests, hopes, and pride can be roughly subsumed under the reversed categories of common symbolism, economic advantage and fears of British duplicity.[9]

1.   Common Symbolism

Davis and others were concerned to evoke some unifying,

rather than divisive, symbols. Songs set to music were a valuable device, especially as there was a possibility that they might be absorbed, through a good tune, by both communities. Much of Davis's historical balladry was warlike and hence divisive. He tried, however, to remedy the defect. Two of his best efforts were 'Celts and Saxons' and 'Orange and Green will Carry the Day'. The former, a riposte to the unionist *Dublin Evening Mail*, contained the celebrated lines epitomising the ideal of secular nationalism which welcomed the contribution of all traditions to a generous unity.[10]

> And oh! it were a gallant deed
>   To show before mankind,
> How every race and every creed
>   Might be by love combined —
> Might be combined, yet not forget
>   The fountains whence they rose,
> As, filled by many a rivulet,
>   The stately Shannon flows.

Even more to the point was 'Orange and Green will carry the Day', which was set to the racy tune of the Orange song, 'The Protestant Boys'. The poem epitomised *Nation* editorial prose in rejecting Britain's divide and rule. The futility of the Irish, of either faction, supporting English kings like William III or James II was demonstrated before the poetic peroration which asserted the potency of a united Ireland:[11]

> Tories and Whigs grew pale with dismay,
>   When from North
>   Burst the cry forth,
> 'Orange and Green will carry the day!'
>   No surrender!
>   No pretender!
> Never to falter and never betray —
>   With an amen,
>   We swear it again,
> Orange and Green shall carry the day!

A similar message was propagated by Jean Frazer, who wrote

promiscuously for *The Nation*, the *Dublin University Magazine*, the *Irish Felon* and Barrett's *Pilot*. For 12 July 1843 he pleaded, before the achievement of a united Ireland:[12]

> 'Till then the Orange lily be
> *Thy* badge, my patriot brother
> The everlasting Green for me,
> And — we for one another.

Elsewhere Davis emphasised that the army of William III had carried symbolic green banners to the battle of the Boyne in 1690. Why not carry them again for Ireland? 'Will the Orangemen quarrel with their next-door neighbours, their playmates, and fellow-marketers, to please this foreign and faithless government?' Why not give up the practice of quoting religious texts at each other? MacNevin likewise implored both Repealers and Orangemen to forget James II and William III. John Mitchel, who did not add verse to his other accomplishments, expressed the new counter-myth in racy prose when he declared in 1848 that, were Ireland as united as in 1782, he would gravitate towards the Orange faction. He preferred the support of 5,000 northern Protestants to that of 50,000 French. Four years earlier a *Nation* editorial, reminding Orangemen again on the eve of their annual demonstrations of the green sprigs carried by William III's army, offered to allow the loyalists to festoon Conciliation Hall with Orange lilies, provided they reflected on the exploitation of that 'Whig colour' as the badge of English division which had kept Ireland in poverty. When an Orangeman asked *The Nation* if William III's statue would be removed from Dublin's College Green after Repeal, the paper replied that it was averse to the destruction of historical monuments and that William had written a page of Irish history with a strong hand at the Boyne and Aughrim. Most important was Meagher's importation from Paris in 1848 of the green, white and orange tricolour, ultimately Ireland's flag. There was, however, some grumbling that its French-inspired symbolism implied that Orangemen were half a nation whereas they were at best one-third.[13]

The Liberator also praised Orange ballads, like 'Boyne

Water' which, he declared, was often played during the Emancipation struggle. Catholics should not react to any Orange tunes, nor to the absurd loyalist cry, 'To Hell with the Pope!' *The Nation* agreed wholeheartedly. If ignored, the cry would soon die out. Davis's 'Native Swords', set to the tune of Boyne Water, appropriately contained the lines:[14]

> Religion's name, since then, became
> Our pretext for division.

Unfortunately, the line, 'By knaves and priests divided', was denounced by the ex-Orangeman, Barrett, as an insult to Catholics. In 1845, there seemed some chance that the Orangemen might be interested in revising their symbols. The bitterly anti-Catholic Tresham Gregg astonished a public meeting by praising *The Nation* and Moore's *Melodies*, and asserting a love for the Green as well as the Orange. Davis publicised talk in the conservative *Dublin Evening Mail* of a rendezvous of 100,000 Orangemen and 100,000 Repealers on the banks of the Boyne. Peel's increased Maynooth grant and other would-be conciliatory reforms directed at Catholics aroused easily exploitable Protestant fears of a sell-out. As in 1974, when the threat of a Council of Ireland sent Ulster loyalists groping for the symbols of Irish culture, disillusionment with Britain had surprising results. But nationalists needed to produce hard evidence of economic and political common interest.[15]

2.   An Economic Common Interest?

From the early days of *The Nation*, Young Irelanders like Davis, Duffy and MacNevin denied that Ulster prospered under the Union. Davis, for example, in 1843 described the increase of paupers, decay of manufactures, and the constant drain of taxation and absentee rents which affected the whole country. Duffy's scathing depiction of Belfast has already been mentioned. In a *Nation* editorial MacNevin lamented the 'departed spirit of the linen trade' in Ulster. Though clearly an exaggeration, the linen trade did not reach its predominance till the American Civil War of the 1860s cut off the British cotton supply. Nor did shipbuilding develop till the 1850s.

During the famine years, while Ulster suffered less than the south and the west, northern misery enabled *The Nation* to declare that 'gasping men totter like ghosts along the roads'. Smith O'Brien maintained that there were then more evictions in Ulster than elsewhere. Moreover, the human suffering caused by Belfast industrialisation enabled Duffy to argue that Presbyterian leaders like Henry Cooke exploited the ignorance of the very class most in need of Repeal. Many of these lived in 'small, unventilated, and shockingly filthy tenements, built on a swamp in the suburb of Ballymacarrett'. When they occasionally emerged from 'the foetid air of their dens, strangers are frightened of their spectral appearance, and ask if they are inmates of a fever ward. These poor men work from twelve to fourteen hours a day at their sedentary labours, and subsist almost exclusively upon *starch sowens* — a filthy and nauseous liquid, which Dr Cooke would not give his pigs.' On their few holidays, however, such unfortunates could be relied upon to shout 'No Repeal'.[16]

The Young Irelanders effectively backed up, once more, the Liberator's insistence that, despite Belfast's considerable volume of trade, commerce would greatly increase under the protection of a native parliament. A recent French treaty, for example, had attempted to lower duties on English cutlery at the expense of Irish yarns. Orangemen, said O'Connell, should learn that prosperity was in the interests of all. Sharman Crawford's warning that the north preferred free trade was ignored. Davis extended the argument by relating Ulster prosperity to the retention of taxes now drained away to finance British military adventures in India and China.[17]

In developing the economic argument for unity, Repealers needed to avoid antagonising northern Protestants by hinting at a possible reversal of the seventeenth-century plantations which had dispossessed the Catholic landowners. Already the traditional Orange fear of a revengeful massacre, like 1641, to destroy the plantation, was full blown. O'Connell's 1843 *Memoir of Ireland, Native and Saxon* had sought to allay this fear by denying the historical evidence for any large-scale killing. In his Repeal Association speeches, the Liberator,

with boring reiteration, insisted that Catholics had not persecuted Protestants on the three occasions that they had held
power in Ireland. Davis fully supported the Liberator's efforts,
producing even more evidence against the theory of 1641
genocide and lauding the tolerance of James II's Irish parliament. On the plantations themselves, O'Connell tactfully
ignored the rights of individual planters and concentrated
on the continued exploitation of Ulster by London companies, such as the Fishmongers. When these had been sent
by a Repeal parliament to fish elsewhere the land could be
made available, on easy purchase terms, to small farmers.
Davis added his customary gloss to this argument, drawing
attention to the fact that tenants 'fought for and held the
land, and the Corporations of London received the rents.'
O'Connell agreed that it was the broad swords of the yeomen
and peasantry who conquered Ulster, not the landlords.
The Ulster Protestant, John Mitchel, in the preface to his
Aodh O'Neill, personalised the issue by admitting himself a
non-Milesian planter by blood. He insisted that 'the Anglo-
Irish and Scottish Ulstermen have now far too old a title
to be questioned: they were a hardy race, and fought stoutly
for the pleasant valleys they dwell in.' He saw the sieges of
Derry and Enniskillen as comparable to the O'Neills' great
victories in rooting the settlers deep in the Ulster soil. Though
essentially the nationalism of Davis, this was a statement with
which few Ulster unionists could disagree, and indeed still
forms the basis of their polemic. Symbols were neatly tailored
to economic necessity. The tragedy, then as now, was that
there seemed no means for injecting such clever arguments
into the tribal consciousness of the community for which
they were intended.[18]

Leaving aside basic ownership, Repealers addressed specific
grievances. Eighteen forty-five, with the publication of the
Devon Report which failed to recommend the legislative
protection of the Ulster custom, and Stanley's ambiguous
land bill which followed, proved a crucial year. Davis, in the
last months of his life, after the Colleges bill furore, was
preoccupied with the defence of Ulster custom and appeals
to northern farmers to guard their inheritance. Though no
orator, he used the Repeal Association to issue a solemn

warning: 'He had looked upon the homesteads of Ulster — so peaceful, so happy, so comfortable; and it did seem to him as if he saw something like a British lion skirting round these happy homes — longing to enter in and destroy the peace and comfort that were there [*Cheers*].'[19]

After Davis's death a few weeks later, *The Nation* continued his strategy, emphasising any Orange demands for tenant right or expression of fear at government intentions. As Duffy told O'Brien, this agitation provided an opening to Ulster. *The Nation* supported William Sharman Crawford on the issue in parliament. Duffy effected a liaison with the 'Black Protestant' William McKnight, editor of the *Derry Standard*, who, in advocating tenant right, asserted that human nature was the same in Tipperary and Ulster. The *Belfast Protestant Journal* praised the Young Irelanders for their stand on the same subject. In early 1848 the Somerville land bill was portrayed as another threat to the Ulster custom. On the eve of rebellion, *The Nation* anticipated that fears for their land would inhibit Orange support for the government. Mitchel advised Protestant farmers that their 'man of sin', the pope, 'bring no ejectments in Ireland'. After the failure of the 1848 revolt, Duffy worked with some initial success to create a League of North and South, based on a common defence of tenant right.[20]

3. The Uses of British Perfidy

Though agrarian economics appeared an excellent means of appealing to the northern Protestant's reason and self-interest, if not his pride, there were other politico-religious strings to the Young Ireland bow. *The Nation* did its best to encourage a sense of grievance amongst Presbyterians agitated in 1844 over the government failure to concede full validity to their marriages. In the following year, Peel's conciliatory gestures to Catholicism in Ireland enabled *The Nation* to argue that the government was plotting to discard their Orange dupes as inefficient agents and establish the Catholic religion in Ireland as a means of governing through Castle Catholics. Orangemen should therefore throw in their lot with the Young Ireland section of the Repeal movement, committed as it was against the establishment of a state Catholicism.

Other Repealers, Orangemen were warned, had less aversion to the political endowment of Catholicism. Acting alone, Orangemen were isolated. Could they hope to appoint their own Orange wardens? Their demonstrations were formidable only when they combined with nationalists. Humiliations, such as the dismissal of an Orange magistrate, and the prohibition of marching music, were emphasised. Nor was England's negotiation with the Vatican in early 1848 ignored as an Orange grievance. There was some ambivalence in *The Nation* approach when it also argued that Peel's centralising policy — sweeping away Irish monopolies of church, bench, and executive — helped Repeal in that integration with England would end the 'two nations' division in Ireland. Presumably Orangemen could choose between reduction to ciphers in an Anglicised and Catholicised Ireland, and retention of their tradition as Repeal allies. Again the argument was plausible, if specious.[21]

4. Did Conciliation achieve any success?

Hindsight has demonstrated the futility of such argumentative strategies in winning a community still impervious to national arguments. But failure was not then inevitable. There was ritual insistence at Repeal meetings by the Liberator, and even some Young Irelanders, that Orangemen were joining 'multitudinously'. Sometimes this was based on mere assertion, or the fallacy that relatively small groups of political converts constituted a prospective avalanche. Duffy's claim in 1843 to have obtained Repeal subscriptions from the Orange stronghold of Sandy Row seemed extremely impressive, as did the subsequent location of a John Mitchel Confederate club in the area. O'Connell occasionally confused 'Ulster', where Catholic-Protestant numbers were approximately equal, with 'Protestant Ulster'. Sometimes the claims of northern rapport were feeble. O'Connell was delighted when Orangemen exulted less than expected on his conviction in 1844. Duffy saw it as a promising sign that Henry Cooke needed to warn his followers against Repeal. When the Orange movement appeared to change its name to the Protestant Alliance in 1845, it was hoped that this indicated a softening of its approach. Unsubstantiated claims that bigotry was dying out were made. Much of this can be dismissed either as insincere propaganda or optimistic self-delusion, and sometimes a dash of both.[22]

The Split and the Orangemen

The effectiveness of Repeal propaganda directed at northern Protestants was scarcely enhanced by the Repeal split of July 1846. Though O'Connell's insistence that his Peace Propositions made it safe for Orangemen to join the Association, the seceders' counter-argument, that the north turned towards Repeal after Young Ireland had asserted religious liberty, was no more implausible. *The Warder*, a recognised Orange journal, showed considerable sympathy towards several aspects of *Nation* policy after 1845. In 1848 the brief formation of the Protestant Repeal Association, with which men like the poet Samuel Ferguson were associated, may be regarded as a reaction towards Confederate policy. It was, despite its middle-class character, a possible bridge to the Orangemen, one of whom attended a meeting in full regalia. In Dublin, there was an attempt to fill its meetings with counterfeit Orangemen. Immediately before the rising, *The Nation*, speaking for Duffy and McGee, suggested that the success of two Protestant Repeal deputations to the north were the last chance of averting revolution. W. S. Crawford, who supported Protestant Repeal by letter, accepted this analysis. There were minor indications of divided Orange loyalties. Twenty-nine Orangmen, for example, were expelled from Belfast lodges for advocating Repeal.[23]

Ultimately traditional loyalties reasserted themselves. As Sharman Crawford lamented, Orange demonstrations checked the movement towards tenant right. The failure of Martin's open letter to the Orangemen of Down to contest Lord Roden's assertion that Orangemen supported the government was symbolised by the Dolly's Brae affair on Roden's property. On 12 July 1848, Catholic Ribbonmen, perhaps emboldened by current revolutionary fervour, forced the local Orange march to retreat from the hill. On the following year, however, while troops and police scattered the Ribbonmen, Orange marchers devastated Catholic areas, creating a new myth of violence and division, long celebrated in song and story.[24]

Tragically, for all their good intentions, the Young Irelanders left sectarian tension even greater than they found it. Yet subsequent generations have done little better. Many of the arguments — economic advantage, British divide and rule — have been repeated with no greater effect by later nationalists.

Young Ireland and the Cult of Nationalism

Pearse Determines the Agenda

Young Ireland has been linked with the tradition of mystical revolutionary dates through the Fenian leaders who participated in the 1848 Rising and through the physical survival of Confederate clubs which merged into Fenian units. More important is the literary tradition evoked by Padraic Pearse, the supreme ideologist of 1916. In a celebrated pamphlet, *Ghosts*, and its successors, Pearse associated the three Young Irelanders, Davis, Mitchel and Lalor, with Wolfe Tone to constitute an Irish nationalist apostolic tradition with its own sacred fathers. Davis was credited with providing a spiritual dimension to the republican cult, Mitchel with generating a superb literary hatred of British tyranny and Lalor with incorporating the interests of people on the land. O'Connell, pointedly, does not qualify for the team, though his constitutional successor Parnell joins the squad as a reserve.

Pearse's conscious myth-making is as interesting for what it ignores as for what it includes. Though exalting Davis at O'Connell's expense, Pearse was careful to avoid the chief difference between the two Repealers, their attitude to secular nationalism and its corollary, undenominational education.

The Theory of Secular Nationalism

Paradoxically, Davis, credited with spiritualising Irish nationalism, was determined to secularise it to the extent of excluding contentious religious discussion. As Davis clearly demonstrated in 1844, Repeal did not consider any man's creed, but worked for common secular interests. Doheny pointed out that in Repeal even the word 'tolerate' was objectionable as it implied the superiority of one belief over another. Davis's insistence, derived from Burke, that a nation is 'a spiritual essence', suggests a nationalist alternative to Christianity. But the 'undenominational' interpretation of 'secular' rendered spiritual nationalism a mere undogmatic idealism. Duffy had the same idea in 1847 when declaring a rising nation's need for a policy 'as grand and comprehensive as the sublime system of the Catholic church'. As O'Connell put it in 1843, his movement was religious, not in a sectarian sense, but in its intention 'to feed the hungry, to clothe the naked, to relieve the diseased and afflicted'. O'Connell also asserted that he accepted the authority of Catholic bishops in religion, but not politics. Daunt, possibly more accurately, quoted Burke on a nation as a 'moral essence'. Burke himself, though he died before the union and showed concern at the condition of his native land, had little sympathy with romantic nationalism, which later pervaded Europe in the 1840s.[1]

Clear polarisation between Young and Old Ireland statements on nationalism, particularly before 1845, is difficult to establish. One sign is the Liberator's definition of religion as responsibility for the poor. This is consistent with his challenges to Britain to undermine Repeal by good government. In *The Nation*'s first year such a challenge was categorically rejected by Davis who asserted that nationality was worth any price and that ruin was preferable to provincialism. Dillon, with greater circumspection, likewise insisted that, despite the material benefits certain to flow from self-government, independence was desirable for its own sake. Smith O'Brien, not yet a Repealer, was criticised in a *Nation* article, aimed indirectly at the Liberator, for his emphasis on practical reforms.[2]

Though the Liberator and his son John originally advocated non-denominational Repeal, many Association members were reluctant to merge their defensive 'Catholic nationalism' in a wider, more comprehensive patriotism. Duffy admitted that he required conversion by Davis; his successor on *The Vindicator*, Kevin Buggy, raised a storm by referring to Protestantism as 'a miserable heresy'; Davis's *Nation* prospectus was attacked, *inter alia*, by the *True Tablet* for its failure to see that 'the nationality of Ireland is before all other things, and (please God) will be to the end of time essentially Catholic.' Duffy ignored this criticism in his reply. Eighteen months later the unionist *Warder* probed the division between *The Nation* and the post-Duffy *Vindicator*, arguing that while the former wanted Presbyterians in the Repeal movement, the latter did not. This was partly due to the northern Catholic inability to match their uninvolved co-religionists in the south in magnanimity to Ulster Protestants. However, the Colleges dispute, which transferred the problem of national unity from the orator's platform to the classrooms of the country, inspired more frank statements on Catholic priority. Thus Dillon Browne asserted that nationality and Catholicism were convertible terms. *The Pilot*, regarded as O'Connell's mouthpiece, likewise insisted that Ireland without Catholicism would be no nation. Catholics *were* the Irish nation, while Protestants had no country and were simply agents of the British to keep the Catholics in subjection. Interestingly, Davis and Mitchel endeavoured to turn such reasoning on its head by creating a secular nationalist myth that Irish martyrs in the past had died, nominally for religion, but in reality for their country. Tension between an official belief in national unity and pluralism and private preference for Catholic predominance has remained to the present day.[3]

Was the Liberator a Nationalist?

If a real, though partly masked, difference does appear between Old and Young Ireland on secular nationalism, is it possible to show the Young Irelanders as romantic revolutionaries diverging markedly from the pragmatic, utilitarian Liberator? Given such evidence as a split and a subsequent Young Ireland protest in arms the case appears watertight. But analysis of statements by Old and Young Irelanders in the crucial areas of national identity, national language, national literature (especially poetry and history), and national character makes easy generalisation difficult. As in economics, imperialism, and rapport with Orangemen, divisions inside the Young Ireland party were sometimes greater than those between Young and Old Ireland.

1. National Identity

The crucial issue lay in the advocacy of Ireland as a nation rather than a well governed province. If verbal assertion, particularly in 1843, is the test, then O'Connell was certainly an Irish nationalist. The very title of Davis's famous poem, 'A Nation Once Again', long treated as the anthem of Irish republicans, was a paraphrase of the Liberator's statements in 1843. The latter wanted 'A Nation Again' inscribed on his tomb, and aspired to remove 'filthy Saxon domination', thus leaving his country 'A Nation once more'. France and England, said O'Connell at Tara, were both equally foreign to Ireland. The Liberator, moreover, grounded his nationalism in the mandate of Providence. The youthful Meagher, participating at his first public meeting at Lismore, heard O'Connell declare: 'I want to raise this country to the fiscal and national elevation which nature and nature's God intended her for.' After his imprisonment, the Liberator sounded a more cautious note, but he still demanded Ireland 'a nation again' in late 1844. It is easy to question O'Connell's sincerity. Even during the Repeal Year itself, the unionist *Warder* denied that O'Connell really wanted Repeal, but used the demand to bully Westminster. This is irrelevant to the fact that O'Connell, in the most powerful medium available, encouraged the Irish people to think towards absolute national identity. Young Ireland's task was to deepen the foundation and ensure that it was not overlain by subsequent political expediencies.[4]

2. Linguistic Resuscitation

According to conventional wisdom, O'Connell discouraged the use of Irish, in which he was fluent, on utilitarian grounds, while the Young Irelanders enthusiastically espoused the revivalist cause, thus preparing the ground for the Gaelic League and Pearse. Advocacy of the Irish language was the chief example of spiritual depth with which Pearse credited Davis. A cool examination of the facts suggests, however, that Young Ireland was less enthusiastic for Gaelic, and O'Connell less deprecatory, than is popularly believed.[5]

Davis is again the key. Gavan Duffy had little interest in the Irish language and at best paid it only lip-service. He portrays Davis meeting 'vehement resistance' from his friends when he tried to start Irish classes. Davis's insistence, moreover, on the use of Irish names, such as Dunleary for Kingstown, led to some jocularity amongst his colleagues. Mitchel identified as a Saxon, not a Celt, while MacNevin wanted modern facts, not misty reminders of probably apocryphal kings like Daithi on the Repeal card. Only O'Brien, never an intimate member of *The Nation* set, was really interested. At forty, confessing shame at his ignorance of the ancient language of the people, he put himself, as he said, to school daily to acquire it. He became sufficiently proficient to quote an Irish proverb at a public meeting in Limerick: 'An úair is mó an tanafa is goire an chobhair' (When the storm is greatest, help is nearest), and quote MacNamara's famous poem of exile in Van Diemen's Land. 'I feel as much desire to acquire the old language of our dear fatherland as if I was going home tomorrow.' Language was particularly important to O'Brien in view of his ancestry and residence west of the Derry-Waterford line, beyond which Irish was still regularly spoken.[6]

The evolution of Davis's views on the language can be traced from the 1840 Historical Society address. There, after a plea for the study of modern languages, and English in particular, Davis added Irish as an afterthought in the second rank. In the early *Nation* his first references to Gaelic were in connection with the Trinity College divinity school and Protestant proselytisers like the Rev. Caesar Otway. Davis did not refer to proselytism, but Daunt denounced the translation of the Bible into Gaelic for this purpose. This was indeed one of the reasons why Protestants were likely to become more enthusiastic than their Catholic colleagues about a linguistic revival.[7]

In articles on 'Our National Language' in 1843, Davis's doctrine of Gaelic as an antidote to anglicisation were set forth. The first was written at the height of Repeal Year enthusiasm when all blessings appeared immediately attainable. Ridiculing 'the mongrel of a hundred breeds called English', totally unsuitable for Celts, Davis insisted, in the famous passage apostrophised by Pearse, that 'a people without a language of its own is only half a nation. A nation should guard its language more than its territories — 'tis a surer barrier, and more important frontier, than fortress or river.' Moreover, 'to lose your native tongue, and learn that of an alien, is the worst badge of conquest — it is the chain on the soul. To have lost entirely the national language is death; the fetter has worn through.' So much for the ideal, but Davis was a little doubtful of his hope that the 'sweet old language' would ever again be spoken in 'college, mart and senate'.[8]

The second article, written in the aftermath of the Clontarf fiasco, was more cautious. Davis warned that if Irish were imposed on English-speaking people in eastern Ireland the adverse reaction 'might extinguish it altogether'. Instead it should be taught to the upper classes as a second language and its influence might filter down to the middle classes who now considered Gaelic vulgar. In the Irish-speaking west, however, teachers should know Irish and be equipped with Irish translations of the schoolbooks. He still regarded English as the main language. Thus, in the eyes of modern Gaelic enthusiasts, Davis' ultimate conclusion failed to keep pace with his dramatic rejection of English in early 1843. As a result, Davis's views on the language have been castigated as inadequate by Daniel Corkery, and the Young Irelander's admirers have been constrained to make excuses for their hero.

But what of the Liberator in 1843? Davis hoped that speaking of Gaelic by great Irishmen from Brian Boru to O'Connell would allay middle-class prejudice. During the Repeal Year O'Connell had professed a similar linguistic interest. Duffy, no Gaelic enthusiast, depicts O'Connell at a monster meeting at Skibbereen talking Gaelic to confuse government reporters. The suggestion is absurd. O'Connell responded appropriately to a speech in Irish by a supporter, Fr Hogan. The Liberator described Gaelic as 'the heartfelt, the heart-abiding Irish', your 'proper language' as opposed to 'the vulgar Saxon tongue'. This was, in effect, much the same message as Davis's enthusiastic eulogy in *The Nation* some weeks before. Nor was it the only occasion when O'Connell used Irish at public meetings. At a banquet in his honour at Loughrea the dining hall was covered with inscriptions in Irish. O'Connell thanked another banquet in Irish in Kerry several years later. Irish tags and phrases were quite common in his speeches. The Liberator's sincerity can always be questioned, but his statements are on record. Significantly, O'Connell's strongest repudiation of the utility of Irish was made at a private gathering in England. The Irish scholar, John O'Donovan, expressed similar views to Davis.[9]

Both Davis and O'Connell were operating in a milieu in which Irish was respected as a hallmark of nationality. If O'Connell believed English the language of Ireland's future, Davis thought much the same. His Historical Society address, placing Irish definitely in second place, was published in *The Nation* as late as 1848.

Did Davis's death mark a change in *The Nation* and Young Ireland? In his last weeks Davis favourably reviewed O'Donovan's Irish grammar, insisting that the variety of Irish dialect was not greater than in other countries. In a *Nation* article published a day before the onset of his fatal illness on 7 September, Davis gave some extracts from O'Donovan, but was almost in despair at the decline of the spoken language in the West. A year later when a correspondent complained that English misrule was eliminating the remnant (1/6th) of Irish who still spoke Gaelic, *The Nation* was almost sarcastic: 'Not Irish, but English is our mother tongue; yet do we claim to be Irishmen, and to have some interest in our country's hopes and prospects. We desire to be no better than Grattan was, and he spoke no Irish.' A free Ireland did not have to be entirely Celtic, a physical impossibility in any case. Nevertheless, an obligation was recognised to preserve the language, and practical suggestions for an Irish model school were welcomed. The answer represented the views of both Duffy and Mitchel. No practical proposals appear to have been forthcoming. The Repeal split and the famine concentrated attention on other matters. Smith O'Brien continued his daily study. But a useful Irish Society lapsed through lack of interest. Though bitterly opposed to *The Nation*, Barrett's *Pilot* did not differ fundamentally in its attitude to Gaelic. The diffusion of English, it believed, could not be stopped, yet Irish must be preserved a valuable 'historical monument'. Davis was a rare Young Ireland enthusiast, but even his belief in Gaelicisation should not be exaggerated. His most powerful statements can be read as a gloss on some of the Liberator's rhetoric.[10]

3. The Poetry of Nationalism

While Young Ireland's views on the Gaelic revival contained some ambiguities, there were no reservations about the movement's conscious programme for creating a patriotic literature in song and poetry. Davis saw new songs as a substitute for lost Gaelic culture. He was extremely frank about the practicality of his own poetic objectives. The starting-point was Thomas Moore, still recognised in the 1840s as Ireland's supreme patriotic poet. His relations with O'Connell were interesting. Moore's *Irish Melodies* were a considerable help to the Liberator in the Emancipation struggle. Later Moore became disillusioned with O'Connell's new movement and refused to stand for parliament on his behalf. In 1834 Moore showed his feelings in 'The Dreams of Those Days'. Though no names were mentioned, the Liberator is said to have wept and raved at the foul attack on him.[11]

> The dream of those days when first I sung thee is o'er,
> Thy triumph hath stain'd the charm thy sorrows then wore,
> And ev'n of the light which Hope once shed o'er thy chains
> Alas, not a gleam to grace thy freedom remains.

This was certainly a powerful indictment. Moore considered that the Liberator had slighted Moore's United Irish friends, such as Thomas Addis Emmet and Robert Emmet. O'Connell, on the other hand, disliked Moore's practical abandonment of the Irish cause to fawn on Whig grandees in London. Personal relations were, however, patched up. During the Repeal campaign the Liberator spiced his most flamboyant speeches with quotations from at least seven of the *Irish Melodies*. Moore's 'Remember Thee' gave the Liberator a powerfully nationalist peroration:

> Wert thou all that I wish thee, great, glorious, and free,
> First flower of the earth, and first gem of the sea.

Though these lines appealed to the Rev. Tresham Gregg, others had a more controversial impact and enabled opponents to ridicule the Liberator's alleged 'moral force'. 'The Song of O'Ruark', dealt with the Norman invasion of Ireland,[12]

> Onward the green banner bearing,
> Go flesh every sword to the hilt;
> On our side is virtue and Erin —
> On theirs is the Saxon and guilt.

This stanza provided the motto of O'Connell's 1843 *Memoir of Ireland*. The *Boston Pilot* used it to celebrate the coming rebellion of 1848. Another favourite, sounding like Moore, but not included in the *Melodies*, aroused tremendous cheers at the Lismore monster meeting in September 1843:[13]

> Oh, Erin, shall it e'er be mine,
> To wreak the wrongs in battle line —
> To raise my victor head and see
> Thy hills, thy dales, and people free?
> That glance of bliss is all I crave
> Between my labours and my grave.

Similarly portentous lines were derived from Moore's friend, Lord Byron, whom the Liberator considered the 'most beautiful of the English poets' and a castigator of the Act of Union:[14]

> Hereditary Bondsmen know ye not,
> Who would be free themselves must strike the blow.

The use of such quotations demonstrates the Liberator's mastery of calculated ambiguity. At enthusiastic public meetings their use certainly seemed to demonstrate warlike intentions; on the other hand, as at his trial in 1844, O'Connell could minimise quotations from Tom Moore who was not even a Repealer. Unionists and Young Irelanders persistently complained of the Liberator's inconsistency. Duffy ridiculed attacks on *The Nation* for quoting Danton when O'Connell himself admired an infidel, voluptuary and physical-force revolutionary, Lord Byron.[15]

The Old Irelanders were not abashed by such repartee. When *The Nation* later published an article on Shelley, *Old Ireland* stigmatised the pagan rites with which Byron had buried him. The Liberator denied that Byron's 'blow' implied physical force. Rather it was an example of the principle, dear to Repealers, Young and Old, 'Ourselves Alone'. This phrase, subsequently regarded as an inaccurate translation for Arthur Griffith's Sinn Fein of the early 1900s, preceded its Irish version. Applied to situations ranging from opposition to the Whig alliance to a readiness to persist in revolutionary preparation without French help, 'Ourselves Alone' in the 1840s implied a vigorous nationalism. At a Thurles banquet for O'Connell in late 1845 Fr Heffernan, responding to a toast on behalf of the Irish hierarchy, translated 'Ourselves Alone' as 'Shin fane'. Thus the Griffith slogan, far from denoting a separatism totally divorced from constitutionalism, was in fact a revival of O'Connell's Repeal.[16]

When they created their new Irish poetry, which was to arouse so much interest in *The Spirit of the Nation*, Duffy and Davis had a convenient model in 'Glorious' Moore. But as Davis pointed out, Moore was 'too delicate and subtle' for the middle and lower classes. He was also too abstract, lacking narrative, popular idiom or local colour. As the Irish, losing their language, had no popular national culture, it was essential to create one quickly. Archbishop MacHale's efforts to translate Moore into Irish were unsuccessful; his Irish was as stilted as Moore's verse. Davis consciously set out to de-anglicise the country with something rougher and bolder. *The Spirit of the Nation*, whatever its limitations as pure poetry, was successful, at least in arousing the middle classes. Many of the poems were set to rousing music, an art where Davis believed Ireland to reign supreme. As an American reviewer said, *The Spirit of the Nation* was quite unlike the 'lacrymose *boudoir* sentimentalities of Moore'.[17]

In the controversies on physical force after 1846, Old Irelanders tried to portray *The Spirit of the Nation* as dangerously provocative. Yet the warlike anti-Saxon images were also found in Moore and quoted by O'Connell. The Repeal Association did not officially recognise *The Spirit*, and O'Connell seems never to have quoted its verse, but it could not be so easily dismissed. Moore himself was believed to have written some of the poems, and Davis's verse was attributed by one paper to the Liberator's daughter Kate. When Maurice O'Connell attacked *The Spirit* in 1847, Smith O'Brien referred him to his own sabre-rattling contribution to the collection, 'Recruiting Song for the Irish Brigade', which celebrated those who 'many a Saxon's life-blood shed'. Though O'Connell in late 1843 promised to drop the term 'Saxon', all Repealers happily continued to use it. Both Duffy and the Liberator argued that it was a response to English contempt for Ireland. If the O'Connells had some misgivings, so too did *The Nation* which, on several occasions rebuked contributors for their perpetual glorification of violence. The evidence suggests that no hard and fast lines can be drawn between Moore, O'Connell and Davis in the strength of their literary patriotism, except that as a more forceful product, Davis's poems were a greater threat to the government.[18]

4.   Propagandist History?

Moore was a historian of Ireland as well as its great poet. However, his history received no praise from Davis and his colleagues who argued that it was dry, colourless and too dependent on conservative predecessors like Leland. Davis considered national history in much the same category as national poetry. He followed up discussion of Moore: 'Exact history is needful, not only as the best school of politics, but as the purifier and protector of tradition, the basis of fiction, and the arsenal of the song writer.' This catalogue would horrify modern scientific historians. It contains a basic inconsistency between the aim of 'exact' history, which implies detailed objective research, and history as an instrument for raising national consciousness. In Davis's time the dichotomy was less obvious as the problem was to write the history of the Irish people, using new sources, as opposed to the history of their rulers. Moore failed on this count. Davis, like modern exponents of women's history, disclaimed bias but insisted on treatment of groups hitherto ignored by traditional historians. Following O'Connell's *Memoir*, Davis wished to use all available sources to destroy old calumnies against the Irish people. O'Connell's book, which was little more than an extended footnote, was a practical effort to destroy the myth that Catholics persecuted. Davis had the same objective in his treatment of James II's Irish parliament, a work which demonstrates a flair for historical research without satisfying the criteria of modern analysts. His lesser known 'India — her own and another's' was more interesting in that it transferred the method to a distant country. With the limited sources at his command, Davis analysed the British seizure of India, not from the viewpoint of a superior civilisation overcoming barbarians, but from that of traditional native cultures themselves. The method, which has affinity with modern interests, was effectively applied in the Young Ireland 'Library of Ireland' series, with notable contributions from Mitchel on Aodh O'Neill, Fr Meehan on the Confederation of Kilkenny, and MacNevin on the Irish Volunteers. There was a certain naive belief that the facts would speak for themselves, as indicated by Mitchel, whose lively *History of Ireland* was prefaced by his claim to be a mere chronicler. Augustin Thierry was a foremost foreign model providing attractively presented history of the common people. Again, we find the pattern of O'Connell laying down the principle, in what Davis privately described as a deplorably written book, while the Young Irelanders developed it with verve and skill.[19]

Celtic Racialism?

Repealers agreed on many of the basic characteristics of nationhood; division lay in degrees of emphasis. Was this equally true of their depiction of Irish racial characteristics? In recent years Davis, especially in his poetry, has been castigated by Alf MacLochlainn for a narrow-minded Celtic nationalism leading to hatred and xenophobia. The issue was extensively debated in the 1840s; the standard Irish reply was *tu quoque*. As Duffy said, it is difficult to oppose oppression without some hatred of the oppressor. Davis denied that he used the word 'Saxon' as a word of offence, and O'Connell pretended to drop it. But the issue went deeper than mere terminology and verse commemorating past victories. O'Connell's Repeal stock-in-trade included regular assertion of Irish physical, moral and spiritual superiority over the English. As proof the Liberator regularly cited authorities arguing that the Irish were taller than their English counterparts, the superb Irish response to Fr Mathew's temperance crusade, and the traditional loyalty to the Catholic religion. The obverse of this argument was a full-scale denigration of the English, in which Duffy sometimes joined. Thus the English, whose physical deficiencies had been proved by scientific evidence, were depicted as living in outrageous conditions of moral and spiritual squalor. Reports were cited of communities which knew no God and practised disgusting sexual perversions. *The Nation*, despite some lapses of its own, sounded an early warning against such bombast.

Davis in particular advised against false disparagement of opponents and over-estimation of Irish capacities. Even in the heady days of 1843 he often sounded a sour note, suggesting that the people at monster meetings needed more discipline. While O'Connell talked as if independence was there for the taking, the Young Irelanders, especially after Clontarf, saw a long period of national regeneration and education as essential before the Irish were truly fit for freedom. On temperance, as Elizabeth Malcolm has shown, Davis was more sceptical than O'Connell. If drunkenness was 'the Saturnalia of slaves', continued temperance for the masses would always pose problems, certainly before independence was achieved. Was national regeneration a precondition of freedom, or was freedom the only means to regeneration? After the shattering experience of the famine, the latter response prevailed. Even in 1844 it was asserted that empty bellies equalled slavery. The problem was too subtle for the Liberator's platform rhetoric. In the Repeal Year itself *The Nation* demanded that the 'quickness and vivacity' of the Celt be married to the patience and perseverance of the Saxon. This approximated the English stereotype of the flighty Celt. In his history of Young Ireland, written after personal success overseas, Gavan Duffy used such racial language in depicting his own people. He was thus trapped into accepting the disparagement of the oppressor; Davis, in one of his last statements, was wiser in condemning the 'pestilent and lying distinction' between Celt and Saxon.

Thus Young Ireland confronted, to a much greater extent than O'Connell, the question which was to agitate Gandhi in India: is independence worth having before the people have disciplined themselves for it?[20]

Ultimate Objectives?

This study of the national cult has indicated that Young and Old Ireland on most issues started from the same assumptions, but the former, though often divided amongst themselves, were more thoughtful in developing their positions. It is the same story with ultimate objectives. Were the Young Irelanders republicans? Was O'Connell a true nationalist? Such questions are often asked, but are of little help in unravelling a complex debate. At the split in 1846, *The Nation* claimed that it had never advocated separatism, while O'Connell vehemently asserted that it did. Not till 1848 was republicanism seriously advocated by anyone, even Mitchel. Davis himself had been more than flexible on the federal issue, signing *Nation* articles as 'A Federalist', using Sismondi to demonstrate the value of the idea, and seeing the policy as a useful stepping-stone which would attract conservatives. Arthur Griffith, a great admirer of Davis, was to adopt similar reasoning over the Anglo-Irish Treaty in 1921. Duffy's vehement rejection of the idea may have been, as J. A. O'Neill later revealed, the result of an earlier quarrel with O'Connell. Even after Davis's death, Young Irelanders like McGee advocated apparently eccentric ideas, such as the defence of an Anglo-Irish dual monarchy on the ground that Henry VIII had been effectively recognised as king by the Irish people. This idea was also borrowed by the magpie Arthur Griffith. In short, Repealers of all varieties aspired to a relatively limited independence until the dramatic developments of early 1848.[21]

Revolutionary Strategy

Although economics, imperialism, Orangemen and the cult of nationality have shown the Young Irelanders playing variations on O'Connell's tunes, revolutionary strategy suggests total antagonism. After splitting the Repeal Association in 1846 on theoretical force, the Young Irelanders, as their opponents had warned, did indeed attempt a totally ineffective rebellion in 1848. The Young Irelanders, with the endorsement of several historians, Professor Maurice O'Connell excepted, maintained that physical force was not the real cause of the split. In the years immediately following, the Liberator's early speeches were subjected to prolonged debate. The problem is central in Irish historiography, which, like Pearse, used to divide nationalism into watertight compartments: constitutionalism, emanating from O'Connell, and physical force deriving from Young Ireland. Popularly, means appear more important than ostensible ends in assessing patriotism.

Several questions present themselves. What was the exact line of demarcation on violence between Young and Old Ireland? Was there any truth in Young Ireland's contention that they merely took O'Connell literally in 1843? If so, did they formulate new ideas after the split? How far were ideas such as passive resistance and the blood sacrifice, taken up by Griffith and Pearse later, the product of debate in the 1840s? The Repeal Year of 1843 is again crucial. Was Old Ireland right in maintaining that irresponsible *Nation* articles had undermined the Liberator, or did Young Ireland insist correctly that it had been misled by O'Connell's bellicosity?

O'Connell and Young Ireland before the Repeal Year

O'Connell's long-term principle, 'England's difficulty is

Ireland's opportunity', was the point of departure. As Young
Irelanders subsequently pointed out, this principle could not
be squared with the 'Quakerism' which the Liberator liked to
assert. England's difficulties, convenient in 1782, were
emphasised by the Liberator after 1842. He persistently
enumerated England's problems at home and abroad. Evoking
threats of theoretically repudiated 'hard men' is a perennial
expedient of constitutional politicians. *The Nation* in its first
few weeks inadvertently disrupted this strategy by naive
enthusiasm.[1]

What did O'Connell mean in the Repeal Year, 1843?

The problem was exacerbated when O'Connell, with
Young Ireland stimulation behind the scenes, launched his
massive 1843 demonstrations. At the trial of the Repeal
traversers in 1844, the attorney-general maintained, with
some justification, that there was no substantial difference
between *The Nation* pages reporting O'Connell's speeches
and the editorial section. *The Nation* had indeed undertaken
to amplify and expand the Liberator's comments. There was
certainly some correlation between O'Connell's remarks at
Mallow, Tara and Roscommon, and *Nation* editorials such
as 'The Morality of War', 'The March of Nationality', and
'The Crisis is upon us'. Herein lay the difficulty. On 13 May
Davis told the people to stand on the constitution while there
was a shred left; in his famous Mallow defiance O'Connell
repeated the message. *The Nation*, moreover, emphasised
order and obedience to the leader. In July 1843 Davis
specifically warned against expecting direct help from France
and the USA. Ireland was not on the verge of war, but would
defend itself if attacked.[2]

Defence or Aggression?

As the 1846 Peace Proposals permitted defensive violence
these remarks by Davis are significant. Though this was later
challenged to some extent by Young Irelanders, O'Connell's
speeches in 1843 do appear fairly consistent in maintaining
the broad defensive loophole. At Mallow he challenged the

British to trample his dead body under foot and delighted in the idea of giving his life in so noble a cause. At Dundalk he admitted to sometimes hoping that the British would attack. If they did, the issue would not be doubtful. At Roscommon he evoked tremendous cheers by asking his audience if any man would fail to fight if attacked. Dillon abbreviated his own speech in honour of O'Connell's 'music'. At Lismore, the Liberator admitted that he had had to check 'an aspiration' which 'came over me at Mallow', before rousing his audience to tremendous cheers with the 'battle line' stanza. Though O'Connell at the Repeal Association partially rebuffed a suggestion of physical support from the French radical, Ledru-Rollin, he admitted that force 'in the last extremity' was legitimate. If attacked he would be prepared to receive help from any source.[3]

The Liberator, moreover, despite his no drop of blood disclaimer, was particularly lavish with his personal vital fluid. At Mullaghmast, he offered his 'own heart's stream' for Ireland. At an Association meeting in Dublin, O'Connell dared not, in the face of God, shed any blood but his own. At Rathkeale he told his audience that those who deserved to live for Ireland, 'if the occasion existed, would be ready to die for her [*cheers*].'[4]

The evidence of such extracts, and the audience reaction, suggests that O'Connell, like Padraic Pearse, was propagating an ideal of 'blood sacrifice'. The hero of Pearse's *The Singer*, who, with bare hands, seeks to redeem the country by individual sacrifice, had something in common with the Liberator. O'Connell's ideas were never clearly formulated; he hoped for success by bluff rather than by violence; in the last resort, however, he suggested redemptive sacrifice.

O'Connell's defensive criterion seemed to separate him from Pearse, who was prepared to take the initiative in 1916. Yet Pearse was clearly unhappy about this initiative and cogitated on it in the GPO during Easter Week, 1916. The difficulty lies in the definition of defensive. As Fr Kenyon, who denied that O'Connell had indeed used the defensive argument in 1843, subsequently pointed out, any just war could be classified as defensive.[5]

What indications did O'Connell give to his meaning in

1843? The last shred of the constitution, as his opponents later pointed out, and subsequent Ulster unionists discovered, was a tricky concept. As Duffy showed in *The Nation*, with the supremacy of the queen in parliament and no written constitution, definition was purely subjective. O'Connell also declared that the Act of Union should have been resisted to the death. Force was thus justifiable to maintain political rights, but not to recover them when lost. John O'Connell's attempt to catalogue minimum rights, including the collection of Repeal rent and the continued freedom of the Repeal meetings, was hardly convincing. Few contemporary European countries enjoyed such privileges. It was, said Smith O'Brien, more than he personally would have considered reasonable to justify revolution. O'Connell's own list, itemising foreign and British aggression, suspension of parliament, and abolition of trial by jury, was more conservative. Did this apply to packed juries? Mitchel's supporters thought so in 1848 when the *United Irishman* declared that he would be transported on the last plank of the constitution. Traditional Catholic concepts of a just war, deriving from theologians like Aquinas and Ligouri, were always difficult to apply in a particular historical context. Intolerable wrong, under which denial of Repeal rent might be classified, the probability of success, emphasised by Kenyon, and universal popular support, provided scope for debaters like Duffy. Old Irelanders demonstrated some confusion on policy. Daunt, who like Duffy and O'Brien considered 'defence' infinitely elastic, believed all would support war with a good chance of success. A compromise on this basis was suggested by O'Connellites to Mitchel in early 1847.[6]

In 1843, as Kenyon insinuated, O'Connell was not entirely consistent in limiting physical force to defence. He certainly promised not to attack barracks; the police would have to come out and find their opponents. He also talked of Ireland as an excellent terrain, with its numerous roads and enclosed fields, for guerrilla warfare. Even the hordes of Russia could be flung into the sea by determined Irishmen. Davis, attributed with articles on guerrilla warfare in the *Morning Register* of 1841, took up the same issue in a subsequent issue of *The Nation*. The 'War of the Flea' may be 'defensive' in a strategic sense, but hardly tactically as it is considerably more ruthless than the standard 'battle line'. After 1843 little more was said on guerrilla warfare till 1848 when both *The Nation* and the *United Irishman* had series of articles compiled from military handbooks on fighting in ditches and hedges, the setting up of ambushes, throwing vitriol on soldiers, the blowing up of bridges, and operating with small bodies of mobile men. Though not then practised to any great extent, the implications of revolutionary war were certainly placed before the public. Even after the Ballingary disaster, for several months Tipperary remained tense with rumours of astonishing guerrilla feats, using 'flying columns', by Doheny and John O'Mahony.[7]

O'Connell's position in 1843 was scarcely articulated. If the constitution were destroyed could the strategic initiative be taken, or must the government physically attack? The question was not faced. Analysis would destroy the propagandist effect of O'Connell's bluff. Unfortunately, the Young Irelanders were victims of the rhetoric; Davis and his friends believed O'Connell on the verge of leading the Irish in rebellion. O'Brien's friend, Denis Shine Lawlor, later associated with the Confederates, subsequently maintained that he had refused to join the Association in 1843 as the monstrous meetings and O'Connell's rhetoric both pointed to bloodshed.[8]

Real Differences between O'Connell and Young Ireland

It is impossible, however, to argue that there was no difference between *The Nation* and O'Connell at this time. *The Nation*, especially Davis, did exalt the ideal of military glory more openly, though usually with the proviso that moral force was the current policy. Sometimes there were hints that resistance need not be purely defensive. When the Polish rebellion collapsed in 1846, *The Nation*, possibly Mitchel, declared, 'better a little blood-letting to show that there is blood'. More important was the rejection of the pacifist view of James Haughton and D. O. Madden, sometimes voiced by the O'Connells, that real liberty could never result from war. On the contrary, *The Nation* discerned positive advantages in violent resistance. With no Bannockburn in Irish history, the

English treated the Irish with greater contempt than the Scots. Even in Ireland, Wexford, the county most resistant in '98, was one of the most prosperous. It was the same story in the Empire. Akbar Khan in Afghanistan and Hone Heke in New Zealand were respected for their resistance, while the yielding Chinese were despised. These conflicts could be included within the parameters of national defence, but they also implied that moral force might prove psychologically insufficient. If, as Davis said in 'The Morality of War', there was 'more of self-restraint, more contempt of bodily suffering, more of high impulse, more of greatness achieved for its own sake – more, in short, of heroism, in war than in almost any other human occupation', it could be regarded as a means to national regeneration in itself. O'Connell had only obliquely hinted at such a possibility in 1843.[9]

There was less talk of force after Clontarf; even the Young Irelanders turned to regeneration through education, not war. According to Davis, this was the only true moral force; the rest was either bullying or preparation for war. At this time the misleading view was abroad that the Repeal Association was divided between those opposed to force in all circumstances and advocates of violence. *Tait's Magazine*, however, suggested that both 'the pacific O'Brien section' and the war section were equally patient and practical. O'Brien repudiated the notion that he opposed force in all circumstances, but confused the O'Connells about his intentions. O'Connell and some Old Irelanders, however, still maintained that foreign war would soon compel England to grant Repeal. John O'Connell's poem on this theme appeared in *The Nation* on 27 April 1844.[10]

Eighteen forty-five was devoted predominantly to the Colleges dispute, but in October O'Connell asserted that Irish independence would be conceded as soon as England required Irish help. His cousin, Captain Broderick, graphically insisted that the first shot in a foreign war would grant Ireland her demands. Such sentiments, though couched in moral force terms, were further tacit blackmail. O'Connell's declaration in early 1846 that there would be bloody rebellion after his death if Ireland were denied justice was a classic example of this. O'Connell's dismay at Mitchel's notorious railway article was not logical. Mitchel simply enumerated practical measures, such as pulling up rails and hurling projectiles down cuttings, to meet the type of unjust aggression which O'Connell always believed to justify physical force. The Liberator himself had talked of guerrilla warfare, and an earlier *Nation* article, possibly by Davis, had discussed the disruption of railways, if used as a 'weapon of warfare' by the government. Again the real problem was that the Young Irelanders persisted in naively detailing the violence which the Liberator preferred to suggest obliquely.[11]

What did the Peace Proposals Really Mean?

The confused debate over O'Connell's Peace Proposals which led to the split in July 1846 justifies the foregoing contention. The Liberator, as Professor Maurice O'Connell maintains, was genuinely fearful, especially after his trial in 1844, that something might be said or written which could incur prosecution. He reeled off a list of legal precedents — Lord George Gordon in 1781, Holt, C. J., in 1696, Ellenborough on Watson's case, Eyre on Horne Tooke — of more relevance to the British government than to Irish patriots facing a moral dilemma. The object was to stifle discussion, not achieve a Repeal consensus. Accordingly, the Old and Young Irelanders were generally at cross-purposes. Was Meagher's 'sword speech' less defensive than Dillon Browne's utterance several weeks later? Did O'Connell rule out endorsement of force in the past? *The Pilot* and Fr Richard Power thought not. Was violence in other countries tolerable? The O'Connells were later prepared to accept this in a subsequent attempt at conciliation. But who was to demarcate defensive from aggressive violence? None of these questions were consistently answered. The Young Irelanders had some justification for dismissing the entire issue as camouflage for a new Whig alliance. On the other hand, Daunt was surprised that the Young Irelanders did not exploit the ambiguity of the defence loophole. To adapt the Liberator's own boast, they could surely have driven a coach and four through it.[12]

Young Ireland and Defence: 1848

Neither the famine nor the establishment of the Confederation succeeded in laying the issue to rest. John O'Connell still pontificated to his dwindling Repeal Association on constitutionalism and defensive violence. While the Confederates used the mobilisation of Pope Pius IX against Austria as support for their position, John O'Connell depicted the French February 1848 Revolution as basically defensive. As excitement mounted in 1848, Old Irelanders like M. R. Leyne used the shattered last constitutional plank to justify rebellion. He accordingly aligned himself with Smith O'Brien in Tipperary. Across the Atlantic, the hitherto O'Connellite *Boston Pilot* argued likewise that it would be 'moral feebleness', not moral force, to submit to famine. The *Tribune* cited Robert Holmes against any remaining constitutional last plank. The *Irish Felon* and the *United Irishman* further denied the existence of a constitution in Ireland.[13]

While such arguments justified an immediate 'defensive' rebellion, there remained, even amongst the Young Ireland Confederates, a reluctance to contemplate a tactical initiative. Mitchel talked originally of arms to resist eviction. His *United Irishman* declared that the people must await attack and avoid shedding the first blood. Meagher, whose 'sword speech' had apparently triggered the split, was cautious in practice. After calling for the barricades if the constitutional demand failed, Meagher declared that the object was not to draw blood from the government, but to prevent it from being drawn from the people. The Liberator had said much the same in 1843. John Pigot, who compiled *The Nation* articles on guerrilla warfare, warned against any unnecessary breach of the law. John Martin also felt that the people should stand to arms but attack no one. It was John Dillon, however, who explained the position most clearly. All Repealers, he declared in April, accepted the principle of arms for defence. The government must be compelled to strike or surrender. If they chose the former, the clergy would support the people. Only weeks before his armed protest, O'Brien, discussing the best moment to strike, pointed out that moral force advocates had promised to be first in the field when their rights were invaded. He implied that a unified Repeal movement should progress through a constitutional phase before British provocation ensured general resistance. He almost certainly agreed with Dillon's public letter to supporters in Tipperary. The latter linked Repealers' union, the support of the clergy and arming as the prerequisites for a 'bloodless moral force revolution'.[14]

The Liberator's 1843 strategy of what Davis called success by the threat of force rather than force itself remained the aspiration of some Confederate leaders in 1848. Not realising this, others sought a particular *casus belli*. What particular governmental action — jury packing, the famine itself, the suspension of habeus corpus, dissolution of the clubs — justified a defensive rebellion? Was it essential to wait passively for the crown forces to attack, or could a pre-emptive strike take place? There were almost as many answers to these problems as there were Repealers.

Secrecy versus Preparation

Two issues of particular interest for the future emerged. The first has been identified in the dispute between Duffy and Mitchel over revolutionary preparation. Duffy, once one of the most conservative Confederates, lurched after the French Revolution to a surprising radicalism, enabling his enemy Barrett to jeer.

> Fixed thoughts from Duffy! it were vain to seek,
> Who from himself is varying every week.[15]

To Duffy in spring 1848, with no foreign war to distract, unorganised masses could not withstand regular forces. Secret preparations were therefore an essential prelude. Duffy had never accepted O'Connell's defence argument, and appeared untroubled by the avoidance of tactical initiative. More relevant was Devin Reilly's insistence that Davis had repudiated the secrecy of '98. This had also been the Liberator's position. O'Connell, with full backing from Davis and Young Ireland, had continually condemned Ribbonism as the tool of British *agents provocateur*. Mitchel's apparently absurd challenge to the government in the *United Irishman*

was in line with the early Repeal tradition. He did accept the
need for some preparation, pointing out that the Americans
had drilled before challenging George III. He also maintained
that when Milan, Berlin and Vienna rose initially in 1848,
the citizens had possessed few arms. Years later, reflect-
ing on the European experience of 1848, O'Brien accepted
Mitchel's contention that revolution cannot be prepared in
advance. To Duffy this was all nonsense deriving from
Carlyle's *French Revolution*. Controversy with Lucas of *The
Tablet*, however, revealed that Duffy himself was no less
naive. He argued that the Celtic character required a short,
sharp war and that Charles Trevelyan had maintained in 1843
that all the Irish police barracks could be captured in a single
night. Ironically, Duffy's conspiratorial ideas came closer to
subsequent Fenianism, which he repudiated and Mitchel
assisted. Though there was clearly a Ribbon element in some
of the rural Confederate clubs, McGee's attempt, almost
unique amongst Confederate leaders, to liaise with a Ribbon
chief in Sligo was rebuffed on the ground that the rebellion
had little chance of success.[16]

Catholic Principles of Justification or Blood Sacrifice?

This Catholic principle that a justifiable rebellion must
have a reasonable chance of success was enunciated and practised by Fr Kenyon in 1842. Duffy retrospectively argued
that there was indeed a reasonable chance, despite Mitchel's
sabotage of class unity. O'Brien likewise maintained that he
believed success possible when he raised his standard in
July 1848. But, and this is the second important facet of the
1848 debate, there were simultaneous hints of a totally
different attitude, namely the idea a sacrificial revolt to
redeem the country from its lethargy. O'Brien's own poem
and Meagher's post-sentence remarks have already been
quoted, and similar sentiments have been discerned in
O'Connell's 1843 speeches.[17]

The concept, as Pearse demonstrated more effectively than
O'Brien, was best expressed in verse. Moore's *Irish Melodies*
contained a number of examples of this genre. The spirit of
the minstrel boy rose above the chains of the oppressor;

Robert Emmet looked to posterity to 'reverse the decree' of his executioners. Though Davis had generally sung of victory rather than heroic defeat, the Young Irelanders of 1848 often spoke in redemptive tones. Mangan, best of their poets, declared early in the year:

> Is the last hope, then, gone? Must we lie down despairing!
> No! there is always hope for all who will dare and suffer.

Similarly, Speranza's ambition, 'Tis to die with cheers heroic,/ lifting Freedom's standard high', and D'Arcy McGee,

> Oh, we will go forth with pike and gun,
> To keep our own or fall.[18]

The Nation declared that the opportunity provided by the French Revolution 'warms our blood like wine'. Though this can be seen as genuine hope for victory, rather than sacrifice, the imprisoned Duffy's invocation to 'naked hands and an armed soul' suggests an appeal to posterity. Similarly the failed Polish revolt was depicted as preferable to cowardice. Meagher apostrophised Mazzini's sedition for recalling the soul of the Italian people. Sometimes the sacrificial idea was combined with the defence notion. *The Nation*, for example, promised that O'Brien would return to France as an Irish representative when his cause was 'consecrated to force by the blood of brave men shed in defence'. The most celebrated of such statements was Lalor's last contribution in the *Irish Felon* on 22 July, when he declared that it might not always be possible to wait for an opportunity: 'somewhere, and somehow, and by somebody, a beginning must be made. Who strikes the first blow for Ireland? Who draws the first blood for Ireland? Who wins a wreath that will be green for ever?' Speranza's leader on the same day similarly proclaimed the message: 'Strike! Strike!'[19]

There was no formulation of the blood sacrifice ideal as persuasive as that of Pearse before 1916; O'Brien's satirical verse on the tribulations of his voyage to Van Diemen's Land was less compelling than Pearse on his own execution. The basic ingredients, if confused with incompatible notions, were all present in 1848. The Rising was as literary as its successor, though the quality of its verse and prose was much inferior. There was another important parallel. In 1916 Griffith's non-violent Sinn Fein movement was confused with the Irish Volunteers, whose overlapping membership contained many believers in defensive activity. Sinn Fein proper represented a divergent nationalist tactic. In early 1848, before the French Revolution, Duffy himself outlined a passive resistance programme.

The Young Irelanders and Passive Resistance

In 1843 O'Connell had developed an integrated programme with a Council of 300 (later categorised by Griffith as the Liberator's only statesmanlike idea), the non-consumption of British goods, and arbitration courts. The third, in which Duffy participated, was attempted before Clontarf. Meanwhile, Smith O'Brien, not yet an official Repealer, supported non-consumption in parliament. Davis, in an open letter to the Duke of Wellington, outlined as an alternative to guerrilla warfare a programme of legal resistance based on the evasion of acts and proclamations and the refusal of rents and taxes. This he believed would ensure government by the sword leading to the physical expulsion of the British from Ireland. Young Ireland's failure to back William Conner's Repeal Association motion for non-violent passive resistance based on refusal of rents appears inconsistent with a belief in Davis's suggestions. Disillusionment and the regrouping of the movement after Clontarf rendered such daring projects impossible. O'Connell was denounced for abandoning the Council of 300 but the subsequent Confederation was no more successful in its implementation. Some areas elected their representatives in 1848. There were occasional *Nation* articles which fostered the idea of passive resistance. Immediately before Davis's death the municipalities were suggested as the 'nucleus and embryo of natural freedom'. Efforts were made during the famine to use Poor Law Unions, and encourage consumer preference for Irish goods. O'Brien was imprisoned in 1846 by parliament for his attempt to practise selective abstentionism, an idea promoted by Davis. O'Brien and other Irish MPs at Westminster also adopted obstructive tactics.[20] Towards the end of 1847 the debate on means intensified with the increasing divergence between Mitchel and Duffy. Lalor's ideas of agrarian passive resistance, which so influenced Mitchel, suggest Davis's 1843 proposal. A *Nation* article, possibly by Mitchel, 'The Coming Year', hinted at full scale passive resistance when everything English, protection, laws, reliefs, titles, would be rejected. To counteract Mitchel's resistance to the poor law, which would develop into guerrilla warfare, Duffy outlined a comprehensive plan, immediately overtaken by the French Revolution, but of great interest as a possible basis for Arthur Griffith's subsequent Sinn Fein.[21]

Duffy demanded the exploitation of Ireland's free speech and franchise. He sought the election of a strong Irish parliamentary party to obtain the balance of power at Westminster and thus enforce Irish demands. Obstruction was another valuable weapon. If expelled, Irish MPs could return home to participate in a great council of all representatives, including corporations, grand juries and Poor Law Unions. The latter might act immediately as Irish representative bodies encouraging Irish manufactures and development. Duffy believed that Ulster would be enticed in. On the precedent of Canada in 1842, he considered that the British would have to capitulate to what was in fact an Irish assembly. Nor was it necessary to begin with a general election; individual Irish MPs could start at once. Many of the proposals clearly derived from Davis.   .

The plan differed from Griffith's *Sinn Fein Policy* of 1905 in that the latter was more rigidly abstentionist. However, Griffith's hope that the new General Council of County Councils would form the nucleus of the Irish authority, to which Irish MPs could adhere when they were persuaded to leave parliament, was very close to Duffy's thinking. Parnell, whom Griffith greatly admired, had already endeavoured to exploit obstruction and the Westminster balance of power. His successor, John Redmond, appeared to have permanently undermined Sinn Fein by securing the Home Rule bill of 1912 by balance of power tactics. Nevertheless, Griffith's chance to implement part of the programme came with Sinn Fein's election victory of 1918.

Moral Insurrection

Both Duffy and Griffith appear to have envisaged bloodless victory in their original passive resistance programmes. Fintan Lalor in the *Irish Felon* attempted, however, to merge physical and moral force into an amalgam which he called 'moral insurrection'. This was close to Davis's suggestion in 1843. It also incorporated the O'Connellite notion of defence. Lalor envisaged an initial movement of passive resistance, based on refusing recognition to usurped authority and obstruction of every effort to exercise it. Meanwhile nationalists peacefully assumed and defended the rights of government. To Lalor this differed from 'true military insurrection' only in 'the difference between the *defensive* and the aggressive use of physical force — a difference, however, which is often important, whether as regards moral right or mechanical efficacy.' Lalor's moral insurrection was revived by Griffith's Sinn Fein opponents in the early years of the twentieth century to evade the latter's apparently pacifist conclusions.[22]

Thus the revolutionary wheel had completed its circle back to O'Connell's contested 'defensive' distinction. Young Ireland and Repeal as a whole failed to produce a consistent and coherent revolutionary strategy, violent or non-violent, beyond the bluff which successive governments were ready to call. There were hints of consistent non-violent resistance, of the type later practised by Mahatma Gandhi in India, from William Conner, James Haughton, Isaac Varian, and even John Mitchel, but these were never developed. However, there was ample scope for subsequent nationalists to isolate their own nostrums as the real message of the movement. Analysis again reveals the symbiotic relationship between O'Connell and the young men to be as persistent as ever.

Conclusion

In late 1849 Michael Doheny assaulted William D'Arcy McGee in a New York street; the two men had to be separated by police. Though the affray was triggered by McGee's public assertion that Doheny wasted his days and nights in public houses, the causes lay deeper. It represented a final breach between the conservative Confederates, led by Duffy and McGee, and the more radical school of Mitchel, Doheny and Reilly. More trouble followed. Bitterness, resentment and suspicion took many years to evaporate. Duffy and Mitchel savagely attacked each other's honour in 1854. Meagher warned Duffy of the dishonesty of McGee in the same year. Stephens long believed that O'Brien had cruelly deserted him after Ballingary. Mitchel and Martin found Stephens untrustworthy. O'Brien and Martin engaged in public controversy in 1861. Even the brothers-in-law, Mitchel and Martin, disagreed strongly on constitutional action in the 1860s and 1870s. Though never a tightly integrated body of opinion, Young Ireland, with most of its leaders in voluntary or involuntary exile, degenerated after 1849 into backbiting factions.[1]

Ostensibly, little had changed in Ireland. In January 1849, *The Irishman*, dedicated to Mitchel's philosophy, began publication. Duffy re-established *The Nation* in September 1849; in the following month John O'Connell at last succeeded in reviving the Repeal Association. An Irish Alliance, backed by Duffy, several Protestant Repealers and some radical Old Irelanders, attempted to carry on the work of the defunct Irish League. *The Irishman*, condemning both the revived Association and the new Alliance, encouraged more radical Democratic Clubs. Emboldened by the victory of reaction in Europe and further papal repudiation of the Colleges, John O'Connell's denunciation of violence and infidelity rang out again. Nor was he more willing for union than in 1848. However, lack of support forced the final closure of the Repeal Association in July 1850. In the following month the Tenant Right League, with Frederick Lucas of *The Tablet* as chief progenitor, and Duffy as an important member, was established after negotiation between the Alliance and the Democratic Clubs. As John O'Connell endorsed the new movement, it appeared that the long-term Confederate demand for unity through a new organisation had been finally achieved.

History unfortunately repeated itself. Initial attempts to unite the farmers of both north and south, as Davis had suggested, were overtaken by Catholic religious grievances. Though Duffy, winning a seat in parliament for New Ross, tried to implement the constitutional policy he had devised before the French Revolution, the new movement collapsed over the great cause of dissension between Old and Young Ireland in 1846 – place-hunting. Meanwhile, with Archbishop Paul Cullen dominating the Irish Catholic church in place of Drs Crolly and Murray, pressure for separate education and denunciation of infidelity intensified. Here John O'Connell was victorious. Duffy was glad to remove himself to greener pastures in Australia. His subsequent conclusion, that 'in Ireland hitherto history has repeated itself with the fidelity of a stock piece at the theatre, where nothing is changed from generation to generation but the actors', was endorsed by a unionist contemporary. It sarcastically portrayed Duffy's final contest with John O'Connell as the resuscitation of an old Punch and Judy show, complete with antiquated props. Though Duffy maintained that he had been consistent, opponents on both left and right denounced what T. D. Reilly called Duffy's 'constant tergiversations', enabling him to glide from conservatism to insurrection, and finally revert to tepid constitutionalism in 1849.[2]

If Young Ireland by 1849 was clearly defunct as a coherent movement, what exactly had it been in its prime? The preceding chapters have not located any single set of principles, or any consistent tactical process which clearly distinguishes it from Repeal as a whole. This was strongly maintained by

The Irishman. It accused the Irish Confederation of being the Repeal Association 'with a new coat on it'. The Confederation, 'while it abjured the slavish doctrines of its predecessor, it imitated its acts.' Though *The Irishman* had its Mitchelite axe to grind, there is some truth in its polemic. Both in theory and practice there was total diversity amongst Young Irelanders, who were, however, never able to emerge finally from the colossal shadow cast by the Liberator.[3]

Young Ireland began and ended as a group of intellectuals associated with *The Nation* newspaper. Though *The Nation* was an integral part of Daniel O'Connell's Repeal movement, and developed the undenominational nationalism he asserted on many platforms, a constant rivalry was maintained between Duffy's *Nation* and Barrett's *Pilot*. To a considerable extent, this destructive conflict was based on competition for subscribers, Barrett in particular insisting that Duffy's sole motive was economic gain and affluent living. A very important difference of principle nevertheless emerged. *The Pilot*, edited by a Protestant, advocated Catholic nationalism, with Protestants reduced to a subordinate role, while *The Nation*, edited by a Catholic, demanded a comprehensive pluralist nationality. The Liberator, a consummate politician, could speak both languages, and nonchalantly played the rivals off against each other. Had *The Pilot* possessed a large circulation, and *The Nation* a small one, the situation would have been stable. Catholic clergy, vital to the movement, would have been heartened by *The Pilot*, while *The Nation* might have been tolerated as a useful auxiliary, appealing mainly to liberal Protestants. *The Nation*, however, because of the infectious enthusiasm and literary flair of its contributors, achieved a massive success which *The Pilot* was unable to match. This created a serious problem. Churchmen, especially those linked with MacHale, grew uneasy and discovered heterodoxy or 'infidelity' in *Nation* articles. The Liberator, an adept judge of the pragmatic limits to pluralist advocacy and hints of violence, found *The Nation*, with its independent circulation, hard to control. John O'Connell's bid for the Association succession, in the face of Smith O'Brien's aristocratic appeal, was another complicating factor. O'Brien had at first few links with *The Nation*, apart from the essential fact that neither was a creature of O'Connell's and both obtained direct endorsement from the community.

Tension finally exploded in disputes over education and violence. Mixed education was basic to Davis's pluralist nationalism already confronting Barrett's Catholic variant; unfortunately the political issue was confused by the long-standing battle within the Catholic hierarchy between the Murray-Crolly bishops and the MacHale group. Had the specific needs of John O'Connell, Barrett and MacHale not intensified the issue, a compromise was obviously achievable. As Doheny later claimed, no Young Irelander actually supported Peel's bill. Even Davis, sometimes tactless and provocative, accepted the bishops' ambiguous amendments, which the government refused to incorporate. The overkill of the bill's opponents, with their blistering insistence on 'godlessness' and infidelity provoked renewed assertions of the desirability of 'mixed education' for Protestants and Catholics. Ironically, the Young Irelanders accepted many of the key claims later advocated by Catholic educational separatists. The educational contest thus appears an aspect of a power struggle as well as a contest of philosophies.[4]

The same argument may be applied to the debate on violence. Contemporaries like Daunt were unable to comprehend why the defence loophole, with its almost infinite scope, was not used for compromise. The Liberator, unlike the Young Irelanders, knew how to approach the brink of physical force without being submerged and needed the Peace Proposals to curb the latter. The Proposals were also an answer to a general, if masked, threat to his leadership and his son's succession. His desire to do non-Repeal business with the Whigs — indistinguishable from the exercise of some patronage, or place-hunting — was unacceptable to the young men.

Yet, like children, the Young Irelanders, even after the secession, were unable to throw off O'Connell's paternal influence. The story of the next years, even after Ballingary, is an attempt to regain Repeal unity on favourable terms. The Confederation, as a device for effective bargaining, makes better sense than an opposition party. The negotiations persistently failed because the Repeal Association, despite its own weakness, retained the trump card of clerical support and the magic name of O'Connell. When the Irish League appeared on the verge of providing conditional clerical approval for Young Ireland, John O'Connell held back. In any case, the episcopal supporters of the League hoped to neutralise Young Ireland rather than be manipulated by it. Ballingary marked less the failure of Smith O'Brien as an insurgent leader than the limitations of Young Ireland policy since its inception.

Davis had earlier insisted that Protestant assistance was a prerequisite for independence. By 1848, however, the Young Irelanders, despite their enthusiasm and the backing of the influential Smith O'Brien, had failed to make any impact on the Protestant gentry or the working-class Orangemen of the north. Dolly's Brae symbolised the collapse of the argument that the new generation of northern Protestants were abandoning the anti-Catholicism of their fathers. Young Ireland discovered no more effective argument for reconciling Protestants than those of the Liberator. For a time, however, with unionist papers like *The Warder* praising Young Ireland, it appeared that genuine progress was being made. This proved short-lived when Davis's alternative prerequisite, distraction of England overseas, was wrongly identified in the French Revolution of February 1848.

Meanwhile the famine, instead of nationalising the gentry, turned them away from the people and called into existence radical Confederates like Lalor and Mitchel who apparently wished to base revolution on the agrarian masses. Conservatives like Duffy and O'Brien were closer to the Old Irelanders in economics than they were to their own radicals. Yet even Mitchel and Lalor did not seriously threaten the existing class system, being populist rather than socialist. Ostensibly, the Young Irelanders, influenced on both left and right by Carlyle, rejected the utilitarian, free trade opinions of the Liberator. In reality, however, O'Connell advocated similar protective duties to foster Irish industry. He was more hostile to the existence of a poor law than Smith O'Brien and the Young Irelanders; otherwise Old Ireland's prescription for the famine differed only marginally from that of Young Ireland.

Both Young and Old Ireland were concerned with problems of empire, denouncing British advance in India and lauding Canada's progress towards responsible government. Some Young Irelanders rejected the British Empire in toto and demanded an alliance with its enemies. Smith O'Brien, no less than O'Connell, was prepared to support Britain after justice had been conceded to Ireland. Duffy ended his career as a Knight Commander of the Order of St Michael and St George, earmarked for colonial politicians. Smith O'Brien, his treason conviction notwithstanding, never abandoned the ideas of Wakefield's school of 'Colonial Reformers' for whom he had been a parliamentary spokesman in the 1830s. In their assertion of universal freedom and lukewarm opposition to slavery, the Young Irelanders appeared to the right of O'Connell, though even the latter could use racist language on occasion. Mitchel moved from a pragmatic refusal to offend supportive American slaveowners to a full-blooded justification of the institution of slavery itself. In so doing he was strongly influenced by Carlyle, and partly by Davis who distinguished races by their courage in resisting oppression. Davis, however, was one of the few Young Irelanders dimly aware of cultural relativity.

On the development of Irish cultural nationalism, Young Irelanders were divided between those, like Davis and O'Brien, who stressed the need for linguistic revival, and others, like Duffy, MacNevin and Mitchel, who were mildly contemptuous. The latter appear to have differed little in their attitude from the Liberator, who, in a suitable environment, applauded Gaelic culture and denounced the debased life-style of the Saxon. Even Davis stopped short of advocating Irish as the main spoken language of the whole country.

If there was considerable doubt amongst Young Irelanders as to the ultimate ends of their movement, there was corresponding inconsistency on strategy. Confused by the Liberator's calculated bluff, the group moved from warlike exhilaration in 1843 to passive constitutionalism in 1844, followed by insurrectionary aspirations in 1848. After Ballingary it was each man for himself: disillusioned unionism, constitutionalism, or armed conspiracy. Though there were hints of it, neither O'Connell nor the Young Irelanders fully developed the non-violent, non-constitutional alternative later made famous by Mahatma Gandhi. Had they done so, the future of Ireland might have been very different.

Young Ireland, therefore, remains elusive but firmly locked into the organisational and ideological forcing-house of O'Connell's Repeal movement. The variety of opinion loosely associated under the 'Young Ireland' banner achieved practical disaster in the 1840s but developed into a potent myth in subsequent years. Every cause or opinion found justification in its ideological stockpile. Republicans and dual monarchists, physical-force men and pacifists, socialists and capitalists, could all claim plausibly to be the inheritors of the authentic Young Ireland tradition. It is forgotten that the Liberator's intellectual versatility was equal to theirs. But O'Connell, and to a lesser extent his son John, had no real competitors after the departure of the Young Irelanders from the Association. In the Confederation, despite their inconsistencies and errors of judgment, the creative tension between men as spirited and energetic as Charles Gavan Duffy, Thomas Davis, William Smith O'Brien, John Mitchel, and John Dillon gives their movement an abiding interest. The Catholic-Protestant pluralism they advocated in theory and practised amongst themselves is perhaps their finest legacy to Ireland at the end of the twentieth century.

Abbreviations

Books

Colleges = Denis Gwynn, *O'Connell, Davis and the Colleges Bill*, Cork, 1948.

DD = C. G. Duffy, *Thomas Davis: The Memoirs of an Irish Patriot, 1840-1846*, London, 1890.

D.O'C = K. B. Nowlan and M. R. O'Connell, eds, *Daniel O'Connell, Portrait of a Radical*, Belfast, 1984.

Fitz = W. J. Fitzpatrick, ed., *Correspondence of Daniel O'Connell, the Liberator*, 2 vols., London, 1888.

FT = M. Doheny, *The Felon's Track*, Dublin, 1951.

FY = C. G. Duffy, *Four Years of Irish History, 1845-1849*, Melbourne, 1883.

GwynnYI = Denis Gwynn, *Young Ireland and 1848*, Cork, 1949.

LC = J. Mitchel, *The Last Conquest of Ireland (Perhaps)*, Glasgow, n.d.

M.O'C = M. J. O'Connell, *The Correspondence of Daniel O'Connell*, 8 vols., Dublin, 1980 (vol. 8).

O'S = T. F. O'Sullivan, *The Young Irelanders*, Tralee, 1944.

POR = Kevin B. Nowlan, *The Politics of Repeal*, London, 1965.

RY = L. McCaffrey, *Daniel O'Connell and the Repeal Year*, Lexington, Kentucky, 1966.

2Hem = C. G. Duffy, *My Life in Two Hemispheres*, 2 vols., London, 1898.

W.O'C = D. McCartney, ed., *The World of Daniel O'Connell*, Dublin, 1980.

YI = C. G. Duffy, *Young Ireland; a fragment of Irish history, 1840-45*, London, 1896.

YI vols = C. G. Duffy, *Young Ireland*, final revision, 2 vols., London, 1896.

Newspapers

BP = *Boston Pilot*	N = *Nation*
DEM = *Dublin Evening Mail*	OI = *Old Ireland*
DUM = *Dublin University Magazine*	P = *Pilot*
FJ = *Freeman's Journal*	TV = *Tipperary Vindicator*
IC = *Irish Citizen*	UI = *United Irishman*
IF = *Irish Felon*	V = *Vindicator*
IT = *Irish Times*	W = *Warder*

Private Papers

Aut = Young Ireland Autographs (Trinity College, Dublin)
Conf = Minutes of Irish Confederation (Royal Irish Academy)
Clarendon = Clarendon (Bodleian, Oxford)
Daunt = W. O'Neill Daunt Correspondence (National Library of Ireland)
DauntJ = W. O'Neill Daunt Journal (NLI)
Davis = Thomas Davis (NLI)
Dillon, TCD = John Dillon Papers
Duffy = C. G. Duffy (RIA)
DuffyN = C. G. Duffy (NLI)
Farrell = Michael Farrell (TCD)
Hardiman = James Hardiman Papers (RIA)
Hickey = Hickey Papers (NLI)
Lalor = J. F. Lalor (NLI)
Larcom = Larcom Papers (NLI)
Len = Maurice Lenihan (NLI)
Martin = John Martin (PRO Northern Ireland)
O'B = William Smith O'Brien (NLI)
O'D = P. O'Donohoe on '48 Rising (NLI)
O'M = J. O'Mahony's Personal Narrative (NLI)
Outrage [Dublin or Tipperary] = Outrage Papers, 1848 (State Paper Office)
Reports, TCD = Report Books of Government Agents, 1848
Wyse = Thomas Wyse (NLI)

References

Introduction (pp. 1–5)
1. YI, 284, 373 & 787; N, 25.2.43; FY, 57.
2. POR; M. R. O'Connell, 'O'Connell, Young Ireland, and Violence', *Thought*, Vol. 52, No. 207, December 1977.
3. GwynnYI; Colleges; D. A. Kerr, *Peel, Priests and Politics: Sir Robert Peel's Administration and the Roman Catholic Church in Ireland, 1841-1846*, Oxford, 1982; D. Bowen, *Paul Cardinal Cullen and the Shaping of Modern Irish Catholicism*, Dublin, 1983.
4. A. MacLochlainn, IT, 20.11.73, and *Journal of Irish Literature*, 5.5.76; O. MacDonagh, *States of Mind*, London, 1983, 76-7; M. R. O'Connell, IT, 6.8.74.

Chapter 1. The Establishment of 'The Nation' (pp. 9–36)
1. J. G. Kohl, *Travels in Ireland*, London, 1844; O'C's use, N, 16.3.44, 15.3.45, 2.5.45, etc.
2. N, 12.8.43 & 19.8.43 — Baltinglass and Mountmellick.
3. Fitz, ii, 178 & 156.
4. A. Boyd, *Holy War in Belfast*, Tralee, 1969, 9-10 — riots 1839 & 1843, but really serious 1857; Sharman Crawford, YI, 10.
5. E. Strauss, *Irish Nationalism and British Democracy*, London, 1951, 102-3; M.O'C, vii, 168.
6. R. Kee, *The Green Flag*, 260-73; W. M. Thackeray, *Collected Works*, v, 356; J. Nichol, *Thomas Carlyle*, London, 1926, 102; but for *Punch*, see M. Tierney, ed., *Daniel O'Connell, Nine Centenary Essays*, Dublin, 1949, 227.
7. E. Malcolm, 'The Catholic Church and the Irish Temperance Movement, 1838-1901', *Irish Historical Studies*, xxiii, 89, 2.82, 1-5.
8. Spring ramble, YI Aug — Davis, 527; summer N, 4.10.45; Davis YI 49-50, DUM, 29, 40, 2.45, 198; Dillon, YI 60-61; C. G. Duffy, *Conversations with Carlyle*, London, 1892, 3; L. O Broin, *Charles Gavan Duffy: Patriot and Statesman*, Dublin, 1967, 137.
9. 2Hem, i, 3-21; P, 21.12.46.
10. [T. D. McGee], *Memoir of Gavan Duffy*, Dublin, 1849, 7; YI, 46; 2Hem, i, 59 ('dogmatic and self-conceited'); YI 527-9.
11. IC, 7.3.68; Dillon, TCD, 6455, 121, to Ady 26.6.49; J. Barrow, *A Tour Round Ireland*, London, 1836, 158.

12. YI, 58 and 526; N, 4.10.45 (possibly Doheny).
13. Duffy, 12 P, 19.
14. MacNevin (1844) & Davis to Duffy (21.4.44) DuffyN, 5756.
15. T. W. Moody, 'Thomas Davis and the Irish Nation', *Hermathena*, 1966, 103, 6.
16. Davis, 'An Address delivered before the Historical Society, Dublin', in T. W. Rolleston, ed., *Prose Writings of Thomas Davis*, London, 1890, 1-43; M. G. Buckley, 'Thomas Davis: A Study in Nationalist Philosophy', University College, Cork, Ph.D. thesis, 1980, 20-21, argues that Davis never visited the Continent.
17. N 4.10.45; Moody, 6.
18. Rolleston, 1-43.
19. *Morning Register*, 20 & 21.4.41.
20. M.O'C vii, 78, 29.5.41; DD, 88.
21. DD, 81 (Davis to Waddy, 6.7.42).
22. M.O'C vii, 172 (O'C to Ray) 6.8.42.
23. YI, 527, 30.4.44.
24. V, 17.8.42.
25. P, 17.1.48; YI 49; O'S, 43; Daunt, 10,507, 18.10.42.
26. O'Connell to Cullen, 9.5.42; M.O'C, vii, 155-161; P, 14.4.47 and 21.11.42, OI, 31.10.45.
27. P, 21.11.42.
28. P, 14.4.47; DauntJ, 340, 1843; P, 20.2.43.
29. DD, 102; N, 24.12.42.
30. YI, 169-70; N, 11 & 18.2.42, 18.3.43 (Lover's Rory O'More), 10.6.43 (Duffy v. Lever) & 12.8.43 (O'C & Prout).
31. [McGee], *Memoir of Gavan Duffy*, 11; YI, 172.
32. YI, 179; IC, 2.11.67.
33. N, 3.5.43.
34. DD, 95 & 133; 2Hem, i, 65; YI, 166; MacNevin (1844) in DuffyN, 5756.
35. 2Hem, i, 64-5; DD, 93 (6th number); YI, 182.
36. N, 19.11.42, 22.7.43 & 9.9.43; DD, 142; 2Hem, i, 70.
37. YI, 49 & 527; DD, 91 & 94.
38. N, 3 & 17.12.42.
39. N, 17 & 31.12.42, 14.1.43, 25.2.43, 24.6.43 & 23.12.43; P, 8.5.43.
40. N, 9.11.42 & 25.3.43.
41. N, 14.1.43 & 25.2.43.

Chapter 2. *Towards Confrontation – Old and Young Ireland, 1843-45* (pp. 37–81)

1. RY, 31 & 39; N, 21.1.43 & 4.2.43.
2. N, 7.1.43, 18.2.43 & 4.2.43; G. Broeker, *Rural Disorder and Police Reform in Ireland, 1812-36*, London, 1970, 178.
3. N, 4.3.43 & 11.3.43.
4. RY, 39; N, 22.4.43, 29.4.43, 6.5.43 & 18.2.43; O'B, 437, 1677.
5. YI, 299-302.
6. YI vols, i, 140; N, 10.6.43 & 17.6.43.

7. 2Hem, i, 89; FT, 20.
8. W, 27.5.43; N, 20.5.43.
9. W, 17.6.43; N. 3.6.43.
10. RY, 59.
11. IC, 12.11.67; O'S, 249 & 407; YI, i, 112.
12. N, 16.9.43; YI, i, 167-8; N, 19.8.43 (The crisis is on us) & 26.8.43 (Rubicon).
13. N, 12.8.43.
14. N, 26.8.43 & 30.9.43.
15. N, 7.10.43.
16. N, 30.9.43, 7.10.43 & 14.10.43.
17. YI, i, 181-2; FT 27; N, 25.3.48.
18. DEM, 16, 20 & 23.10.43.
19. N, 11.3.43.
20. N, 29.4.43 & 10.6.43.
21. N, 16.12.43 & 30.12.43; DEM, 18.12.43; DuffyN, 575-6 (MacNevin, 1844).
22. O'B, 464, Retrospect, 15; O'S, 175; O'B, 8655; O'B, 443, 2563 (O'B to Lucy 19.9.49).
23. O'B, 426, passim; D. Gwynn, 'William Smith O'Brien, *Studies*, 12.46, 448-458; O'B, 429, 459.
24. Mitchel on O'B, IC, 2.11.67.
25. O'B, 432, 966, (9.5.43, and other items).
26. N, 26.10.43.
27. O'B, 433, 1071 and 1093 (24.10.43 & 25.12.43); W, 27.1.44.
28. O'B, 433, 1072-3 & 1084.
29. O'B, 433, 1076 & 1083 (22.11.43).
30. N, 16.3.44, 13.4.43.
31. N, 16.3.44.
32. N, 27.1.44 & 3.2.44.
33. YI vols, ii, 32-3; FT, 41; 2Hem, i, 107; N, 15.5.47 (J. O'Neill).
34. N, 24.2. & 2.3.44; W, 9.3.44.
35. N, 13 & 27.5.43; W. Dillon, *Life of John Mitchel*, i, London, 1888, 49.
36. N, 30.3.44, 31.5.45 & 22.3.45; FT, 32; Davis, 2644 (20.9.43); W, 30.3.44 & 1.6.44; O'B, 2642, 3456 (26.11.46); FY, 291; P, 4.5.45.
37. Kee, 221; N, 9.3.44 & 13.4.44.
38. W, 1.6.44 & 20.7.44.
39. N, 15.6.44 & 22.6.44.
40. FT, 35-36.
41. O'B, 434, 1224 (E. M. Caulfield 11.8.[44]); N, 6.7.44 & 3.8.44 (Tait's 8.44).
42. O'B, 433, 1121 (15.2.44); 433, 1152; 440, 2145.
43. M.O'C, vii, 258; W, 15, 22, & 31.8.44; DauntJ, iii, (O'Loghlen, 13.3.48).
44. *Irish Monthly*, 'A Batch of "Young Ireland" Letters', xi, 1883, 376-382.

45. P, 17.1.48.
46. N, 14.9.44.
47. N, 28.9.44.
48. N, 10.3.43.
49. N, 23.3.44, 14.9.44 & 19.10.44.
50. P. S. O'Hegarty, *A History of Ireland Under the Union*, London, 1952, 200; YI vols, ii, 108; N, 17.10.46 (O'Neill in FJ, 28.10.44), 19.10.44.
51. YI vols, ii, 121.
52. W, 26.10.44 & 9.11.44; N, 12.10.44.
53. GwynnYI, 28-31; P, 26.2.47; YI vols, ii, 115, 117; O'B, 441, 2244, (Duffy [1847]).
54. FT, 38; J. D. Frazer thought Duffy's letter 'matchless', DuffyN, 5756, 21.10.44; DD, 270; N, 2.11.44; M.O'C, viii, 287, 30.10.44.
55. P, 20.11.46; DauntJ, iii, 3040.
56. *The Spirit of the Nation; or Ballads and Songs by the Writers of "The Nation"*, 59th ed. [1st 1843], Dublin, 1934, 74; DauntJ, iii, 3040, (O'B, 10.1.48).
57. P, 10.1.45; N, 18.1.4; YI, 32.
58. Colleges, 39; YI vols, ii, 185; O'B, 440, 2162 (John O'Connell attacks bill); Daunt, 10,507, 16 (O'Loghlen, 20.3.48); M.O'C. vii, 304 & 306.
59. N, 17.5.45; Colleges, 48.
60. Colleges, 51-2.
61. O'B, 435, 1383 (29.8.45); YI vols, ii, 172.
62. Kerr, 313; Davis, 2644 (Griffin, 2 & 15.6.45).
63. Colleges, 77-79, (15.6.45 & 17.6.45); N, 19.7.45 & 13.9.45; P, 21.7 & 22.8.45.
64. Colleges, 80 & 87; N, 15.11.45; O'B, 435, 1377 (30.7.45 – J.O'C).
65. N, 1.2.45.
66. N, 8.2.45 & 18.1.45; Davis, 2644 (Cane, 14.3.45).
67. YI vols, ii, 151; W, 4.1.45 & 8.2.45 (poem); N, 29.3.45.
68. N, 19.4.45.
69. FT, 49.
70. IC, 2.11.67.
71. N, 31.5.45.
72. N, 28.6.45.
73. J. M. Hone, *The Love Story of Thomas Davis, told in the letters of Annie Hutton*, Dublin, 1945.
74. DuffyN, 5756 (13.4.46); YI vols, ii, 197.
75. Fitz, ii, 17.9.45; DauntJ, iii, 3040, 1313 (O'Loghlen 12.3.48.)
76. Duffy, 5756, passim; O'B, 435, 1397; Doheny in N, 27.9.45; W, 20.9.45.
77. W, 20.9.45; N, 4.10.45 (complains of maligning Davis & attacks Barrett).
78. O'Hegarty, *History*, 219.

Chapter 3. Repeal Splits, 1845-46 (pp. 82—116)
1. Duffy, 5756 (Pigot 4.11.45); N, 4.10.45.
2. 2Hem, i, 127.
3. Duffy, 5756, 24.9.[45]; IC, 30.11.67.
4. W. Stokes, *The Life and Labours in Art and Archeology of George Petrie*, London, 1868, 97 (quotes Wakeman on Mangan); YI, 297 (Mangan); N, 18.4.46; P, 9.11.46.
5. Speranza, O'S, 458; N, 3.1.46.
6. N, 22.11.45.
7. O'S, 458; N, 29.11.45, & 10.1.46.
8. N, 20.6.46.
9. W, 21.2.46.
10. GwynnYI, 59-60; FT, 74 & 76; N, 22.3.45 (Dillon Browne).
11. (Davis) Wyse papers, 15,026, 93, 10.7.43; N, 4.4.46.
12. N, 18.4.46, 25.4.46 & 2.5.46 (O'B v. O'C in parliament on Corn Laws & outdoor relief, 17 & 21 April).
13. M.O'C, viii, 15-16; IC, 23.11.67.
14. N, 2.5.46; O'B, 436, 1560 (29.4.46); P, 1.5.46.
15. M.O'C, viii, 17-18; McNevin's Minutes of Repeal Committee, O'B, 434, 1199.
16. O'B, 436, 1569, 1580 & 1605; 437, 1642; 440, 2135; 441, 2243, & 2251.
17. IC, 23.11.67.
18. M.O'C, viii, 21-3, 9.5.46; W, 9 & 23.5.46.
19. N, 9.5.46 & 16.5.46; DuffyN, 5756, 23.1.46.
20. N, 6.6.46 & 30.5.46; W, 23.5.46.
21. N, 30.5.46.
22. N, 6 & 13.6.46; M.O'C, viii, 34 (19.5.46).
23. N, 6, 13, 20 & 27.6.46; M.O'C, viii, 55 (J. A. Quigley, 22.6.46); P, 24.6.46.
24. FY, 170-71, N, 27.6.46.
25. N, 7.6.45 & 11.7.46.
26. N, 11.7.46.
27. LC, 114; FT, 108-9; M.O'C, *Thought*, 52, 207, 390.
28. O'B, 441, 2254, & 437, 1660.
29. O'B, 439, 2060.
30. P, 9.2.46 & 15.7.46.
31. N, 18.7.46; FT, 103; P, 15.7.46; O'B, 439, 2060.
32. W, 25.7.46.
33. N, 25.7.46.
34. DuffyN, 5756; LC, 114; M.O'C, viii, 70.
35. N, 25.7.46.
36. N, 1.8.46.
37. N, 24.2.44, 2.3.44.
38. O'B, 437, 29.6.46 (MacHale), 13.7.46 (Bp Kennedy also dissatisfied with Repeal cause); IC, 23.11.67.
39. 2Hem, i, 167; O'B, 441, 2250; P, 20.7.46; W, 31.5.45.
40. P, 28.8.46 & 28.9.46. Nowlan, *Charles Gavan Duffy*, 10.

272   *The Young Ireland Movement*

41. O'B, 2642, 8.12.46.
42. IC, 23.11.47; N, 22.8.46.
43. N, 8.8.46; O'B, 2642, 3445, 15.10.46.
44. N, 15 & 22.7.46.
45. N, 8.8.46, 12.9.46 & 19.9.46; FY, 285; GwynnYI, 82.
46. P, 3.8.46.
47. P, 12.8.46, 14.9.46, 31.5.46, 21.9.46 & 28.9.46.
48. N, 22.8.46, 5.9.46, 19.9.46, 12.9.46 & 16.10.46; P, 14.9.46; W, 19.9.46.
49. N, 26.9.46; P, 5.10.46 & 28.8.46.
50. N, 3.10.46; FY, 352; W, 10.10.46; O'B, 2642, 3443, 21.9.46.
51. O'B, 437, 1690 (8.10.46) & 2642, 3447 & 3448 (29.10 & 2.11.46) & 2642, 3446 (20.10.46); Reports, TCD, 2038 & 2040; O'D, 770; Dillon, TCD, 6455; N, 3.10.46 & 7.11.46; P, 28.9.46 & 30.10.46; FY, 299.
52. W, 7.11.46; N, 7.11.46.
53. P, 4.11.46; N, 31.10.46.
54. N, 7.11.46; W, 7.11.46.
55. IC, 7.3.69; O'B, 440, 2220.
56. N, 31.10.46.
57. N & W, 5.12.46.
58. P, 4 & 7.12.46; FY, 337-8; O'Loghlen agreed with Duffy, DauntJ, iii, 3040, 13.3.48, that O'Connell, not John, wanted agreement; N, 3.1.46; W, 28.11.46.
59. GwynnYI, 92; O'B, 1738; N, 19.12.46 & 26.12.46; W, 19.12.46; O'B, 437, 1691; 440, 2212; 441, 2276.
60. N, 12.12.46.
61. O'B, 2642, 9.12.46.
62. O'B, 438, 1737; 437, 1714; 441, 2237.
63. N, 26.12.46.
64. GwynnYI, 92; O'B, 438, 1737-8 (16.12.46); P, 21.12.46.
65. N, 26.12.46; P, 30.11.46.
66. GwynnYI, 93; O'B 3458; P, 1.1.47.
67. GwynnYI, 89; N, 2.1.47.
68. (Mitchel to O'B, 30.12.46) O'B, 438, 1738; GywnnYI, 92.

Chapter 4. The Irish Confederation United, 1847 (pp. 117–139)
1. O'B, 441, 2241; N, 16.1.47.
2. FY, 359-60, McGee, *Memoir of C. G. Duffy*, 22; J. Hill, 'The Role of Dublin in the Irish National Movement, 1840-48, Ph.D. Leeds, 1978, 346.
3. N, 6.3.47 & 10.4.47 (Conf, £23.3.3., Assn. £6); O'B, 438, 1875 & 1928.
4. P, 18.1.47; Dillon, 6455, 33, (Pigot wants less meetings, 8.5.47).
5. O'S, 209.
6. P, 15.1.47; W, 16.1.47; N, 16.1.47.
7. N, 23.1.47.
8. P, 26.2.47 & 1.3.47; N, 30.1.47 & 20.2.47.

9. IC, 7.3.68; O'B, 437, 1774; 438, 1845; 441, 2271 & 2273; N, 20.2.47; P, 22.2.47.
10. GwynnYI, 106 & 108-9; O'B, 438, 1845, 1856 & 1867; 2642, 18.12.46.
11. GwynnYI, 111 & 113; O'B, 441, 2248 (25.4.47) & 1881 & 1888.
12. O'S, 383; Samuel Haughton, *Memoir of James Haughton*, Dublin, 1877; N, 9.1.47 (Haughton letter to Duffy), 16.1.47, 6.3.47 & 13.2.47.
13. Conf, 13 & 21.4.46; N, 10.4.47 & 1.5.47.
14. O'B, 441, 2233; (Steele) N, 13.2.47; W. Dillon, *Life of John Mitchel*, ii, 44; P, 24.2.47, 26.2.47, 24.3.47 & 12.4.47.
15. Conf, 12.
16. P, 22.2.47; YI, 114; FY, 387; O'B, 438, 1880, 24.4.46; N, 3.4.47.
17. W, 3.4.47; FY, 385; GwynnYI, 113; O'B, 1888.
18. N, 10.4.47; P, 12.4.47.
19. O'S, 272-3; RY, 66.
20. N, 8.5.47 (report), 15.5.47 (confed. mtg.); O'B, 440, 2191; P, 10, 17 & 19.5.47; O'B, 438, 1893, 1900 & 1908.
21. N, 15.5.47.
22. N, 22.5.47.
23. O'B, 438, 1878 & 1899; Conf, 26.5.47; N, 29.5.47.
24. P, 31.5.47; Conf, 4.6.47.
25. Duffy, *Letter to John Mitchel*, Dublin, 1854; UI, 26.2.48; N, 5.6.47; FY, 402-3; W, 12.6.47; P, 2 & 9.6.47.
26. P, 28 & 31.5.47.
27. O'B, 440, 2218.
28. O'B, 441, 2249; N, 14.8.47.
29. O'B, 438, 1918-19 & 447, 2240; FY, 426.
30. N, 14 & 21.8.47 & 4.9.47; GwynnYI, 128.
31. FT, 116; FY, 409; N, 31.7.47.
32. N, 17.7.47 & 20.11.47; O'B, 449, 3399; IC, 16.11.67 (no Kentish fire).
33. W, 28.8.47, 20 & 27.11.47 & 13.11.47; N, 2.10.47.
34. N, 18.9.47; N, 10.7.47, 14.8.47 & 23.10.47; see also 'Italy and Ireland', 11.9.47.
35. N, 10.6.48, 8.8.46 & 11.10.45; O'B, 439, 1985 (McGee), 440, 2203 (9.9.47 Meagher); N, 3 & 10.7.47; Conf, 28.6.47.
36. N, 10.7.47, 23.10.47, 25.9.47, 16.10.47 & 28.8.47; FY, 482.
37. O'B, 441, 2231; W, 23.10.47; Conf, 30.7. & 17.8.47; O'B, 442, 2443 (4.5.48).
38. N, 21 & 28.8.47.
39. N, 23.10.47 & 18.9.47.
40. O'B, 438, 1896, 24.5.47; FY, 422-3; N, 13.11.47.
41. O'B, 441, 2272 (6.12.47), 24.12.47.

Chapter 5. The Confederation in 1848: A Road to Fiasco? (pp. 140-168)

1. FT, 118; N, 5.2.48, 8.1.48 (Letter to Duffy). The Irish Council was an unrepresentative upper-class body.

2. O'B, 441, 2235 (11.12.47), 2033 & 2642; GwynnYI, 144.
3. GwynnYI, 144-5; O'B 1751; N, 8.1.48 (Mitchel also in FJ).
4. O'B, 441, 2355, 18.1.48 & 439, 2040, 30.12.47; N, 22.1.48; GwynnYI, 146 (O'B, 2298); P, 10.1.47 & 27.3.48.
5. O'B, 441, 2347, 3.1.48; GwynnYI, 145 (2234), 147-8 (O'B 2351 & 2039) & 150.
6. O'B, 441, 2347 (3.1.48) & 2367 (15.1.48, Pigot).
7. FT, 122.
8. UI, 12.2.48.
9. N, 12.2.48.
10. FT, 127; W, 19.2.48.
11. O'B, 442, 2374 (22.2.48).
12. W, 19.2.48; POR, 194-6.
13. O'B, 438, 1788; 2642, 3477 (28.2.48); UI, 19.2.48; N, 4.3.48 (Cuddihy).
14. N, 6.5.43 & 25.3.48; UI, 11.3.48.
15. O'B, 449, 3399; 442, 2394 (12.3.48) & 2396 (14.3.48) & 2383 (4.3.48); 444, 2711.
16. O'B, 440, 2221; 442, 2394, 12.3.48; N, 4.3.48.
17. FY, 540.
18. O'B, 2642, 3479 (1.3.48); N, 11.3.48; 2Hem, i, 261-2.
19. LC, 166.
20. N, 25.3.48; UI, 18.3.48; O'B, 449, 3399.
21. LC, 167; N, 29.4.48.
22. UI, 22.4.48.
23. N, 10.6.48; UI, 13 & 6.5.48.
24. W, 3.6.48.
25. T, 17.6.48; IF, 8.7.48; FT, 141, 148-9; Reports, TCD, 2038.
26. UI, 29.4.48.
27. UI, 13.5.48; IF, 24.6.48.
28. FT, 148; N, 17.6.48 & 15.7.48; O'B, 442, 2490, 12.7.48 & 2480 (20.6.48); T. D. McGee, *A Life of the Rt. Rev. Edward Maginn*, New York, 1863, 153-8.
29. N, 22.7.48; O'B, 442, 2484 (29.6.48); McGee, *Maginn*, 158.
30. FY, 608-9.
31. N, 29.4.48; FY, 637-8.
32. FT, 155; POR, 213 (28.7.48).
33. GwynnYI, 280, 284, 230 (O'Brien) & 282 (Meagher); Farrell Papers, TCD, 9786, 27.
34. *Correspondence between John Martin and William Smith O'Brien, relative to a French Invasion*, Dublin, 1861, 32.
35. GwynnYI, diff. accounts; FY, 655-692. Two peers sympathetic to Young Ireland, Lords Cloncurry and Wallscourt, were as reluctant to participate as Kenyon.
36. GwynnYI, diff. accounts; O'M, 868; O'D, 770; O'B, 444, 2711 (Anstey); J. G. Hodges, *Report of the trial of William Smith O'Brien for High Treason ...*, Dublin, 1849, 148.
37. *NY Herald*, 1 & 30.9.48, 1.10.48; R. V. Comerford, *The Fenians*

in Context: Irish Politics and Society, 1848-82, Dublin, 1985, 18; Outrage Tipp., 9.48.
38. GwynnYI, 234; Speech of William Smith O'Brien at Clonmel on Friday, October 29, 1858, Dublin, 1858, 10.
39. O'B, 441, 2316 (quoted by Grace O'Brien).
40. W, 14.10.48 & 12.8.48; O'B, 441, 2315; 442, 2506-7 (14.10 & 27.10.48); BP, 28.10.48.
41. IC, 14.12.67.

Chapter 6. Religion, Education and Secularism (pp. 171—184)
1. N, 3 & 17.12.42.
2. *Weekly Register*, 19.10.44; N, 8.9.44.
3. (Miracle) *Tablet*, 14.9.44; (Davis) Colleges, 21; (Duffy admission) P, 28.10.44; (O'B to Davis) Colleges, 22-3; Duffy, SR 12/P/19, (Doheny, 5.9.[44 or 45]); (Hely Hutchinson) Davis, 2644, 29.10.44; (Frazer) DuffyN, 5756, 21.10.44; (Dillon) DuffyN, 5736, n.d.; Dillon, TCD, 6455, 34 (7.47).
4. Colleges, 11; N, 1.3.45.
5. Colleges, 25.
6. Colleges, 15-16, 23-24.
7. M.O'C, vii, 159, 304 (2.2.45), 306 (19.2.45), 287 (30.10.44).
8. P, 4.5.46.
9. N, 17.5.45.
10. N, 14.6.45.
11. N, 19.7.45; P, 21.7.45 & 22.8.45.
12. J. Mitchel, *An Apology for British Government in Ireland*, Dublin, 1905, 65.
13. N, 18.12.47.
14. OI, 24.10.45.
15. N, 13.9.45 & 7.6.45.
16. *Victorian Parliamentary Debates*, 1869, viii, 1286-7 (6 July). Reference from Eugene J. Doyle & Professor Maurice O'Connell.
17. YI, 725-6; 2Hem, ii, 294.
18. DD, 303.
19. Dillon, TCD 56457b.

Chapter 7. The Economics of Young Ireland (pp. 185—200)
1. OI, 28.11.45.
2. Rolleston, 44-5; J. M. Hone, *Thomas Davis*, London, 1934, 61; N, 15.6.44.
3. N, 27.6.46, R. D. C. Black, *Economic Thought and the Irish Question, 1817-1870*, Cambridge, 1960, 144.
4. N, 5.11.42.
5. N, 17.5.45 & 3.12.42; O'B, 2642 (15.2.51); *Speech of William Smith O'Brien, Esq., M.P., on the Causes of Discontent in Ireland (4.7.43)*, Dublin, 1843, 45; N, 7.1.43 (Duffy), 28.1.43 (Dillon), 24.12.42 (Davis).

6. *Weekly Freeman*, 3.11.55; O'B, 441, 2232 (for Duffy and O'Brien).
See POR, 151, Black, 24 (Conner), T. P. O'Neill, 'The Economic
and Political Ideas of James Fintan Lalor', *Irish Ecclesiastical
Record*, 74, July-Dec. 1950, 398-409.
7. N, 24.12.42, 15.8.46, 3.4.47, 3.7.47, 16.8.45, 3.1.46 & 4.4.46;
Lectures on America, Dublin, 1860, 46; UI, 11.3.48; O'B, 441,
2228 & 441 (24.12.47).
8. N, 22.4.48 & 27.5.47; O'B, 442, 2377 (28.2.48 Manchester); T,
10.6.48.
9. N, 21.1.43, 18.2.43, 11.2.43, 8.11.45 & 25.5.44.
10. W. 25.5.48 & 1.3.45; (Daunt) N, 12.10.44 & 15.2.45.
11. N, 11.2.43, 12.11.42, 16.3.44, 31.12.42 & 17.8.44.
12. N, 17.8.44 & 24.7.47.
13. N, 31.8.44, 3.4.47 & 27.11.47.
14. O'B, 438, 1856, 24.3.47.
15. N, 22.5.47 & 17.10.46.
16. N, 25.10.45, 19.6.47, 24.7.47 & 4.9.47.
17. N, 10.10.46, 31.10.46, 4.4.46 & 25.4.46.
18. N, 24 & 31.1.46 & 7.2.46; O'B, 439, 1984, 8.9.47.
19. N, 3.10.46, 12.9.46, 24.10.46, 13.2.47, 10.10.46 & 9.1.46; O'B,
438, 1878, 23.4.47 (O'G).
20. N, 13.3.47.
21. W. S. O'Brien, *Principles of Government; or Meditations in Exile*,
Dublin, 1856, i, 333-359, and *Plan for the relief of the Poor in
Ireland*, London, 1830; Black, *Economic Thought*, 100; O'B, 440,
2224.
22. N, 11.4.46 & 18.3.48.
23. *Thomas Davis: Essays & Poems & a Centenary Memoir, 1845-1945*,
Dublin, 1945, 7.

Chapter 8. Young Ireland and British Imperialism (pp. 201—214)
1. N, 10.12.42 & 7.1.43.
2. *Citizen*, 5.40; N, 29.10.42, 26.11.42, 3.12.42 & 9.10.47.
3. N, 27.7.44; *Morning Register*, 25.5.41.
4. V, 19.3.42; N, 25.1.45.
5. N, 15.4.43.
6. N, 9.5.46, 13.2.47, 15.6.44 & 16.1.47.
7. N, 18.5.44; O'B, 436, 1544, 10.4.46.
8. N, 11.2.43, 6.4.44, 27.6.46, 30.8.45, 3.4.45 & 26.12.46; UI,
8.4.48.
9. N, 15 & 27.11.47.
10. N, 5.11.42 & 4.11.43.
11. YI, 746; N, 9.8.45, 24.1.46 & 25.4.46 (Merus Hibernicus), &
25.3.48; UI, 11.3.48.
12. N, 23.10.42, 26.8.43, 25.3.43, 7.2.46 & 2.9.43.
13. N, 10.6.43 & 25.3.43.
14. *Lectures on America*, 18-21, *Principles of Government*, i, 291-2.
15. BP, 22.4.43; N, 25.3.43, 23.3.44, 13.1.44, 9 & 16.8.45.

16. N, 5.4.45 & 9.8.45; BP, 14.6.43 & 5.7.45.
17. N, 5.11.42.
18. N, 22.10.42, 12.11.42; FJ, 25.10.41.
19. W, 11.2.43; N, 22.10.42.
20. YI, 303; N, 22 & 29.1.48.
21. N, 13.1.44, 6.1.44, 20.4.44, 30.11.44, 3.11.45, 3.4.47 & 14.8.47; *Lectures on America*, 15.
22. *Principles of Government*, i, 301; Alan J. Ward, 'Exporting the British Constitution: Responsible Government in New Zealand, Canada, Australia and Ireland', *Journal of Commonwealth and Comparative Politics*, xxx, 1, March 1987, 12.

Chapter 9. Orange and Green will Carry the Day? (pp. 215—229)

1. N, 1.4.43 & 1.7.43; W, 13.5.43.
2. N, 13.4.44, 30.3.44 (O'C estimate, 752,000).
3. N, 31.12.42.
4. N, 20.5.43, 8.7.43, 9.3.44 (Argument for Ireland), & 30.8.45; P, 15.9.54; OI, 31.10.45.
5. N, 27.5.43, 23.3.44, 21.9.44, 12.7.45, 22.6.44, 2.1.47, 14.9.44, 20.12.45, 26.7.45 & 6.11.47; O'B, 435, 1372, 27.7.45.
6. OI, 2.1.46; P, 20.7.46; N, 22.4.43, 18.7.46 & 8.4.48.
7. N, 1.7.43, 20.5.43, 14.12.44 (Davis?), 2.5.46, 27.6.46, 29.7.43.
8. N, 17.12.42.
9. O'B, 437, 1717, 3.12.46, & 436, 1493, 28.1.46 (B. Molloy).
10. N, 13.4.44.
11. N, 14.12.44.
12. N, 8.7.43.
13. N, 17.6.43, 27.5.43, 6.7.44, 8.4.48, 4.7.46 & 29.4.48 (Meagher brings tricolour).
14. N, 26.7.45 & 1.11.45.
15. N, 15.2.45 & 2.8.45.
16. N, 29.7.43, 23.9.43, 27.3.47, 5.2.48 & 22.7.43.
17. N, 17.6.43 & 29.7.43.
18. N, 15.7.43 & 12.7.45; John Mitchel, *The Life and Times of Aodh O'Neill*, Dublin, 1845, vii-viii.
19. N, 28.6.45.
20. O'B, 441, 2257; N, 18.7.46, 6.11.47, 11.9.47, 19.2.48 & 26.6.48; UI, 22.4.48.
21. N, 13.4.44, 16.8.45, 9.8.45, 23.5.46, 16.8.45 (Watson), 8.7.48, 1.7.48 & 4.7.46.
22. N, 18.2.43, etc., 25.5.43, 15.7.48, 3.5.45, 21.9.44, 22.7.43, 29.11.45 & 13.11.47.
23. N, 18.7.46, 1.1.48, 15.7.48, 22.7.48, 8.7.48, (see also Lurgan) 29.4.48; O'B, 440, 2221, & 442, 2410; McGee, *Maginn*, 150.
24. N, 22.7.48; IF, 15.7.48.

Chapter 10. Young Ireland and the Cult of Nationalism (pp. 230—243)

1. N, 12.10.44, 17.12.42, 17.4.47 (just 'essence'), 6.5.43 & 21.12.44.

2. N, 8.7.43, 22.7.43.
3. V, 21.9.42; W, 30.3.44; N, 18.10.45 & 27.5.43; P, 4.5.46 & 15.2.47.
4. N, 13.7.44, 19.8.43, 26.8.43, 16.9.43, 30.9.43 & 23.11.44; W, 29.4.43.
5. W. J. O'N. Daunt, *Personal Recollections of the late Daniel O'Connell, M.P.*, London, 1848, 14-15 (O'Connell talks of Tower of Babel at Edward Bulwer's, 1833.).
6. YI vols, ii, 98; Rolleston, 158; O'B, 441, 2289; 433, 2597; N, 3.8.44, 17.4.44, 30.5.46 & 30.12.43.
7. N, 12.11.42 & 15.4.43.
8. N, 1.4.43 & 30.12.43.
9. N, 1.7.43, 16.9.43 & 11.10.45. D. Corkery, in M. J. McManus, ed., *Thomas Davis and Young Ireland*, Dublin, 1945, 14-23. See also J. A. Murphy in D. O'C, 32-52 and G. Ó Tuathaigh in W. O'C, 30-41.
10. N, 23.8.45, 9.9.45 & 5.9.46; P, 10.7.46.
11. T. de V. White, *Tom Moore, the Irish Poet*, London, 1977, 238; R. Welch, *Irish Poetry from Moore to Yeats*, Gerrards Cross, 1980, 43.
12. N, 15.2.45.
13. BP, 29.4.48; Devoy version, John Devoy, *Recollections of an Irish Rebel*, New York, 1929, 8.
14. N, 13.12.45.
15. N, 1.8.46; *Childe Harold's Pilgrimage*, Canto ii, lxxvi.
16. OI, 26.12.43; N, 27.9.45.
17. N, 15.4.43 & 4.1.45; *NY Truth Teller* in N, 13.7.44.
18. N, 31.7.47.
19. N, 15.4.43; B. Farrell, ed., *The Irish Parliamentary Tradition*, Dublin, 1973, 272, quoted in Buckley, 'Thomas Davis', 260.
20. N, 11.2.43, 22.4.43, 20.5.43, 30.9.43, 18.5.44, 1.6.43 & 6.9.45; YI, 42 & 507; FY, 2.
21. N, 27.6.46, 25.4.46, 23.5.46, 9.1.47 & 2.10.47.

Chapter 11. Revolutionary Strategy (pp. 244—257)

1. N, 17.12.42.
2. N, 10.6.43, 12.9.43, 26.8.43, 17.6.43 & 15.7.43.
3. N, 17.6.43, 1.7.43, 26.8.43, 30.9.43, 5.8.43 & 22.7.43.
4. N, 7.10.43, 11.3.43 & 22.4.43.
5. N, 8.8.46.
6. FJ, 5.11.42; N, 7.11.46; UI, 27.5.48; O'B, 441, 2348 & 2342 (5 & 14.1.48 Daunt); 438, 1845 (19.3.47 Mitchel).
7. N, 30.9.43, 18.2.43 & 6.5.43; TV, 16.9.48; Outrage, Tipp., 27, 1133-2726.
8. DEM, 27.7.46; W, 25.7.46; O'B, 437, 1677 (7.9.46).
9. N, 4.4.46, 20.4.44, 26.7.45, 14.2.46 & 10.6.43; YI, 574.
10. YI, 673; N, 6.7.44 & 28.12.44.
11. N, 4.10.45 & 30.8.45.
12. N, 5.9.46; P, 10.8.46.
13. N, 11.3.48 & 15.7.48; BP, 5.5.48; T, 10.6.48 & 8.7.48 (sophistry); UI, 12.2.48; IF, 1.7.48.

14. N, 5.2.48, 18.3.48, 1.4.48, 8.4.48 & 17.6.48; UI, 18.3.48; IF, 22.7.48, TV, 5.4.48.
15. R. Barrett, *History of the Irish Confederation*, Dublin, 1849, 19.
16. N, 12.2.48 & 24.6.48; UI, 1.4.48; O'Brien, *Correspondence*, 1861, 34; GwynnYI, 320.
17. FY, 230 & 559.
18. N, 1.1.48, 15.1.48 & 15.7.48.
19. N, 4.3.48, 22.9.48, 1.4.48, 13.5.48 & 17.6.48.
20. N, 6.5.43 & 6.9.45.
21. N, 9.10.47 & 26.2.48.
22. L. M. Fogarty, *James Fintan Lalor, Patriot and Political Essayist*, Dublin, 1918, 75-6; IF, 1.7.48. My italics in Lalor quote.

Conclusion (pp. 258—264)
1. TV, 19.12.49.
2. FY, vii; DEM, 3.10.49.
3. *Irishman*, Dublin, 8.9.49.
4. (Pigot) DuffyN, 5756 (24.11.46); TV, 28.10.4.

Bibliographical Note

The literature relating to Young Ireland is vast, and only pointers to further reading can be given here. The massive retrospective works, beginning in the 1880s, by C. G. Duffy, (see abbreviations) anticipated by contributions from other Young Irelanders such as John Mitchel and Michael Doheny, remain the starting point for serious study. The rise of the Sinn Fein movement after 1905 made Young Ireland a valuable precedent and Arthur Griffith produced idiosyncratic editions of Mitchel's *Jail Journal* (1913), *Thomas Davis: The Thinker and Teacher* (1914), Doheny's *The Felon's Track* (1914) and *Meagher of the Sword* (1916). After the Revolution the approach of the Young Ireland centenary created a further interest. G. Randall Clarke broke new ground with his 1936 Queen's University M.A. thesis, 'The Political and Social Teachings of the Young Irelanders, 1842-1848' and 'The Relations between O'Connell and the Young Irelanders', *Irish Historical Studies* (IHS), iii, 9, March 1942, 18-30. T. F. O'Sullivan's *The Young Irelanders* (1944) remains a mine of biographical information. R. Dudley Edwards, 'The Contribution of Young Ireland to the Development of the Irish National Idea', in S. Pender, *Feilscribhinn Torna*, Cork, 1947, 115-133, showed how O'Connell 'tuned the instrument on which the Young Irelanders were to play'. Denis Gwynn's *Young Ireland and 1848* (1948) is valuable, especially for its extracts from the Smith O'Brien papers. So too are his numerous *Studies'* articles on Young Irelanders. K. M. McGrath's 'Writers in the Nation 1842-5', IHS, vi, 23, March 1949, enables the identification of many *Nation* articles, at least to 1844.

More recently, interest in O'Connell has revived and enthusiasm for the Young Irelanders as a group has waned in

Ireland. In Australia, Canada and the United States, where the post-1848 contribution of individual Young Irelanders was very extensive, considerable enthusiasm exists amongst both scholars and popular writers. Kerby Miller's monumental *Emigrants and Exiles: Ireland and the Irish Exodus to America*, OUP, 1985, gives considerable space to the Young Ireland diaspora, while Patsy Adam Smith's *Heart of Exile*, Melbourne, 1986, is a good example of the popular romantic genre.

The best recent analysis of Young Ireland, 1842-48, has appeared in more general volumes. R. B. McDowell, *Public Opinion and Government Policy in Ireland, 1801-1846*, London, 1952, has a valuable section on O'Connell and Young Ireland. Kevin Nowlan's description in *The Politics of Repeal* (1965) is unlikely to be superseded. Robert Kee's *The Green Flag*, London, 1972, also takes a detached look at the Young Irelanders. Gearoid Ó Tuathaigh's *Ireland Before the Famine, 1798-1848*, Dublin, 1972, gives an excellent short survey. T. N. Brown's *The Politics of Irish Literature from Thomas Davis to W. B. Yeats*, Seattle, 1972, provides a lively account of the movement, like Kee making good use of *The Nation*'s files.

There is an abundance of work on Daniel O'Connell. The eight volumes of Maurice R. O'Connell's *The Correspondence of Daniel O'Connell*, Dublin, 1972-80, with their detailed footnotes, are an invaluable source, supplemented by the editor's other extensive writings on this subject. Fergus O'Ferrall's *Daniel O'Connell*, Dublin, 1981 is a handy distillation of more detailed research. Two books of essays, Donal MacCartney, ed., *The World of Daniel O'Connell*, Cork, 1980, and Kevin B. Nowlan and Maurice R. O'Connell, eds., *Daniel O'Connell: Portrait of a Radical*, Belfast, 1984, provide some of the most recent conclusions on O'Connell. The first volume of a definitive life of O'Connell by Oliver MacDonagh is awaited.

Despite Davis's central role in Young Ireland there has been no full-scale biography since that of Gavan Duffy. J. M. Hone, *Thomas Davis*, London, 1934, is short. T. W. Moody, *Thomas Davis, 1814-45*, Dublin, 1945, is equally brief but supplemented by his 'Thomas Davis and the Irish Nation', *Hermathena*, 1966, 5-31, which contains a full bibliography.

E. Sullivan, *Thomas Davis*, New Jersey, 1978, summarises his main prose and poetry. M. G. Buckley, 'Thomas Davis: A Study in Nationalist Philosophy', Ph.D. NUI, Cork, 1980 covers more ground.

John Blake Dillon, despite his importance in Young Ireland and the profusion of his papers in the TCD archives, still awaits a serious biography. Charles Gavan Duffy, almost as important in the history of Australia as in that of Ireland, is more fortunate. Kevin Nowlan, in the short space of an O'Donnell Lecture, *Charles Gavan Duffy and the Repeal Movement*, Dublin, 1963, provides a valuable analysis of the contrast between Duffy's political role and the impression provided by his writings. León Ó Broin, *Charles Gavan Duffy: Patriot and Statesman*, Dublin, 1967, is a short popular account. A longer popular biography, without detailed references, is Cyril Pearl, *The Three Lives of Gavan Duffy*, Sydney, 1979.

William Smith O'Brien lacks a full modern biography. Blanche Touhill's *William Smith O'Brien and His Irish Revolutionary Companions in Penal Exile*, Missouri, 1981, deals mainly with the post-1848 period. However, Gwynn's *Young Ireland and 1848* is virtually an O'Brien biography. J. M. Hone, 'William Smith O'Brien', *The Dublin Magazine*, xii, 3, Sept. 1937, 37-46, is perceptive. See also D. Gwynn, 'Smith O'Brien and the Secession', *Studies*, xxxvi, 142, June 1947, 129-140.

John Mitchel is more fortunate. William Dillon, *Life of John Mitchel*, 2 vols, London, 1888 contains much primary material. Seamus MacCall, *Irish Mitchel: A Biography*, London, 1938, is one popular account. A new edition of the *Jail Journal*, (1954) introduced by Thomas Flanagan, was published by the University Press of Ireland, 1982. The author of an early Mitchel biography, P. A. Sillard, wrote *The Life and Letters of John Martin*, Dublin, 1893.

T. F. Meagher and Thomas D'Arcy McGee, who played important roles in the United States and Canada, are well publicised. Meagher has three American biographers, W. F. Lyons (1870), M. Cavanagh (1892) and R. G. Athearn, whose *Thomas Francis Meagher: an Irish Revolutionary in America*, Colorado University Press, 1949, is, like the others, centred on the USA. Denis Gwynn's extended O'Donnell lecture, *Thomas Francis Meagher*, Cork, 1961, is still the best introduction. McGee has inspired several biographies, the most recent being Josephine Phelan, *The Ardent Exile*, Toronto, 1951 and W. Kirwan, *Thomas D'Arcy McGee: Visionary of the Welfare State in Canada*, Calgary, 1981. Kirwan's 'The Radical Youth of a Conservative: D'Arcy McGee in Young Ireland', *The Canadian Journal of Irish Studies*, x, 1, June 1984, 51-62, argues for the continuity of McGee's politics.

Lalor and Fr Kenyon have had their writings collected by L. Fogarty in *James Fintan Lalor, Patriot and Political Essayist*, Dublin, 1919, and *Father John Kenyon: a Patriot Priest of Forty-Eight*, Dublin, 1921. Lalor myths have been dissipated by T. P. O'Neill in Irish in *Fiontan O Leathlobhair*, Dublin, 1962, and in English in 'Economic and Political Ideas of James Fintan Lalor', *Irish Ecclesiastical Record*, lxxiv, July-Dec. 1950, 398-409, and 'Fintan Lalor and the 1849 Movement', *An Cosantoir*, x, 4, April 1950, 173-179. Fr Kenyon has been served by the indefatigable Denis Gwynn's 'Father Kenyon and Young Ireland', *Irish Ecclesiastical Record*, lxxi, 975 & 978, March & June 1949, 226-246 & 508-532. Gwynn does not find Kenyon's abandonment of revolution in 1848 convincing.

Several of the Young Ireland poets have merited biographical studies. Mangan, the best, is the centre of an academic debate for which James Kilroy's *James Clarence Mangan*, New Jersey, 1970, may serve as an introduction. Terence de Vere White's *The Parents of Oscar Wilde*, London, 1967, wittily examines Speranza's career.

The Famine background of Young Ireland is provided by the essays (especially that by Kevin Nowlan) of T. D. Williams and R. D. Edwards, eds., *The Great Famine*, Dublin, 1956 and 1976, and Cecil Woodham-Smith, whose *The Great Hunger: Ireland 1845-9*, London, 1962, contains a detailed account of the 1848 Rising. Interest is reviving in the latter with current attempts to preserve Widow McCormack's 'Warhouse' at Boolagh, near Ballingary, and the republication of Fr P. Fitzgerald's eye-witness accounts, *Personal Recollections of the Insurrection at Ballingary*, Dublin, 1861 and *A Narrative of the Proceedings of the Confederates of '48. . .*,

Dublin, 1868. See also Thomas Trant (police inspector besieged in Warhouse), *Reply to Father Fitzgerald's Pamphlet...*, Dublin, 1862. Nearly all the leading participants left an individual description, and those of the future Fenian leader, John O'Mahony, and the lesser-known Patrick O'Donohoe, who contrived to edit the *Irish Exile* in Van Diemen's Land, are ripe for publication. James Stephens, *Personal Recollections* in the Weekly Freeman, 6.10.83 to 3.11.83, contains important material on O'Brien. John O'Leary's *Recollections of Fenians and Fenianism*, i, Shannon, 1969, takes the story to the Rising in 1849. Another participant in this latter action, John Savage, has left *'98 and '48: Irish Revolutionary History and Literature*, New York, 1860.

Such memoirs are now backed up by local studies such as T. G. McGrath, 'The Catholic clergy and Popular Politics in the Diocese of Cashel and Emly, 1823-48', M.A., UCD, 1980: Brendán Ó Cathoir, 'John O'Mahony, 1815-1877', *The Capuchin Annual*, 1977, 180-193; and Georgina Flynn, 'The Young Ireland Movement in Waterford, 1848', *Decies*, xviii, Sept. 1981, 41-49 and xix, Jan. 1982, 53-60. For the metropolis there is Jacqueline R. Hill, 'The Role of Dublin in the Irish national movement, 1840-48', Ph.D., Leeds, 1973, and accompanying studies such as 'Artisans, Sectarianism and Politics in Dublin, 1829-48', *Saothar*, 7, 1981, 16-24.

Index